Dark Web Markets

Illegal Goods, Services, and the Fight Against Cybercrime

Anaya Patel

ISBN: 978-1-77890-600-8
Imprint: darkside.exe

Contents

Introduction to Dark Web Markets

What is the Dark Web

Definition of the Dark Web

The Dark Web refers to a hidden part of the internet that is not indexed by search engines and requires specific software or configurations to access. It is a subset of the Deep Web, which encompasses the parts of the internet that are not accessible through traditional search engines.

The Dark Web is often associated with illicit activities, such as the buying and selling of illegal goods and services, including drugs, weapons, counterfeit documents, hacking tools, and stolen data. However, it is essential to note that the Dark Web is not inherently illegal, and it can also be used for legitimate purposes, such as protecting privacy and promoting free speech in countries with oppressive regimes.

The anonymous and encrypted nature of the Dark Web makes it attractive to those seeking privacy and anonymity online. Users can access the Dark Web using software like Tor (The Onion Router), which routes internet traffic through a network of volunteer-operated servers to conceal a user's identity and location.

One of the key characteristics of the Dark Web is its decentralized nature. It lacks the central authority and control typically associated with the Surface Web. As a result, it has become a breeding ground for various illegal activities that pry on this absence of governance.

The Dark Web can be accessed through various layers, each providing a different degree of anonymity. The most common layer is Tor, but other networks like I2P (Invisible Internet Project) and Freenet also contribute to the Dark Web ecosystem.

It is important to distinguish between the Dark Web and the Deep Web. The

Deep Web includes all parts of the internet that are not accessible through search engines, such as private databases, subscription-based websites, and intranets. While the Deep Web is often misunderstood as a haven for illegal activities, the majority of its content consists of legitimate, albeit not publicly accessible, information.

The term "Dark Web" should not be confused with the term "Darknet." A Darknet refers to a network that is separate from the public internet and requires specific software, configurations, or authorization to access. The Dark Web is a subset of Darknets and specifically refers to the part of Darknets where illicit activities typically occur.

In summary, the Dark Web is a hidden part of the internet that requires specific software or configurations to access. It is known for its anonymity and encryption, making it a platform for both illegal and legitimate activities. The Dark Web is not inherently illegal, but its decentralized nature and lack of regulation contribute to its association with illicit activities. It is important to understand the Dark Web and its implications to address the challenges it poses to society.

How the Dark Web differs from the Surface Web

The Dark Web and the Surface Web are two distinct parts of the internet with significant differences. While the Surface Web is the portion of the internet that is accessible through search engines like Google and can be easily accessed through regular web browsers, the Dark Web is a hidden network of websites that cannot be accessed using standard web browsers. In this section, we will explore the key differences between the Dark Web and the Surface Web, including their content, access, and anonymity.

Content

One of the main differences between the Dark Web and the Surface Web is the nature of the content that can be found on each. The Surface Web comprises websites and web pages that are indexed by search engines and available for public access. These websites provide a wide range of information, including news, educational resources, e-commerce platforms, social media networks, and more.

On the other hand, the Dark Web is known for hosting illegal activities and hidden services. This includes illicit goods and services such as drugs, weapons, fake passports, hacking tools, stolen data, and even hired hitmen. While not all content on the Dark Web is illegal, it has gained notoriety for being a hub for criminal activities due to its anonymity and privacy features.

Access

Accessing the Surface Web is straightforward and accessible to anyone with an internet connection. Websites on the Surface Web can be accessed using search engines or by directly entering the website's URL into a web browser. Most websites on the Surface Web are designed to be user-friendly and easily navigable.

However, accessing the Dark Web requires specialized software and configurations, making it far less accessible to the average internet user. The most common method of accessing the Dark Web is through a network called Tor (The Onion Router). Tor anonymizes internet traffic by routing it through multiple servers, making it difficult to trace the origin of the connection. This additional layer of encryption and anonymity allows users to access hidden services on the Dark Web while maintaining their privacy.

Anonymity

Anonymity is a key distinguishing feature of the Dark Web. On the Surface Web, most websites collect user data such as IP addresses, browsing history, and personal information. This data can be used to track and identify users, allowing for targeted advertising and behavioral analysis.

In contrast, the Dark Web offers users a higher level of anonymity. The Tor network used to access the Dark Web encrypts and relays internet traffic, making it extremely difficult to trace the source of the connection. This anonymity attracts individuals who wish to operate outside the boundaries of the law, as they can conduct illegal activities without fear of being identified.

It is worth noting that while the Dark Web provides anonymity to its users, it does not guarantee absolute security. Sophisticated law enforcement techniques and cybersecurity measures can still uncover the identities of individuals involved in illegal activities on the Dark Web.

Summary

In summary, the Dark Web and the Surface Web are distinct parts of the internet with significant differences. The Surface Web consists of publicly accessible websites and offers a wide range of legitimate content. In contrast, the Dark Web hosts hidden services and illegal activities, and its access requires specialized software and configurations. The Dark Web provides a higher level of anonymity through the use of the Tor network, attracting individuals involved in criminal activities. However, it is important to note that the Dark Web does not provide absolute security, as law enforcement agencies and cybersecurity professionals continue to develop techniques to combat illegal activities on the Dark Web.

Anatomy of the Dark Web

The Dark Web is a complex and layered part of the internet that operates on the principles of anonymity, privacy, and secrecy. Understanding the anatomy of the Dark Web is crucial for comprehending its structure and functioning.

At its core, the Dark Web is a network of websites and online platforms that are not indexed or easily accessible through traditional search engines like Google. These websites are hidden from the view of ordinary internet users and can only be accessed through specific tools and protocols.

The structure of the Dark Web is based on a decentralized network known as the Tor network. Tor, short for "The Onion Router," is a system that allows users to navigate the internet anonymously by encrypting their internet traffic and routing it through multiple volunteer-run servers called Tor relays. Each relay removes a layer of encryption, similar to peeling an onion, hence the name. This multi-layered encryption ensures that the source and destination of internet traffic remain hidden.

To access the Dark Web, users need to install and configure the Tor browser, which is a modified version of Mozilla Firefox. The browser routes all internet traffic through the Tor network, providing anonymity and privacy to users.

The Dark Web consists of three main layers: the surface layer, the deep web, and the darknet. Each layer has its own characteristics and serves different purposes.

The surface layer, also known as the "clearnet," is the visible part of the internet that can be accessed by anyone using standard browsers. This layer includes popular websites like social media platforms, news sites, online shopping sites, and banking portals.

Beneath the surface layer lies the deep web, which refers to the parts of the internet that are not indexed by search engines. This includes private databases, password-protected websites, academic resources, and other content that is not intended to be accessed by the general public. The deep web is not inherently illegal or malicious, but it provides a foundation for the hidden services on the Dark Web.

The darknet, also known as the "overlay network," is the hidden part of the internet that is only accessible through specific software, configurations, and authorization. It consists of websites, forums, marketplaces, and other platforms that operate within the Tor network. The darknet forms the backbone of the Dark Web and is predominantly associated with illegal activities, such as the sale of drugs, weapons, stolen data, hacking services, and other illicit goods and services.

It is important to note that not all activity on the Dark Web is illegal. The same anonymity and privacy features that attract criminal elements also provide an essential space for journalists, activists, whistleblowers, and individuals living under repressive regimes to communicate, share information, and exercise their freedom of expression.

However, the anonymous nature of the Dark Web also poses challenges for law enforcement agencies and cybersecurity professionals. Tracking, identifying, and prosecuting individuals involved in illegal activities on the Dark Web is a complex task, often requiring sophisticated techniques, collaboration between international agencies, and the development of advanced technologies.

In the next section, we will explore the different types of Dark Web marketplaces and their evolution over time, shedding light on the goods, services, and impact they have on society.

The Tor network and other Dark Web access methods

Accessing the Dark Web is not as simple as typing a URL into a web browser. To navigate this hidden part of the internet, users rely on specialized tools and networks designed to provide anonymity and security. One such network is the Tor network, which stands for "The Onion Router." In this section, we will explore the Tor network and other access methods used to interact with Dark Web markets.

The Tor network

The Tor network is a decentralized network of volunteer-operated servers, known as nodes or relays, that allow users to browse the internet anonymously. The network redirects internet traffic through a series of randomly selected relays before reaching its destination. Each relay only knows the previous and next hop in the network, ensuring that no single relay can trace the entire network path.

How the Tor network works

To understand how the Tor network provides anonymity, let's look at the steps involved in establishing a connection:

1. **Client-side setup:** Users must install Tor software, such as the Tor Browser, on their devices. The Tor Browser is a modified version of Mozilla Firefox that routes all internet traffic through the Tor network.

2. **Creating a circuit:** When a user wants to access a website, the Tor software establishes a circuit by selecting a series of relays. Each relay in the circuit encrypts the data it receives and forwards it to the next relay.

3. **Data transmission:** The client's data is broken into encrypted chunks, or layers, like the layers of an onion. Each relay decrypts only the outermost layer, revealing the address of the next relay in the circuit. This process ensures that no single relay can see both the source and destination of the data.

4. **Exit relay:** The final relay in the circuit, known as the exit relay, decrypts the final layer of encryption and sends the data to the destination website. It appears as if the data is originating from the exit relay rather than the client, enhancing anonymity.

5. **Response retrieval:** The response from the website follows the same circuit back through the network, ensuring that the entire connection remains anonymous.

Advantages of using the Tor network

The Tor network offers several notable advantages for accessing the Dark Web:

- **Anonymity:** By routing internet traffic through multiple relays, the Tor network makes it difficult to trace the origin and destination of data, providing users with a higher level of anonymity than traditional internet browsing.

- **Censorship resistance:** The decentralized nature of the Tor network makes it resistant to censorship and surveillance. It allows users to bypass internet restrictions imposed by certain governments or organizations.

- **Secure communication:** The Tor network provides encryption between relays, ensuring that data remains secure and protected from eavesdropping or tampering.

Other Dark Web access methods

While the Tor network is the most well-known and widely used method for accessing the Dark Web, there are alternative access methods available:

- **I2P (Invisible Internet Project):** Similar to the Tor network, I2P is an encrypted overlay network that allows users to access the Dark Web anonymously. It uses a distributed peer-to-peer architecture with multiple encrypted tunnels to transmit data securely.

- **Freenet:** Freenet is another decentralized network that enables users to share information and access the Dark Web anonymously. It utilizes a distributed data store that replicates and encrypts content across the network, providing high levels of privacy and censorship resistance.

- **ZeroNet:** ZeroNet is a more recent addition to the Dark Web access methods. It uses a combination of Bitcoin cryptography and BitTorrent technology to create a decentralized, uncensorable network. Websites and content on ZeroNet are served via peer-to-peer connections, making them highly resilient to takedowns.

Choosing the right access method for Dark Web markets

When accessing Dark Web markets, the choice of the access method depends on various factors, such as the level of anonymity desired, the reliability of the network, and the specific market being accessed. While the Tor network is the most established and widely used, exploring alternative access methods can provide additional options for users seeking different degrees of privacy and security.

Caveats and precautions

While the Tor network and other Dark Web access methods provide anonymity and security, it is important to note some caveats and take precautions:

- **Endpoint security:** While the Tor network may protect the user's identity during browsing, it does not protect against malware, phishing attacks, or exploits targeting the user's device. Users should employ good security practices, such as using up-to-date antivirus software and being cautious of downloading files from unknown sources.

- **Trustworthiness of marketplaces:** Although accessing Dark Web markets through the Tor network may provide anonymity, it does not guarantee the trustworthiness of the marketplaces themselves. Users should exercise caution and only engage in transactions on reputable and trusted platforms.

- **Legal implications:** Accessing Dark Web markets may expose users to illegal activities and potentially violate local and international laws. It is essential to understand the legal implications and risks associated with engaging in Dark Web transactions.

Summary

The Tor network and other Dark Web access methods play a crucial role in allowing users to explore the hidden corners of the internet. With its decentralized nature and layered encryption, the Tor network provides users with anonymity and security. Alternative access methods like I2P, Freenet, and ZeroNet offer additional options for users seeking different degrees of privacy and censorship resistance. However, it is important to exercise caution, maintain endpoint security, and be aware of the legal implications when accessing Dark Web markets. In the next section, we will delve into the different types of Dark Web markets and the evolution of their operations.

Understanding the different layers of the Dark Web

The Dark Web is a complex network that operates within the hidden corners of the internet. It is important to understand the different layers that make up this hidden world in order to grasp its structure and functionality. In this section, we will explore the various layers of the Dark Web, providing insights into its intricate architecture.

The Surface Web

Before delving into the layers of the Dark Web, it is essential to understand its distinction from the Surface Web. The Surface Web refers to the portion of the internet that is readily accessible and indexed by search engines like Google, Bing, and Yahoo. This includes websites, web applications, and other online content that can be easily found through traditional web browsers.

The Surface Web is the part of the internet that most people are familiar with and use on a daily basis. It encompasses a wide range of legitimate websites, including social media platforms, news sites, online shopping portals, and more. It is estimated that the Surface Web represents only a small fraction of the entire internet, with the majority of the network residing in the depths of the Dark Web.

The Deep Web

The Deep Web refers to the vast portion of the internet that is not accessible through traditional search engines and requires specific authorization or knowledge to access. Unlike the Dark Web, the Deep Web is not inherently illegal or nefarious. It consists of databases, private websites, academic resources, government intranets, and other secure online platforms.

A significant portion of the Deep Web is comprised of password-protected sites, online banking systems, email platforms, and other secure channels where users require login credentials to access their accounts. The content within the Deep Web is generally not indexed by search engines, making it more challenging to discover and navigate.

The Dark Web

Beneath the Deep Web lies the enigmatic realm of the Dark Web. The Dark Web is a part of the internet that is intentionally concealed and requires specific software, such as Tor (The Onion Router), to access. It is characterized by anonymity, encrypted communication, and the facilitation of illegal activities.

The Dark Web consists of hidden websites and online marketplaces that trade in illicit goods and services, including drugs, weapons, stolen data, counterfeit goods, and hacking tools. These websites typically have complex URLs and are not indexed by search engines, making them difficult to discover without prior knowledge.

Onion Routing and Layers

At the core of the Dark Web's architecture is a network of computers that employ a technique called onion routing to ensure anonymity and security. Onion routing involves encrypting and redirecting internet traffic through a series of volunteer-operated servers known as Tor relays. This process makes it nearly impossible to trace the origin and destination of internet traffic, providing a high level of privacy.

The concept of layers is integral to understanding the architecture of the Dark Web. Each layer in the Tor network represents a different level of encryption and redirection, making it increasingly challenging to track users' activities. As data passes through each layer, a layer of encryption is peeled off, revealing the next destination. The final layer is stripped off at the exit node, where the data is sent to its intended recipient.

In this layered approach, the Dark Web achieves a remarkable level of anonymity, ensuring that transactions and communications are shielded from surveillance and censorship. However, this anonymity also provides a conducive environment for illegal activities, as it becomes difficult for law enforcement agencies to identify and prosecute criminals operating within the Dark Web.

Challenges and Limitations

Understanding the different layers of the Dark Web is crucial for comprehending the complexities associated with combating cybercrime in this hidden landscape. However, it is important to acknowledge that this knowledge alone is not sufficient to overcome the challenges posed by the Dark Web.

Law enforcement agencies face significant obstacles when trying to infiltrate and dismantle Dark Web marketplaces. The extensive use of encryption, anonymous communication tools, and cryptocurrencies makes it difficult to trace transactions and identify individuals involved in illegal activities. Furthermore, the global nature of the Dark Web presents jurisdictional challenges, as criminals can operate across borders, evading prosecution.

Moreover, the layered structure of the Dark Web makes it challenging to monitor and track malicious activities effectively. While law enforcement agencies and cybersecurity professionals employ various techniques and technologies to identify and combat cybercrime, the constantly evolving nature of the Dark Web requires constant adaptation and innovation.

In the next sections, we will explore the various participants and components of the Dark Web market ecosystem, shedding light on their roles and the strategies employed in the ongoing fight against Dark Web markets.

Types of Dark Web Markets

Overview of different Dark Web marketplaces

Dark Web marketplaces have emerged as a thriving underworld economy, providing a platform for the buying and selling of illegal goods and services. These markets operate in hidden corners of the internet, where anonymity and privacy are paramount. In this section, we will provide an overview of different Dark Web marketplaces, shedding light on their unique features and the products they offer.

Silk Road: The pioneer

One of the most notorious Dark Web marketplaces in history is Silk Road. Launched in 2011 by Ross Ulbricht, also known as Dread Pirate Roberts, Silk

Road gained popularity for its focus on drug trade. It offered a wide range of illegal narcotics, from marijuana to heroin, allowing buyers and sellers to transact using Bitcoin. Silk Road pioneered the use of escrow services, providing a level of trust and security.

Despite its notoriety, Silk Road was shut down in 2013 by law enforcement agencies, who arrested Ulbricht and seized the website. However, its downfall did not mark the end of Dark Web marketplaces. Instead, it catalyzed the evolution and proliferation of other platforms.

AlphaBay: The successor

After the demise of Silk Road, a new marketplace called AlphaBay emerged as its main successor. AlphaBay quickly gained popularity and became the largest Dark Web marketplace at its peak. It offered not only drugs but also a wide range of other illicit goods and services, including stolen data, counterfeit documents, hacking tools, and weapons.

What set AlphaBay apart was its intuitive user interface, advanced search functionalities, and an extensive network of reputable sellers. These features allowed buyers to navigate the marketplace efficiently and find what they were looking for. Additionally, AlphaBay introduced a multi-signature escrow system, enhancing security and reducing the risk of scams.

In 2017, the downfall of AlphaBay came as a result of a joint operation by international law enforcement agencies. The marketplace was seized, and its alleged operator, Alexandre Cazes, was arrested. However, the shutdown of AlphaBay did not mark the end of Dark Web marketplaces. It only fueled the existence and growth of other platforms.

Dream Market: The resilient

Dream Market is another prominent Dark Web marketplace that emerged as a successor to Silk Road. Since its launch in 2013, Dream Market has been one of the most resilient marketplaces, surviving various takedown attempts and law enforcement operations.

Dream Market offers a broad range of illegal products, including drugs, stolen data, counterfeit items, and hacking tools. It gained a reputation for its high level of security, user-friendly interface, and strong community presence. Dream Market utilizes an escrow system to ensure secure transactions, with multisig functionality available.

While Dream Market has weathered numerous storms, it eventually succumbed to the pressure of law enforcement. In 2019, it announced its decision to shut down, citing security concerns and mounting pressure. However, the closure of Dream Market does not imply the end of Dark Web marketplaces, as new platforms continue to emerge.

Evolution and diversification

The landscape of Dark Web marketplaces is constantly evolving, with new platforms emerging and existing ones adapting to counter measures by law enforcement. As one marketplace shuts down, another rises to take its place, leading to a cycle of innovation and change.

Beyond the pioneers and successors, several other marketplaces have emerged, each with its own unique features and offerings. Some notable examples include Wall Street Market, Empire Market, and Berlusconi Market. These marketplaces specialize in various illegal goods and services, catering to the diverse needs of their customers.

It is worth noting that Dark Web marketplaces are not limited to the buying and selling of illegal products. Some platforms focus on providing forums for hackers to exchange information and share techniques, while others offer services such as hacking, malware development, and DDoS attacks as a form of cybercrime-as-a-service.

The ever-evolving nature of Dark Web marketplaces poses significant challenges to law enforcement agencies and cybersecurity professionals. As marketplaces continue to diversify and adapt, it is crucial for efforts to combat these illicit platforms to keep pace with the changing landscape.

Summary

In this section, we provided an overview of different Dark Web marketplaces. We explored the pioneering Silk Road, the successor AlphaBay, the resilient Dream Market, and the evolving landscape of marketplaces. Despite the crackdown on marketplaces by law enforcement, new platforms continue to emerge, demonstrating the persistent nature of the Dark Web economy. Understanding the dynamics and unique features of these marketplaces is critical in the fight against cybercrime and the protection of online security.

The evolution of Dark Web marketplaces

Dark Web marketplaces have undergone significant evolution since their inception, adapting to changes in technology, law enforcement efforts, and the demands of their users. Understanding this evolution is crucial in comprehending the current state of Dark Web markets and predicting their future trajectory.

The early days of Dark Web marketplaces can be traced back to the launch of Silk Road in 2011. Silk Road was the first prominent online marketplace that operated on the Dark Web, allowing users to buy and sell various illicit goods and services anonymously. Its founder, Ross Ulbricht, created a platform that utilized the Tor network, enabling users to access the site and conduct transactions without revealing their identity or location.

Silk Road quickly gained popularity and became synonymous with Dark Web markets. It facilitated the exchange of a wide range of illegal products, primarily drugs. This success spurred the development of numerous similar marketplaces, such as AlphaBay, Dream Market, and Hansa Market, which further expanded the reach and variety of goods available on the Dark Web.

As Dark Web marketplaces gained traction, law enforcement agencies began to take notice and initiated efforts to dismantle these illicit platforms. The takedown of Silk Road in 2013 marked a significant victory for law enforcement, but it also sparked the evolution of Dark Web marketplaces.

In response to the Silk Road seizure, the Dark Web market ecosystem adapted by implementing new strategies to enhance security, privacy, and resilience. Marketplaces started adopting decentralized infrastructure, utilizing features like multi-signature escrow systems and cryptography to ensure safer transactions and protect users' identities. The previously centralized model of Silk Road gave way to a more distributed and resilient network of marketplaces, making it increasingly challenging for law enforcement to target specific platforms.

However, as law enforcement crackdowns intensified, marketplaces faced a constant battle to maintain trust and security. Frequent exit scams, where marketplace administrators suddenly shut down their platforms and absconded with users' funds, eroded trust among buyers and sellers. To counter these issues and improve reliability, marketplaces began introducing reputation and feedback systems, allowing users to rate and review sellers based on their experiences. These systems played a vital role in establishing trust within the Dark Web market community and weeding out unreliable vendors.

The evolution of Dark Web marketplaces also saw the expansion of their product catalog beyond drugs. While drugs remain a significant portion of the goods traded, marketplaces started offering a wider range of illicit products, including counterfeit documents, stolen data, hacking tools, firearms, and even malware-as-a-service. This diversification catered to the demands of a growing user base seeking various illegal goods and services.

Furthermore, the evolution of Dark Web marketplaces has been intertwined with advancements in cryptocurrencies. Originally, Bitcoin was the primary payment method on these platforms, as it provided a pseudo-anonymous means of conducting transactions. However, the increasing scrutiny from law enforcement led to the emergence of privacy-focused cryptocurrencies like Monero and Zcash. These privacy-enhanced cryptocurrencies gained traction and became widely accepted on Dark Web markets, further solidifying the connection between the Dark Web and the cryptocurrency ecosystem.

Looking forward, the evolution of Dark Web marketplaces is expected to continue. As law enforcement techniques improve, marketplaces will likely adopt more sophisticated security measures, making it even harder for authorities to infiltrate and dismantle these platforms. Additionally, technological advancements such as blockchain-based marketplaces and decentralized finance may shape the future landscape of Dark Web markets, introducing new challenges for law enforcement and cybersecurity professionals.

In conclusion, Dark Web marketplaces have come a long way since the early days of Silk Road. The evolution of these illicit platforms has been influenced by law enforcement actions, user demands, and technological advancements. Understanding this evolution is key to combating the threats posed by Dark Web markets and staying ahead in the fight against cybercrime.

Popular illegal goods and services on Dark Web markets

Dark Web markets have gained notoriety for hosting a wide range of illegal goods and services. These hidden online marketplaces, shielded by layers of encryption and anonymity, provide platforms for the buying and selling of illicit and forbidden items.

1. Drugs: One of the most prevalent and profitable categories on Dark Web markets is the sale of drugs. These online platforms have transformed the drug trade by enabling anonymous transactions and global distribution. A variety of drugs, including synthetic narcotics, prescription medications, and recreational substances like cocaine and marijuana, can be found on these marketplaces. The availability of drugs on Dark Web markets has allowed users to purchase substances without the risk associated with traditional street dealing. This has fueled concerns among law enforcement and governments worldwide due to the

challenges they face in regulating and controlling the drug trade in this hidden realm.

2. Weapons and firearms: Dark Web markets also serve as hubs for the sale of illegal firearms and weaponry. Buyers can access an assortment of firearms, ammunition, explosives, and other dangerous weapons. The anonymity provided by these platforms makes it difficult for law enforcement agencies to track and seize these illicit items. The sale of weapons on Dark Web markets poses significant risks, as it enables individuals with malicious intent to access deadly weapons easily.

3. Stolen personal information: Dark Web markets have become a hotbed for the illicit trade of stolen personal information, such as credit card details, social security numbers, and login credentials. Cybercriminals can sell and purchase this valuable data to carry out identity theft, financial fraud, and other nefarious activities. Such trade in stolen personal information not only compromises the security and privacy of individuals but also has severe financial consequences for victims.

4. Hacking tools and services: The Dark Web is teeming with listings for hacking tools, exploits, and hacking services. Cybercriminals and technology enthusiasts looking to gain unauthorized access to systems can find a range of specialized software, malware, and hacking tutorials. These tools enable the infiltration of computer networks, theft of sensitive information, ransomware attacks, and other cybercrimes. The availability of such resources on Dark Web markets poses a significant threat to cybersecurity and highlights the need for enhanced defenses against hacking attempts.

5. Counterfeit goods: Dark Web markets also offer a platform for the sale of counterfeit products, including luxury items, electronics, passports, and currency. Sellers use these platforms to distribute fake versions of popular brands, taking advantage of the anonymity provided to evade enforcement authorities. The trade in counterfeit goods not only hurts legitimate businesses but can also put consumers at risk, as these knock-off products may be of inferior quality and compromise health and safety standards.

It is important to note that the illegal goods and services mentioned here are just a fraction of the activities present on Dark Web markets. Other items and services found on these platforms range from stolen artworks and endangered wildlife products to human trafficking and hitman-for-hire services. The Dark Web market ecosystem is constantly evolving, adapting to law enforcement efforts, and introducing new items that cater to the demands of its user base.

It is crucial to understand the gravity of the illegal activities on Dark Web markets and the potential implications they hold for society. Law enforcement agencies, cybersecurity professionals, and legislative bodies are continuously working towards combating and mitigating the adverse effects of these illicit markets. By understanding the nature of these illegal goods and services, we can better comprehend the challenges faced in the fight against cybercrime and the importance of innovative strategies and global collaboration.

Examples of famous Dark Web marketplaces

In this section, we will explore some of the most well-known Dark Web marketplaces that have gained significant attention for their illicit activities. These marketplaces have facilitated the sale of illegal goods and services, providing a platform for anonymous transactions and attracting a wide range of buyers and sellers.

1. **Silk Road:** Silk Road is perhaps the most infamous Dark Web marketplace, launched in 2011 by Ross Ulbricht, also known as the "Dread Pirate Roberts." It gained popularity for its user-friendly interface and reputation system, which allowed buyers and sellers to rate each other. Silk Road primarily focused on selling drugs, including cocaine, MDMA, and marijuana. However, it was eventually shut down in 2013 by law enforcement, leading to the arrest and conviction of Ulbricht.

2. **AlphaBay:** AlphaBay emerged as one of the largest Dark Web marketplaces after the downfall of Silk Road. It offered a wide range of illegal goods and services, including drugs, weapons, stolen data, counterfeit documents, hacking tools, and more. AlphaBay became notorious for its robust escrow system, allowing buyers to have confidence in their transactions. However, in 2017, AlphaBay was seized and taken down by law enforcement agencies.

3. **Dream Market:** Dream Market was established in 2013 and quickly became one of the most popular Dark Web marketplaces. It provided a platform for the sale of drugs, counterfeit money, firearms, stolen data, and hacking services. Dream Market had a user-friendly interface and implemented several security measures to protect the identities of buyers and sellers, including relying heavily on the Tor network for anonymity. However, in 2019, Dream Market voluntarily shut down operations, leaving a void in the Dark Web marketplace landscape.

4. **Wall Street Market:** Wall Street Market gained prominence as a Dark Web marketplace specializing in the sale of narcotics, counterfeit documents, hacking tools, and stolen data. It gained popularity due to its multi-language support and user-friendly interface. Additionally, Wall Street Market introduced an innovative feature called "dead drops," enabling sellers to hide physical packages in specific locations for buyers to collect anonymously. However, in 2019, Wall Street

Market was seized by law enforcement agencies from Germany, the United States, and the Netherlands.

5. **Empire Market:** Empire Market is currently one of the largest and most active Dark Web marketplaces. It offers a plethora of illegal goods and services, ranging from drugs and counterfeit money to stolen data and hacking tools. Empire Market operates on the Tor network and implements several security measures, such as mandatory two-factor authentication for user accounts. It has managed to thrive despite multiple law enforcement takedown attempts, showcasing the resilience of Dark Web marketplaces.

These examples only scratch the surface of the numerous Dark Web marketplaces that have emerged over the years. Each marketplace has developed its own unique characteristics, customer base, and risks. It is important to note that accessing and participating in these marketplaces is illegal and highly dangerous. Law enforcement agencies continue to combat these marketplaces and their participants, aiming to disrupt the flow of illegal goods and services.

Key Takeaways

- Silk Road, AlphaBay, Dream Market, Wall Street Market, and Empire Market are some of the most notable Dark Web marketplaces. - These marketplaces facilitated the sale of drugs, counterfeit goods, weapons, hacking tools, and more. - Law enforcement agencies have successfully shut down several of these marketplaces, leading to the arrest and conviction of key individuals involved. - Dark Web marketplaces continue to evolve and thrive, despite ongoing efforts to combat them. - It is crucial to recognize the illegal nature of these marketplaces and the severe risks associated with their use.

The impact of Dark Web markets on society

Dark Web markets have had a profound impact on society, influencing various aspects of our lives. From the economy to public safety, the presence of these underground marketplaces has raised significant concerns and challenges for individuals, communities, and governments. In this section, we will explore the far-reaching effects of Dark Web markets and delve into the implications they have on society.

Economic impact

The economic impact of Dark Web markets is twofold: on one hand, they contribute to the growth of an illegal economy, and on the other hand, they have broader implications for the legal marketplace.

Firstly, Dark Web markets provide a platform for the sale of illegal goods and services, such as drugs, counterfeit documents, stolen data, and hacking tools. These activities generate significant revenue, fueling a shadow economy that can undermine legitimate businesses. The thriving drug trade on Dark Web markets, for example, has disrupted traditional drug distribution networks and caused significant financial losses for law enforcement agencies.

Moreover, the availability of cheap and easily accessible drugs on Dark Web markets has led to increased drug consumption, addiction rates, and associated societal costs. This has strained healthcare systems, law enforcement resources, and rehabilitation centers, having a direct impact on public budgets.

Furthermore, Dark Web markets have indirect economic consequences. Due to the anonymity and convenience they offer, some individuals may choose to purchase goods and services on these platforms rather than through legal means. This can harm legitimate businesses and reduce tax revenue for governments, affecting economic growth and stability.

Social impact

The social impact of Dark Web markets is complex and multifaceted. While they have provided certain individuals with access to goods and services they might not otherwise be able to obtain, their presence has also led to numerous negative consequences.

One significant social impact is the increase in cybercrime. Dark Web markets offer a range of cybercrime-as-a-service offerings, enabling individuals with limited technical expertise to engage in illegal activities such as hacking, identity theft, and ransomware attacks. This has resulted in a surge in cybercrime incidents, posing risks to individuals, businesses, and even national security.

Moreover, Dark Web markets have contributed to the erosion of trust within communities. The anonymity and lack of accountability on these platforms make it easier for scammers, fraudsters, and unscrupulous sellers to operate. As a result, consumers are more wary and skeptical, making it challenging for legitimate businesses to build trust and maintain customer loyalty.

The availability of illegal drugs and other harmful substances on Dark Web markets has also had a devastating impact on public health. The anonymity of online drug purchases has made it easier for individuals to acquire highly addictive substances without fear of legal consequences. This has contributed to the opioid crisis, spreading addiction and causing numerous overdose-related deaths.

Legal and law enforcement impact

The presence of Dark Web markets has presented significant challenges for law enforcement and legal systems worldwide. These underground platforms have become breeding grounds for criminal activities that transcend borders, necessitating international cooperation and legal frameworks to combat them effectively.

One of the main challenges for law enforcement is the difficulty in identifying and apprehending individuals involved in Dark Web markets. The use of encryption, cryptocurrencies, and anonymization tools makes it challenging to trace transactions and link them to real-world identities. This has resulted in a cat-and-mouse game between law enforcement agencies and market participants, with varying degrees of success in apprehending high-profile criminals.

The fight against Dark Web markets has also raised legal and ethical questions surrounding privacy rights and surveillance. Balancing the need for public safety and security with individual privacy poses significant challenges. The use of advanced monitoring technologies on the Dark Web raises concerns about the scope and legality of surveillance practices.

Furthermore, the increasing prevalence of Dark Web markets has prompted governments to revisit existing legislation and develop new strategies to combat online crime. This includes enacting laws that focus on the investigation and prosecution of cybercriminals, as well as providing law enforcement agencies with the necessary tools and resources to keep up with the evolving landscape of illicit online activities.

Conclusion

Dark Web markets have undoubtedly had a profound and far-reaching impact on society. Their influence spans economic, social, legal, and law enforcement domains, shaping the way businesses operate, individuals interact, and governments combat cybercrime. While these markets have provided some individuals with access to goods and services they need, they have also facilitated the growth of illegal activities, increased cybercrime rates, and strained public resources. The fight against Dark Web markets requires collaborative efforts, technological advancements, and ethical considerations to address the risks and challenges they pose to our society.

The Economic Model of Dark Web Markets

How Dark Web markets operate

Dark Web markets provide an online platform for the buying and selling of illegal goods, services, and information. These markets operate on the principles of anonymity, decentralization, and encryption, ensuring a high level of privacy for their users. Understanding how Dark Web markets operate is essential for comprehending the dynamics of illicit online activities and the challenges they pose to law enforcement agencies.

At the core of Dark Web markets is the use of Tor (The Onion Router) network, a network overlay that enables anonymous communication over the internet. The Tor network functions by routing internet traffic through a series of volunteer-operated servers, also known as nodes, to conceal the user's identity and location. This allows users to access Dark Web marketplaces while maintaining their anonymity.

To access a Dark Web market, users typically need a Tor-enabled browser, such as the Tor Browser, that routes their internet traffic through the Tor network. Once connected, users can access various Dark Web marketplaces that are primarily hosted on hidden services within the Tor network. These hidden services use cryptographic keys to establish a secure and untraceable connection between buyers and sellers.

Dark Web markets operate similarly to traditional e-commerce platforms, with sellers creating listings for their products or services and buyers browsing and purchasing these items. However, there are some key differences that set Dark Web markets apart:

1. Anonymity: Dark Web marketplaces prioritize anonymity by allowing users to create pseudonymous accounts. These accounts do not require personal identification or verification, ensuring user privacy.

2. Cryptocurrency transactions: Dark Web markets heavily rely on cryptocurrencies like Bitcoin for transactions. Cryptocurrencies offer a higher level of anonymity and security compared to traditional payment methods, making them the preferred choice for Dark Web transactions.

3. Escrow systems: Dark Web markets often incorporate escrow systems to facilitate secure transactions. These systems hold the buyer's funds in escrow until the buyer receives the purchased item and confirms its satisfactory condition. This helps to mitigate scams and build trust within the marketplace.

4. Feedback and rating systems: Similar to mainstream e-commerce platforms, Dark Web markets utilize feedback and rating systems to provide a measure of trust

and reputation for both buyers and sellers. Positive feedback indicates a reliable and trustworthy user, while negative feedback raises concerns about reliability.

5. Communication channels: Dark Web markets offer encrypted instant messaging features to facilitate communication between buyers and sellers. These communication channels are designed to maintain the privacy of the parties involved and avoid potential detection by law enforcement.

The revenue model of Dark Web markets mainly revolves around collecting a percentage of the transaction fees from the sellers, with some markets also charging fees for premium services. The profit potential of Dark Web markets depends on various factors, including the number of active users, the types of goods and services available, the market's reputation, and the effectiveness of its security measures.

Dark Web markets face several challenges in their operations. These challenges include maintaining security and trust within the marketplace, avoiding scams and frauds, dealing with law enforcement infiltration attempts, and addressing potential vulnerabilities in the encryption and anonymity mechanisms.

It is worth noting that not all activities on Dark Web markets are illegal. Some users seek to access the Dark Web for legitimate purposes such as circumventing censorship or advocating for free speech. However, due to the illicit nature of many transactions, Dark Web markets have gained a negative reputation as hubs for illegal activities.

Overall, understanding the operational aspects of Dark Web markets is crucial for comprehending the strategies employed by cybercriminals, law enforcement's efforts to combat them, and the potential impact on society.

The role of cryptocurrency in Dark Web transactions

Cryptocurrencies, such as Bitcoin, play a crucial role in facilitating transactions on the Dark Web. The decentralized and pseudonymous nature of cryptocurrencies makes them an ideal medium of exchange for illegal goods and services. In this section, we will explore the reasons why cryptocurrencies are widely used on Dark Web markets, the advantages they offer, and the challenges they present to law enforcement agencies.

Anonymity and privacy

One of the key reasons why cryptocurrencies are favored in Dark Web transactions is their ability to provide a certain level of anonymity and privacy. Unlike traditional financial systems where transactions are linked to real-world identities, cryptocurrencies allow users to conduct transactions without revealing their true identities. Instead, transactions are associated with unique cryptographic addresses, which can be created and discarded easily.

This level of anonymity makes it difficult for law enforcement agencies to trace the flow of funds and identify the parties involved in Dark Web transactions. While blockchain technology, which underlies cryptocurrencies, provides a transparent record of all transactions, it does not reveal the real-world identities of the users. This makes it challenging for investigators to pinpoint the individuals behind illicit activities on the Dark Web.

Ease of global transactions

Another advantage of cryptocurrencies in Dark Web transactions is their ability to facilitate seamless cross-border transactions. Traditional financial systems impose various restrictions and regulations on cross-border money transfers, making it difficult for illegal transactions to occur without raising suspicions. However, cryptocurrencies operate on a global scale without the need for intermediaries such as banks or financial institutions.

Bitcoin, the most widely used cryptocurrency on the Dark Web, allows users to send and receive funds instantly, regardless of geographical boundaries. This enables Dark Web market participants to conduct transactions with buyers and sellers from around the world, creating a truly global marketplace for illegal goods and services.

Secure and irreversible transactions

Cryptocurrencies provide a high level of security for Dark Web transactions. Every transaction is secured through cryptography, making it nearly impossible for hackers or other malicious actors to alter or reverse the transaction details. Once a transaction is recorded on the blockchain, it becomes part of a permanent and unchangeable record.

This feature eliminates the risk of chargebacks or fraudulent claims, providing a sense of trust and security to both buyers and sellers on Dark Web markets. Sellers can be confident that once a payment is received, it cannot be reversed, reducing the risk of fraud. Buyers, on the other hand, can trust that their funds will only be released to the seller once the agreed-upon goods or services have been delivered.

Challenges for law enforcement

While cryptocurrencies offer advantages for Dark Web transactions, they also pose significant challenges for law enforcement agencies. The pseudonymous nature of cryptocurrencies makes it difficult to trace the flow of funds and identify the individuals involved in illicit activities. Investigators often face challenges in connecting cryptocurrency addresses to real-world identities.

Additionally, the global and decentralized nature of cryptocurrencies complicates the jurisdictional reach of law enforcement. Unlike traditional financial systems that are regulated by specific countries, cryptocurrencies operate across borders and are not subject to the same level of regulation. This makes it challenging for law enforcement agencies to coordinate efforts and effectively combat Dark Web market activities.

Furthermore, the use of cryptocurrencies in Dark Web transactions has led to the development of various privacy-enhancing technologies, further obfuscating the identities of the parties involved. Mixing services, tumblers, and other techniques are often employed to break the transaction trail, making it more challenging for investigators to trace the funds.

In conclusion, cryptocurrencies have become the preferred medium of exchange on Dark Web markets due to their anonymity, global accessibility, and security features. While they provide benefits to Dark Web market participants, their decentralized and pseudonymous nature presents challenges for law enforcement. As cryptocurrencies continue to evolve, it is crucial for law enforcement agencies to stay abreast of technological advancements and adopt innovative strategies to combat illicit activities on the Dark Web.

Challenges of conducting business on Dark Web markets

Operating a business on Dark Web markets presents unique challenges and risks that are different from traditional brick-and-mortar establishments or even online businesses on the Surface Web. In this section, we will explore some of the major challenges faced by individuals conducting business on Dark Web markets.

1. Trust and Credibility

Establishing trust and credibility is crucial for any business, but it becomes even more challenging on Dark Web markets. Buyers and sellers cannot rely on physical storefronts, face-to-face interactions, or conventional methods of building trust. Instead, they need to rely on alternative mechanisms such as reputation systems and feedback ratings to assess the trustworthiness of potential business partners.

However, building and maintaining trust on Dark Web markets can be difficult due to the anonymity and pseudonymity of users. Users may operate under multiple pseudonyms or have the ability to create fake accounts to manipulate their rating or reputation. This creates uncertainty and skepticism among buyers, making it crucial for sellers to establish a strong and reliable reputation to attract customers.

Example: A seller operating on a Dark Web marketplace selling counterfeit luxury goods needs to establish credibility by consistently delivering high-quality products and maintaining positive feedback from buyers. This can be challenging due to the mistrust associated with such marketplaces.

2. Security and Anonymity

Dark Web markets are known for their emphasis on security and anonymity. While this is beneficial for buyers and sellers seeking to protect their identities and transactions, it also poses challenges for conducting business.

Sellers need to take extra precautions to maintain their anonymity to avoid being traced back to illegal activities or facing legal repercussions. This involves using encryption tools, anonymizing techniques, and secure communication channels to protect their identity and the information they share with buyers.

Conversely, buyers face the challenge of ensuring that they are dealing with genuine sellers and not falling victim to scams or fraud. The inherent anonymity of Dark Web markets makes it easier for malicious actors to deceive buyers, resulting in financial loss or receiving substandard goods or services.

Example: A buyer interested in purchasing illegal drugs on a Dark Web marketplace needs to navigate through the risks of counterfeit products, phishing scams, or purchasing from undercover law enforcement officials. Ensuring anonymity and security while making transactions becomes a crucial challenge in this scenario.

3. Financial Transactions

Dark Web markets predominantly utilize cryptocurrencies as the primary mode of payment. While cryptocurrencies offer a certain degree of anonymity and convenience, they also introduce challenges for conducting business.

The fluctuating value of cryptocurrencies poses a risk to sellers, who need to consider the volatility of prices and the potential impact on their revenues. Additionally, the lack of regulation and oversight in cryptocurrency transactions can make it difficult for sellers to resolve disputes or recover funds in case of fraudulent activities.

For buyers, the challenge lies in understanding and acquiring cryptocurrencies to make purchases. The complexities associated with obtaining and using cryptocurrencies can discourage potential customers or limit their ability to engage in transactions. Moreover, the risk of being scammed or not receiving the purchased goods or services further complicates the financial aspect of conducting business on Dark Web markets.

Example: A seller offering illegal software on a Dark Web marketplace needs to overcome the challenges of cryptocurrency volatility and ensure that buyers understand how to make secure transactions using digital currencies.

4. Competition and Innovation

Dark Web markets are a highly competitive environment, with numerous sellers vying for the attention and business of buyers. The constant demand for new and unique offerings drives sellers to innovate and find ways to differentiate themselves.

However, the challenge lies in maintaining a competitive edge without compromising security or attracting unwanted attention from law enforcement agencies. Sellers need to continuously adapt their products, pricing strategies, or customer service to stay ahead of competitors while navigating the inherent risks associated with operating in the Dark Web ecosystem.

Furthermore, the presence of law enforcement agencies actively targeting Dark Web marketplaces creates an additional challenge for sellers. They need to be cautious about potential infiltration attempts and continuously update their security measures to protect their businesses.

Example: A seller specializing in weapons on a Dark Web marketplace needs to constantly innovate and expand their product offerings while ensuring strict adherence to security protocols to stay competitive without attracting unwanted attention.

5. Branding and Marketing

Establishing a brand and marketing products or services on Dark Web markets can be challenging due to the limited options available compared to traditional marketing channels. Sellers cannot rely on conventional advertising methods or platforms to build brand awareness or attract customers.

Instead, sellers need to leverage alternative marketing strategies within the constraints of the Dark Web ecosystem. This may involve utilizing forum threads, social media platforms specifically tailored for Dark Web communities, or word-of-mouth recommendations within closed networks.

Building a distinctive brand identity and effectively reaching the target audience amidst the vast competition on Dark Web markets can be an ongoing challenge for sellers, requiring creative and unconventional approaches.

Example: A seller offering counterfeit passports on a Dark Web marketplace needs to develop a brand and marketing strategy targeting individuals seeking identity fraud opportunities. They may leverage forums discussing illegal activities and establish trust within these communities to attract potential customers.

In conclusion, conducting business on Dark Web markets presents unique challenges ranging from establishing trust and credibility to ensuring security and anonymity. Overcoming these challenges requires sellers to adapt their strategies, innovate within legal boundaries, and navigate the complexities of the Dark Web ecosystem.

Revenue generation and profitability of Dark Web marketplaces

Dark Web marketplaces generate revenue through various means, primarily through the sale of illegal goods and services facilitated by the anonymity and security provided by the Dark Web. The profitability of these marketplaces is influenced by several factors, including the demand for illegal products, competition among sellers, operational costs, and payment mechanisms.

Demand for illegal goods and services

The demand for illegal goods and services on Dark Web marketplaces is a significant driver of revenue generation. Dark Web marketplaces offer a range of products such as drugs, weapons, counterfeit documents, hacking tools, and stolen data. These goods and services cater to a diverse clientele seeking anonymity and access to illicit products. The underground nature of Dark Web marketplaces creates a niche market where buyers and sellers can conduct transactions discreetly.

The demand for drugs is particularly lucrative on Dark Web marketplaces. The availability of a wide variety of drugs, including opioids, stimulants, and synthetic drugs, attracts a large customer base. The demand for other illegal goods and services, such as stolen credit card information, hacking services, and counterfeit documents, also contributes significantly to the revenue generated by Dark Web marketplaces.

Competition among sellers

The profitability of Dark Web marketplaces is influenced by intense competition among sellers. As the number of sellers offering similar products increases, prices may become more competitive, leading to lower profit margins. Sellers often strive to differentiate themselves through quality, reputation, and customer service to attract and retain buyers. Reputation systems and feedback mechanisms play a crucial role in establishing credibility and trust among buyers, enabling sellers to maintain a steady stream of customers and command higher prices.

Operational costs

Running a Dark Web marketplace incurs several operational costs that impact profitability. These costs include maintaining the infrastructure, managing server expenses, development and maintenance of the marketplace platform, and ensuring reliable and secure communication channels. Dark Web marketplaces may also face additional expenses associated with protecting the anonymity of buyers and sellers through encryption tools, anonymizing networks, and secure payment systems. Additionally, the need for constant innovation and adaptation to avoid detection by law enforcement agencies further adds to operational costs.

Payment mechanisms

One of the key elements that contribute to the revenue generation and profitability of Dark Web marketplaces is the use of cryptocurrencies as a primary payment method. Bitcoin, in particular, is widely accepted due to its pseudonymous nature, making it difficult to trace the flow of funds. Cryptocurrencies offer a degree of anonymity and security to both buyers and sellers, facilitating transactions on Dark Web marketplaces. However, the volatile nature of cryptocurrencies can pose challenges to sellers who need to convert Bitcoin to traditional currencies to realize their profits.

Dark Web marketplaces may also charge fees or commissions for facilitating transactions and providing additional services. These fees are often collected in cryptocurrencies and contribute to the revenue generated by the marketplace operators.

Profitability challenges and considerations

While Dark Web marketplaces can generate substantial revenue, they face several challenges that impact profitability. Law enforcement agencies actively target and shut down these marketplaces, resulting in financial losses for operators and participants. Maintaining the security and anonymity of the marketplace infrastructure requires continuous investment in technology and operational safeguards.

Additionally, the reliance on cryptocurrencies introduces financial risks due to price fluctuations and the potential for funds to be frozen or seized. Market dynamics, including changes in buyer preferences, product availability, and law enforcement interventions, can affect the profitability of Dark Web marketplaces. Sellers must adapt to these shifts to remain competitive and profitable.

It is important to note that engaging in illegal activities on Dark Web marketplaces also poses significant legal and ethical risks. Accessing these marketplaces, participating in illegal transactions, or profiting from such activities can lead to severe legal consequences and damage one's reputation.

Real-world implications and potential solutions

The revenue generation and profitability of Dark Web marketplaces have far-reaching implications. The trade of illegal goods and services on these platforms fuels organized crime, drug addiction, money laundering, and other societal issues. Law enforcement agencies employ various strategies, such as undercover operations, data analysis, and international collaborations, to disrupt, dismantle, and prosecute those involved.

To combat the profitability of Dark Web marketplaces, authorities need to continue investing in technological advancements for monitoring and tracking activities on the Dark Web. Advancements in machine learning, artificial intelligence, and data analysis can help identify patterns and uncover illicit transactions. Collaboration between law enforcement agencies, cybersecurity professionals, and technology companies is vital to developing comprehensive solutions to disrupt and prevent illicit activities.

Furthermore, public awareness and education campaigns can help deter individuals from participating in Dark Web marketplaces by highlighting the legal and ethical consequences of such actions. By empowering individuals with knowledge and resources, they can make informed decisions and protect themselves from the lure of illicit activities on the Dark Web.

In conclusion, Dark Web marketplaces generate revenue and profitability primarily through the sale of illegal goods and services facilitated by the anonymity and security of the Dark Web. Demand for these illicit products, competition among sellers, operational costs, and the use of cryptocurrencies as payment mechanisms all contribute to the financial success of these marketplaces. However, law enforcement efforts, technological advancements, education, and awareness campaigns play essential roles in combating the revenue generation and profitability of Dark Web marketplaces.

Dark Web market dynamics and competition

The world of Dark Web markets is a dynamic and constantly evolving landscape. As the demand for illicit goods and services continues to grow, so does the competition among Dark Web marketplaces. In this section, we will explore the dynamics of Dark Web markets and the factors that drive competition within this underground economy.

Supply and demand dynamics

Dark Web markets operate on the basic principles of supply and demand. The supply of illegal goods and services on these platforms is driven by the incentives and motivations of sellers, while the demand comes from buyers seeking to acquire these illicit items.

The supply side of Dark Web markets is shaped by various factors. Sellers are attracted to these platforms due to the relatively high profits they can earn, the anonymity provided by the Dark Web, and the ability to reach a large customer base. The availability of different goods and services depends on the skills and resources of sellers. For example, vendors with expertise in hacking may offer cybercrime-as-a-service, whereas others may specialize in drugs, weapons, or counterfeit goods.

On the demand side, buyers are motivated by factors such as accessibility, anonymity, and the desire for prohibited items. The Dark Web provides a platform for individuals who may not have access to certain goods and services through traditional channels. Additionally, the anonymity offered by the Dark Web allows buyers to make purchases without the fear of being identified by law enforcement agencies.

The interplay between supply and demand creates a thriving ecosystem of Dark Web markets, with sellers and buyers continuously interacting to satisfy their respective needs. As the demand for specific items increases, more sellers may enter the market, leading to increased competition and further diversification of available goods and services.

Competition among Dark Web marketplaces

Competition among Dark Web marketplaces is intense, driven by the need to attract both buyers and sellers. Just like any other marketplace, Dark Web platforms must differentiate themselves to stand out from their competitors. They do this through various strategies, including:

- **User experience and interface:** Dark Web markets need to provide a user-friendly interface that is easy to navigate and search for desired items. The design of the marketplace can significantly impact user engagement and retention.

- **Security and trust:** Dark Web markets must prioritize security features to gain the trust of both buyers and sellers. This includes implementing encryption protocols, using escrow systems for transactions, and establishing reputation and feedback mechanisms. Marketplaces that can provide a secure environment tend to attract more participants.

- **Product quality and selection:** To stay ahead of the competition, Dark Web markets need to offer a wide range of high-quality products and services. This can include niche items that are not easily found elsewhere, as well as popular illegal goods and services.

- **Pricing and competitiveness:** Dark Web marketplaces need to strike a balance between competitive pricing and ensuring profitability for sellers. Offering lower prices can attract buyers, but marketplaces also need to consider the costs and risks associated with maintaining the platform.

- **Anonymity and privacy:** Dark Web markets that prioritize user anonymity and privacy are more likely to attract individuals who are concerned about their identity being exposed. This involves providing secure communication channels and taking measures to protect user data.

- **Customer support:** Dark Web platforms that offer reliable customer support can differentiate themselves from competitors. Prompt and helpful responses to user inquiries can enhance the overall user experience and build trust among participants.

Successful Dark Web markets often combine these strategies to establish a competitive edge. However, the landscape is constantly changing, and marketplaces must continuously adapt to new technologies and law enforcement efforts that aim to disrupt their operations.

Challenges and risks in Dark Web market dynamics

While competition drives innovation and growth in Dark Web markets, it also presents challenges and risks for market participants. Some of the key challenges include:

- **Law enforcement operations:** Dark Web marketplaces face constant threats from law enforcement agencies that seek to dismantle these illicit platforms. The arrest and prosecution of market administrators and high-profile sellers can disrupt the operations of a marketplace and undermine trust among participants.

- **Exit scams and fraudulent activities:** In the Dark Web ecosystem, exit scams occur when a marketplace administrator suddenly shuts down the platform, taking with them the funds held in escrow. Such scams can cause financial losses for both buyers and sellers and erode trust in the overall Dark Web market ecosystem.

- **Hacking and cybersecurity threats:** Dark Web marketplaces are prime targets for hacking and cyberattacks due to the sensitive nature of the transactions and the potential for financial gain. Successful attacks can compromise user data, disrupt market operations, and expose individuals to legal risks.

- **Volatility and market instability:** Dark Web markets are subject to frequent disruptions and closures, either due to law enforcement operations or internal conflicts among market participants. Marketplaces can quickly disappear, causing financial losses for sellers and affecting buyer confidence.

Navigating these challenges requires a deep understanding of the dynamics of Dark Web markets and a commitment to implementing robust security measures. As law enforcement agencies and cybersecurity professionals continue to refine their strategies, marketplaces must adapt to stay competitive and avoid becoming targets for enforcement actions.

Case study: The Silk Road

One of the most famous examples of a Dark Web marketplace is the Silk Road. Launched in 2011 by Ross Ulbricht, the Silk Road quickly gained popularity as a platform for buying and selling illegal drugs. Ulbricht built a reputation system that allowed buyers and sellers to rate their experiences, which helped establish trust within the marketplace.

The Silk Road's success was attributed to several factors. Ulbricht focused on providing a user-friendly experience, emphasizing security and anonymity, and implementing innovative features like an escrow system. The marketplace attracted a large user base and generated significant revenue through transactions conducted in Bitcoin.

However, despite its initial success, the Silk Road eventually faced the challenges and risks inherent in Dark Web market dynamics. In 2013, law enforcement agencies shut down the Silk Road and arrested Ulbricht, who was found guilty of various charges, including money laundering and conspiracy to commit computer hacking.

The Silk Road case study highlights the evolving nature of Dark Web market dynamics and the challenges faced by both market operators and law enforcement agencies. The marketplace's rise and fall demonstrate the constant struggle for dominance among marketplaces, the risks of criminal activities, and the need for ongoing efforts to combat the illicit trade on the Dark Web.

Key Takeaways

- Dark Web markets operate on the principles of supply and demand, with sellers offering illegal goods and services and buyers seeking to acquire them.
- Competition among Dark Web marketplaces is driven by factors such as user experience, security, selection of products, pricing, privacy, and customer support.
- Successful Dark Web markets differentiate themselves by offering a secure and user-friendly platform, a wide range of high-quality products, competitive pricing, and reliable customer support.
- Dark Web market dynamics also pose challenges and risks, including law enforcement operations, exit scams, cyberattacks, and market instability.
- The Silk Road case study illustrates the dynamics of Dark Web markets, highlighting the rise and fall of a popular marketplace and the inherent challenges and risks in the underground economy.

Discussion Questions

1. How do you think the competition among Dark Web marketplaces affects the quality and pricing of illegal goods and services?
2. In your opinion, do you think law enforcement efforts to target Dark Web marketplaces are effective in combating the illicit trade? Why or why not?
3. What are some potential strategies that Dark Web marketplaces can employ to overcome the challenges and risks in the underground economy?

Exercises

1. Research and identify a recent case of a Dark Web marketplace that has been shut down by law enforcement agencies. Analyze the factors that led to its downfall and discuss the impact it had on the Dark Web market ecosystem.

2. Imagine you are a cybersecurity consultant tasked with advising a Dark Web marketplace on how to enhance its security and trust features. Develop a comprehensive plan that addresses key areas such as encryption, escrow systems, and user authentication.

3. Conduct a survey among your peers to gauge their awareness and understanding of Dark Web markets. Analyze the results and identify any misconceptions or areas that require further education and awareness-building.

Dark Web Market Participants

Buyers on Dark Web Markets

Motivations for using Dark Web markets

In order to understand the motivations behind the use of Dark Web markets, it is important to consider the characteristics and features that distinguish them from traditional online marketplaces. The Dark Web offers users a high level of anonymity and privacy, making it an attractive platform for those seeking to engage in illicit activities. Let's explore some of the key motivations for using Dark Web markets:

Access to Illegal Goods and Services

One of the primary motivations for individuals to use Dark Web markets is the availability of illegal goods and services. These markets provide a platform for the sale and purchase of illicit substances such as drugs, counterfeit currencies, and stolen data. Additionally, individuals can access services related to cybercrime, hacking tools, and even hire hitmen. The anonymity offered by Dark Web markets makes it difficult for law enforcement agencies to track down buyers and sellers of such goods and services.

For example, drug users may turn to Dark Web markets to discreetly purchase controlled substances, bypassing legal restrictions and the risk of arrest. The convenience and variety of drugs available on these platforms can be a strong motivator for individuals seeking to obtain substances that may be difficult to obtain through traditional means.

Desire for Privacy and Anonymity

Another motivation for using Dark Web markets is the desire for privacy and anonymity. On the Dark Web, users can operate under pseudonyms and communicate using encrypted channels, protecting their identities and minimizing the risk of detection. This level of anonymity is particularly appealing to individuals living in countries with oppressive regimes or strict surveillance. By operating within the Dark Web, individuals can evade surveillance and censorship, ensuring their activities remain hidden.

For instance, whistleblowers who want to expose sensitive information without fear of retribution may turn to Dark Web platforms to securely share documents and communicate with journalists or activists. By utilizing encryption and anonymous communication, these individuals can protect their identity and maintain confidentiality.

Availability of Specialized Goods and Services

Dark Web markets also attract users seeking highly specialized goods and services that may not be readily available through legal channels. These range from niche products, such as rare artworks or collectibles, to more illicit items like hacked personal information or forged documents. The Dark Web provides a platform for buyers and sellers to connect and engage in transactions that would otherwise be difficult to facilitate.

For example, individuals interested in acquiring weapons or firearms illegally may find Dark Web markets to be a viable option. These platforms often provide access to a range of weapons that may not be easily purchased through legal means. Similarly, individuals seeking hacker services, ranging from website hacking to social media account hacking, can find providers on Dark Web markets who offer such services for a fee.

Lack of Government Regulation

The absence of government regulation is another factor that motivates individuals to use Dark Web markets. Unlike traditional e-commerce platforms that operate within legal frameworks, Dark Web markets exist in a decentralized and unregulated environment. This lack of oversight and regulatory intervention allows users to engage in activities that would otherwise be prohibited or restricted.

Some individuals may be drawn to Dark Web markets as a means to circumvent government control or avoid taxes. For instance, individuals who wish to engage in tax evasion or money laundering may use Dark Web markets to conduct anonymous transactions without fear of detection by tax authorities or financial institutions.

Curiosity and Exploration

Lastly, curiosity and the desire for exploration can motivate individuals to venture into the Dark Web and use its markets. The clandestine nature of the Dark Web can be intriguing to individuals who are curious about its contents and the activities that take place within it. Some individuals may be driven by a desire to understand the workings of these markets or to satisfy their curiosity about the underground economy.

However, it is important to note that engaging with Dark Web markets carries significant risks, both legal and personal. Users may inadvertently expose themselves to malware, scams, or other forms of cybercrime. Additionally, law enforcement agencies are increasingly cracking down on Dark Web market participants, leading to arrests and prosecutions.

Overall, motivations for using Dark Web markets can vary widely, from seeking access to illegal goods and services to the desire for privacy and anonymity. While the allure of the Dark Web may be strong for some individuals, it is essential to understand the potential risks and consequences associated with engaging in its activities.

Demographics of Dark Web market buyers

Understanding the demographics of Dark Web market buyers is crucial in gaining insight into their motivations and preferences. While it is challenging to obtain precise demographic data for this specific group due to the nature of the Dark Web's anonymity, there have been several studies and reports that provide valuable insights. In this section, we will explore the available information on the demographics of Dark Web market buyers.

Age and Gender

Research suggests that Dark Web market buyers span a wide range of age groups. However, the majority of buyers tend to be young adults and individuals in their 20s and 30s. This age group is often more familiar with technology and comfortable with navigating the Dark Web. The allure of anonymity and access to illegal goods and services can be particularly appealing to this demographic.

In terms of gender, there is limited data available. However, it is believed that Dark Web market buyers primarily consist of males. This could be attributed to the fact that illicit activities, such as drug purchases or cybercrime-related services, are often associated with a predominantly male demographic. It is important to note that this is not a definitive conclusion, as more research is needed in this area.

Geographical Distribution

Dark Web market buyers are distributed globally, with users from various countries participating in these illicit activities. The accessibility of the internet and Dark Web technology allows individuals from different regions to access these marketplaces. However, some regions have been identified as hotspots for Dark Web market activities.

The United States, as one of the largest markets for illegal drugs, has a significant number of Dark Web market buyers. Other countries with notable Dark Web market participation include the United Kingdom, Germany, Australia, and Canada. It is worth mentioning that the dynamics and trends in Dark Web market demographics may change over time as law enforcement agencies target specific regions or as new marketplaces emerge.

Motivations and Preferences

Understanding the motivations and preferences of Dark Web market buyers provides insights into their behaviors and decision-making processes. There are several factors that drive individuals to engage in Dark Web market activities:

1. Anonymity: Dark Web market buyers are attracted to the anonymity offered by these platforms. By leveraging encryption technologies and cryptocurrencies, buyers can maintain a level of privacy and avoid being tracked by authorities.

2. Access to illicit goods and services: Dark Web markets offer a wide range of illegal goods and services that are not easily accessible through conventional means. Buyers are motivated by the availability of drugs, weapons, counterfeit currencies, stolen data, hacking tools, and various cybercrime services.

3. Disruption of traditional markets: Some Dark Web market buyers may be driven by the desire to disrupt traditional markets. For instance, purchasing illegal drugs at a lower cost than street prices or evading restrictive government regulations on certain products.

Preferences among Dark Web market buyers can vary significantly. While drugs remain one of the most sought-after items, there is also demand for counterfeit goods, stolen personal information, hacking services, and firearms. The preference for specific goods or services can depend on cultural factors, regional demand, and individual interests.

Risks and Precautions

Engaging in Dark Web market activities comes with inherent risks, both legal and cybersecurity related. Dark Web market buyers must be cautious and take necessary precautions to safeguard their identities and avoid detection. Some common risks include:

1. Law enforcement operations: Dark Web marketplaces are under constant scrutiny from law enforcement agencies worldwide. Buyers face the risk of being targeted in sting operations or investigations, which can lead to legal repercussions.
2. Fraudulent sellers: Buyers on Dark Web markets must be cautious of fraudulent sellers who may scam them by delivering counterfeit or substandard goods, or not delivering anything at all. Researching sellers, checking feedback ratings, and using escrow services can help mitigate these risks.
3. Cybersecurity threats: Engaging in Dark Web market activities can expose buyers to various cybersecurity risks, including malware, phishing attacks, and identity theft. Employing strong encryption, using trusted devices and networks, and practicing good cybersecurity hygiene can help reduce these risks.

In conclusion, Dark Web market buyers span a wide range of demographics, with young adults being the predominant age group. While limited data is available on gender distribution, Dark Web market activities are believed to be predominantly male-centric. Buyers are motivated by the anonymity, access to illicit goods and services, and the disruptive nature of these marketplaces. However, engaging in Dark Web market activities carries significant risks, and precautions must be taken to protect one's identity and avoid legal and cybersecurity pitfalls.

Buyer personas and their preferences

Understanding the motivations and preferences of buyers on Dark Web markets is crucial for gaining insights into their behaviors and developing effective strategies for combating illicit activities. While it is challenging to obtain comprehensive data on buyer personas, there are common trends and patterns that can be observed based on available information and past investigations.

Motivations for using Dark Web markets

Buyers on Dark Web markets are driven by several motivations that distinguish them from traditional consumers. Some of the main reasons why individuals turn to the Dark Web for their purchases include:

1. Anonymity and privacy: Dark Web markets provide a platform where buyers can maintain their anonymity and privacy. These individuals may have concerns about their activities being monitored on the Surface Web or fear the consequences of being identified by law enforcement agencies.

2. Access to illegal goods and services: Dark Web markets offer a wide range of illegal goods and services that are not easily accessible through traditional channels. This includes drugs, counterfeit documents, hacking tools, stolen data, weapons, and other illicit offerings.

3. Geographical limitations: Buyers residing in countries where certain products or services are unavailable or heavily regulated may resort to Dark Web markets as a means to bypass restrictions. They can purchase restricted products without facing the legal consequences associated with such transactions.

4. Lower prices and increased variety: Dark Web markets often provide competitive prices for goods and services compared to traditional markets. Additionally, buyers can find a wider range of products and services, including unique or rare items that may not be readily available elsewhere.

Demographics of Dark Web market buyers

The demographic profile of Dark Web market buyers is challenging to ascertain due to the encrypted nature of these platforms. Nevertheless, there is some information available based on law enforcement investigations and studies conducted on the subject.

1. Age: Dark Web market buyers span a wide range of age groups, but statistics suggest that the majority are younger individuals, often in their 20s or 30s. This age group is more likely to be technologically savvy and familiar with the use of cryptocurrencies and encryption tools.

2. Technical proficiency: Buyers on Dark Web markets generally possess a certain level of technical knowledge and familiarity with tools like Tor, cryptocurrency wallets, and encrypted communication platforms. They are willing to adopt specialized tools and techniques to access and navigate the Dark Web.

3. Geographic distribution: While Dark Web market buyers come from various countries worldwide, it is challenging to determine the precise distribution due to the anonymous nature of the Dark Web. However, developed countries with high internet penetration tend to have a higher concentration of Dark Web market users.

4. Socioeconomic background: Dark Web market buyers come from diverse socioeconomic backgrounds. They can range from individuals seeking recreational drugs to sophisticated cybercriminals involved in large-scale financial fraud or

hacking activities. Thus, it is difficult to define a specific socioeconomic profile for Dark Web market buyers.

Buyer preferences on Dark Web markets

Understanding buyer preferences is crucial for law enforcement agencies and cybersecurity professionals aiming to disrupt Dark Web markets. By gaining insights into their preferences, investigators can better tailor their approaches to prevent and detect illicit activities. Some notable preferences include:

1. Product quality and reliability: Buyers on Dark Web markets value product quality and reliability. According to feedback and reviews on Dark Web marketplaces, they seek vendors who consistently deliver high-quality products and maintain good communication throughout the transaction process.

2. Vendor reputation: Reputation plays a significant role in buyer preferences on Dark Web markets. Buyers typically prefer to purchase from vendors with positive reviews and established trust within the community. They rely on past buyer experiences and vendor ratings to assess the integrity and credibility of the sellers.

3. Communication and customer support: Buyers appreciate vendors who provide efficient communication and responsive customer support. Prompt replies to queries, clear instructions, and assistance in case of any issues enhance the buyer experience and foster trust.

4. Discretion and stealth shipping: Buyers prioritize vendors who guarantee discreet packaging and reliable shipping methods to minimize the likelihood of detection by law enforcement or customs. Vendors who can effectively conceal the nature of the package and ensure safe delivery are highly valued.

5. Enhanced security measures: Buyers favor vendors who employ robust security measures to protect sensitive information such as transaction details, shipping addresses, and personal data. Techniques such as encryption, multi-signature transactions, and the use of escrow systems contribute to the perception of enhanced security and trust.

Overall, buyer personas and preferences on Dark Web markets are influenced by factors such as anonymity, access to illegal goods, price competitiveness, and a desire for privacy. Law enforcement agencies and cybersecurity professionals must consider these motivations and preferences to effectively disrupt Dark Web market activities and mitigate the associated risks.

Interaction and communication between buyers

In Dark Web markets, buyers engage in various forms of interaction and communication with each other. These interactions play a crucial role in forming a vibrant and bustling marketplace where illicit goods and services are bought and sold. In this section, we will explore the different aspects of interaction and communication between buyers on Dark Web markets.

Motivations for using Dark Web markets

Buyers on Dark Web markets are motivated by several factors that drive their engagement with the underground economy. Some common motivations include:

- **Anonymity and Privacy:** Dark Web markets offer buyers a high level of anonymity and privacy compared to traditional online marketplaces. Buyers who are concerned about their digital footprint and want to avoid surveillance may choose to use Dark Web markets to make their purchases discreetly.

- **Access to Illegal Goods and Services:** Dark Web markets provide buyers with access to a wide range of illegal goods and services that are not easily available through legal channels. These can include drugs, counterfeit goods, stolen data, hacking services, and more.

- **Geographical Restrictions:** Dark Web markets can bypass geographical restrictions that may prevent buyers from accessing certain goods and services in their home countries. This allows buyers to acquire products that are prohibited or heavily regulated in their location.

- **Price and Quality:** Some buyers are attracted to Dark Web markets because they can find products at lower prices than in traditional markets. Additionally, buyers believe they can find high-quality products that may not be available through legal means.

Understanding these motivations is crucial for understanding the dynamics of interaction and communication between buyers on Dark Web markets.

Demographics of Dark Web market buyers

The demographics of Dark Web market buyers are diverse, with people from various backgrounds and locations participating in these marketplaces. However, it is challenging to gather accurate demographic data due to the anonymous nature of Dark Web transactions.

That said, research and investigations have provided some insights into the demographics of Dark Web market buyers. These findings indicate that buyers come from all walks of life and can include individuals from different professions, age groups, and income levels. The allure of anonymity and the potential economic benefits attract a wide range of individuals to Dark Web markets.

Buyer personas and their preferences

Buyers on Dark Web markets can be classified into different personas based on their preferences and purchasing behavior. Understanding these personas can help sellers tailor their offerings and communication strategies to attract and retain customers. Some common buyer personas on Dark Web markets include:

1. **Experimenters:** These buyers are often curious individuals who want to explore the Dark Web and try out different products and services available. They may not have specific preferences and may be willing to explore a variety of offerings.

2. **Regular Consumers:** Regular consumers are buyers who have specific preferences and frequently purchase certain goods or services on Dark Web markets. They have established patterns of purchasing behavior and may be loyal to specific sellers or marketplaces.

3. **Bulk Buyers:** Bulk buyers are individuals or groups who buy large quantities of goods on Dark Web markets. They are often involved in reselling or distributing products and require reliable suppliers who can fulfill their bulk orders.

4. **Sophisticated Buyers:** Sophisticated buyers have in-depth knowledge of Dark Web markets, including the reputation of sellers, quality of products, and prevailing market prices. They may engage in negotiations and seek exclusive deals or rare products.

5. **Risk-Averse Buyers:** Risk-averse buyers prioritize security and privacy over other factors. They may be more cautious when making purchases and prefer sellers with established reliability and strong privacy practices.

Understanding these buyer personas allows sellers to tailor their communication and marketing strategies to attract and cater to specific groups of buyers effectively.

Interaction and communication methods

Communication between buyers on Dark Web markets typically occurs through various methods to facilitate transactions and ensure buyer satisfaction. These methods include:

1. **Messaging Systems:** Dark Web markets provide messaging systems that allow buyers to communicate directly with sellers. These messaging systems often include features such as end-to-end encryption and anonymity to ensure secure communication.

2. **Forums and Discussion Boards:** Buyers can engage in discussions and share information on forums and discussion boards dedicated to Dark Web markets. These platforms serve as a hub for exchanging knowledge, seeking advice, and sharing experiences among buyers.

3. **Vendor Ratings and Reviews:** Buyers can provide feedback and rate their experiences with sellers on Dark Web markets. These ratings and reviews help buyers make informed decisions and build trust within the marketplace.

4. **Escrow Systems:** Escrow systems allow buyers and sellers to conduct transactions securely. Buyers can communicate with sellers through the escrow system to negotiate terms, request additional information, or clarify any concerns before completing a transaction.

5. **Private Channels:** Some buyers and sellers establish private channels of communication outside the Dark Web markets to establish a more personal and secure means of interaction. These private channels can include encrypted messaging apps or virtual private networks (VPNs).

These communication methods facilitate buyer-seller interactions, enable the exchange of information, and contribute to the overall functioning of Dark Web markets.

Risks and precautions for Dark Web market buyers

Buyers on Dark Web markets face several risks and must take precautions to ensure their safety and avoid scams. Some of the risks include:

- **Law Enforcement Monitoring:** Buyers must be aware of the risk of law enforcement surveillance on Dark Web markets. Activities on these platforms can be monitored, and buyers can potentially be subjected to criminal charges and legal consequences.

- **Scams and Fraud:** Dark Web markets are not immune to scams and frauds. Buyers must be cautious and verify the reputation and trustworthiness of sellers before making any transactions. Engaging in thorough research and reading reviews can mitigate the risk of falling victim to scams.

- **Security and Privacy:** Buyers must take steps to protect their security and privacy while engaging in Dark Web market activities. This includes using secure communication tools, maintaining anonymity, and using cryptocurrencies for transactions to minimize exposure of personal information.

To mitigate these risks, buyers must stay vigilant, exercise caution, and educate themselves about best practices for using Dark Web markets safely.

Example: Imagine a buyer, John, who wants to purchase a digital product on a Dark Web market. John researches the seller by reading reviews and checking their reputation on the marketplace's ratings system. Once satisfied with the seller's credibility, John initiates a conversation through the marketplace's messaging system to discuss the product's details, pricing, and delivery methods. After confirming the terms and discussing payment options, John utilizes an escrow system to securely complete the transaction. Finally, John provides a review and rating based on his experience, helping future buyers make informed decisions.

Overall, the interaction and communication between buyers on Dark Web markets are critical elements that contribute to the functionality and success of the underground economy. Buyers leverage different communication methods to engage with sellers, exchange information, negotiate terms, and establish trust. However, buyers must also be aware of the risks involved and take necessary precautions to protect their privacy and security.

Risks and Precautions for Dark Web Market Buyers

When using Dark Web markets, buyers expose themselves to a range of risks due to the illicit nature of the activities taking place. It is important for buyers to understand these risks and take appropriate precautions to protect their identity, finances, and personal safety. In this section, we will discuss some of the major risks faced by Dark Web market buyers and suggest precautions they can take to mitigate these risks.

Risk 1: Law Enforcement Surveillance

One of the primary risks for Dark Web market buyers is the possibility of law enforcement surveillance. Governments worldwide have increased their efforts to combat illegal activities on the Dark Web, and undercover operations are often conducted to identify and apprehend individuals involved in illicit transactions. To mitigate this risk, buyers should consider the following precautions:

- Use Tor and VPN: Dark Web market buyers should always access the Dark Web using the Tor network and a virtual private network (VPN). Tor helps in anonymizing internet traffic, while a VPN adds an extra layer of security by encrypting online activities.
- Use Pseudonyms: Buyers should create unique usernames and never reveal their real identities. It is important to choose a pseudonym that is not linked to any personal information, such as email addresses or social media accounts.
- Secure Communication: Buyers should use encrypted communication channels, such as PGP (Pretty Good Privacy), to communicate with sellers. This ensures that their messages cannot be intercepted or read by unauthorized individuals.
- Discreet Shipping Address: When making purchases of physical goods, buyers should avoid using their home or work addresses. Instead, they should consider using a discreet shipping address, such as a P.O. Box or a friend's address, to maintain anonymity.

By following these precautions, buyers can reduce the risk of being identified and targeted by law enforcement agencies.

Risk 2: Financial Scams and Fraud

Another significant risk on Dark Web markets is the potential for financial scams and fraud. Since transactions on the Dark Web involve anonymous and unregulated payment methods, buyers need to be cautious to avoid falling victim to scams. Here are some precautions to consider:

- Research the Seller: Before making a purchase, buyers should thoroughly research the reputation of the seller. They should look for positive reviews and ratings from other buyers to ensure the seller's legitimacy.

- Escrow Services: Buyers should prefer sellers who offer escrow services. Escrow acts as a third-party intermediary, holding the funds until the buyer receives the product or service, thus providing an additional layer of security and reducing the risk of scams.
- Use renowned cryptocurrencies: While cryptocurrencies like Bitcoin are commonly used on Dark Web markets, buyers should prefer reputable and established cryptocurrencies. These cryptocurrencies have better security measures in place, making it harder for scammers to take advantage.
- Use Tumbling Services: Buyers can use tumbling services, also known as cryptocurrency mixers, to obfuscate the transaction history of their funds. This reduces the risk of being traced back to the buyer.

By taking these precautions, buyers can minimize the risk of financial scams and fraud on Dark Web markets.

Risk 3: Physical Safety

In certain situations, buyers on Dark Web markets may face physical threats if dealing with sellers involved in illicit activities such as the weapons trade or drug trafficking. To protect their physical safety, buyers should consider the following precautions:

- Avoid Personal Meetings: Buyers should never engage in personal meetings or face-to-face transactions with sellers they have encountered on Dark Web markets. Such meetings can be dangerous and increase the risk of being involved in illegal activities unknowingly.
- Secure Packaging: If purchasing physical goods, buyers should ensure that the packaging is discreet and does not reveal the contents. This prevents potential issues at customs or with law enforcement agencies during shipping.
- Personal OpSec: Buyers should practice good operational security (OpSec) by reducing their digital footprint and being cautious about revealing personal information online. This minimizes the risk of being targeted by criminals operating on Dark Web markets.

By being aware of these risks and taking appropriate precautions, buyers can reduce the potential threats to their physical safety.

It is important to note that engaging in any illegal activities on the Dark Web is against the law and can have serious consequences. This section aims to provide guidance to individuals who are curious about the Dark Web but does not condone or encourage its usage for illegal purposes. Buyers should always consider the legal and ethical implications of their actions and prioritize their personal safety above all else.

Sellers on Dark Web Markets

Characteristics of Dark Web Market Sellers

Dark web market sellers play a crucial role in the underground economy by providing a diverse range of illicit goods and services to buyers. These sellers operate on dark web marketplaces to conduct their business while maintaining anonymity and security. Understanding the characteristics of these sellers is essential in comprehending the dynamics of dark web markets and developing effective strategies to combat their activities.

Motivations and Backgrounds of Dark Web Market Sellers

Dark web market sellers are driven by various motivations, primarily centered around financial gain and exploiting the anonymity offered by the dark web. The following are some common motivations for becoming a dark web market seller:

1. Profit: Sellers are attracted to the potential for substantial profits that can be achieved through the sale of illegal goods and services. The dark web provides a platform for sellers to access a global customer base, allowing them to reach a larger audience compared to traditional illicit markets.

2. Technological Proficiency: Many dark web market sellers possess advanced technological skills and use their expertise to navigate the complexities of the dark web and maintain their anonymity. These individuals typically have a deep understanding of encryption, cryptocurrencies, and other tools necessary for conducting business on the dark web.

3. Avoiding Law Enforcement: Some dark web market sellers choose this platform to evade law enforcement agencies and diminish the risk of being detected and apprehended. The dark web's anonymity and encryption features provide a level of protection for sellers, making it difficult for authorities to trace their activities.

4. Ideological Motivation: Certain sellers are motivated by ideological or political beliefs. They may use the dark web to distribute content, communicate

with like-minded individuals, or support causes that are considered illegal or prohibited in the mainstream.

Backgrounds of dark web market sellers vary widely, including individuals with prior criminal records, hackers, technologists, drug manufacturers, and entrepreneurs seeking new revenue streams. The diversity of backgrounds contributes to the range of goods and services available on dark web markets.

Operational Strategies of Dark Web Market Sellers

Dark web market sellers employ specific strategies to ensure the success of their operations. These strategies contribute to their ability to maintain anonymity, evade law enforcement, and attract customers. Some key operational strategies include:

1. Pseudonyms and Online Identities: Sellers create pseudonyms or online identities to operate on dark web marketplaces. These identities help sellers establish a reputation and build trust with buyers while maintaining their anonymity.

2. Reputation and Trust Building: Dark web market sellers rely heavily on reputation and feedback systems to establish credibility and gain the trust of potential buyers. Positive reviews and ratings from previous customers significantly impact a seller's success on the dark web.

3. Stealth Shipping and Packaging: Sellers employ various techniques to ensure the discreet delivery of physical goods. These strategies include using untraceable shipping methods, encrypting addresses, and employing stealth packaging to avoid detection by law enforcement authorities.

4. Vendor Shops and Branding: Some sellers develop their own online shops within dark web marketplaces, allowing them to establish a brand and differentiate themselves from competitors. These vendor shops often feature customized designs, promotional offers, and loyalty programs to attract and retain customers.

5. Price Differentiation and Specialization: Dark web market sellers differentiate themselves by offering unique products or services, competitive pricing, or specialized knowledge. This approach helps them carve out a niche market and attract a specific customer base, increasing their chances of success.

Challenges Faced by Dark Web Market Sellers

Despite the advantages and strategies employed by dark web market sellers, they face several challenges in conducting their operations. These challenges include:

1. Maintaining Anonymity: Sellers must continually adapt to advancements in surveillance technologies employed by law enforcement agencies and cybersecurity professionals. The risks associated with potential exposure and subsequent legal consequences require sellers to stay vigilant and adopt advanced anonymization techniques.

2. Trust Issues and Security Concerns: Dark web market sellers face challenges in building and maintaining trust with buyers due to the inherent risks associated with engaging in illegal activities. Security concerns surrounding payment systems, potential scams, and the reputational risks of operating on the dark web pose significant obstacles for sellers.

3. Competition and Product Differentiation: Dark web markets are highly competitive, with numerous sellers vying for customers' attention. Sellers need to constantly innovate, differentiate their offerings, and adapt to changing market demands to stay ahead of their competitors.

4. Reliability and Consistency: Sellers must maintain consistent supply chains and meet buyers' expectations in terms of product quality, delivery times, and customer service. Any disruptions or inconsistencies in these areas can negatively impact a seller's reputation and success.

5. Legal and Ethical Considerations: Dark web market sellers operate in an illegal and unregulated space. They face potential legal consequences and ethical dilemmas associated with participating in illicit activities, engaging with criminal networks, and potentially causing harm to individuals and communities.

Navigating these challenges requires sellers to adopt a strategic mindset, employ advanced technological tools, and continuously adapt to evolving circumstances in the dark web market ecosystem.

Conclusion

Understanding the characteristics of dark web market sellers sheds light on the dynamics and challenges of dark web markets. These sellers are driven by financial incentives, technological expertise, and the motivation to exploit the anonymity provided by the dark web. They employ various strategies to maintain their anonymity, build trust with buyers, and differentiate themselves in a competitive environment. However, they also face significant challenges related to maintaining anonymity, establishing trust, dealing with competition, ensuring reliability, and navigating legal and ethical considerations. Efforts to combat dark web markets must take into account the characteristics and operational strategies of dark web market sellers to effectively disrupt their activities and reduce the overall impact of illicit online marketplaces.

The process of becoming a Dark Web market seller

Becoming a Dark Web market seller is not a straightforward process. It involves a series of steps and precautions to ensure anonymity and security. This section will outline the process that individuals typically go through to become a Dark Web market seller. It will cover the procedures, challenges, and potential risks involved.

Step 1: Establishing a Presence

The first step in becoming a Dark Web market seller is to establish a presence on the Dark Web. This involves accessing the Dark Web through secure means, such as using the Tor network or other anonymous access methods. The Tor network provides a layer of encryption and anonymity by routing internet traffic through a series of relays.

Once on the Dark Web, an aspiring seller needs to find and select a suitable Dark Web marketplace to operate on. There are various Dark Web marketplaces available, each with unique features and user base. Sellers often choose marketplaces based on reputation, user traffic, and the types of goods or services they wish to offer.

Step 2: Creating a Vendor Account

After selecting a Dark Web marketplace, the next step is to create a vendor account. This step requires careful consideration as it involves establishing a pseudonymous identity. Sellers need to choose a unique username and avatar that will represent their presence on the marketplace.

To maintain anonymity, sellers are advised to create a new email address specifically for Dark Web activities. They should also avoid using any personal information that can be traced back to their real identity. Additionally, sellers may need to provide proofs of their credibility and reliability to gain the trust of the marketplace administrators and buyers.

Step 3: Listing Products and Services

Once a vendor account is created, sellers can start listing their products or services on the Dark Web marketplace. The listings should include detailed descriptions, prices, and any relevant information that potential buyers might need. It is important for sellers to ensure that their listings comply with the rules and regulations of the marketplace.

To protect their identity, sellers often use encryption techniques to safeguard their communications and transactions. They may use public-key encryption to secure their messages, ensuring that only the intended recipients can decrypt and read the content.

Step 4: Managing Orders and Transactions

As sellers receive orders from buyers, they need to manage the entire order fulfillment process. This includes securely communicating with buyers, packaging and shipping goods (if applicable), and providing tracking information. Sellers are responsible for ensuring that the goods or services reach the buyers without compromising their anonymity.

To facilitate transactions, Dark Web markets often make use of cryptocurrencies, such as Bitcoin or Monero. These digital currencies offer relatively high levels of anonymity and can be used to conduct transactions without revealing the identities of the parties involved. Sellers need to understand the basics of cryptocurrency transactions and implement appropriate security measures to protect their funds.

Step 5: Building a Reputation

Building a positive reputation is crucial for Dark Web market sellers. Buyers heavily rely on feedback and reviews left by previous customers when making purchasing decisions. Sellers need to ensure that they provide high-quality products or services, deliver them in a timely manner, and provide good customer support.

To maintain a good reputation, sellers should actively engage with their customers, promptly address any concerns or issues, and continually improve their offerings based on feedback. It is also important for sellers to abide by the marketplace rules and follow ethical practices to avoid negative attention from law enforcement agencies.

Challenges and Risks

Becoming a Dark Web market seller is not without its challenges and risks. Sellers face the constant threat of scams, frauds, and malicious buyers. They need to be vigilant and take precautions to protect their identity, funds, and reputation. Additionally, they need to stay updated on the evolving tactics used by law enforcement agencies to combat Dark Web activities.

Sellers must also be aware of potential cyberattacks targeted at compromising their anonymity and security. Techniques such as phishing, malware, and social engineering are frequently employed to exploit vulnerabilities and gain access to sellers' sensitive information.

Furthermore, sellers face the risk of legal repercussions as engaging in illicit activities on the Dark Web is unlawful in many jurisdictions. Law enforcement agencies actively monitor and investigate Dark Web marketplaces, making sellers vulnerable to prosecution if their identities are exposed.

Ethical Considerations

It is important to highlight the ethical considerations involved in becoming a Dark Web market seller. The activities on Dark Web markets often involve the sale of illegal goods and services, contributing to the societal harms associated with them. Sellers need to carefully consider the consequences of their actions and the potential negative impact on individuals and communities.

Moreover, sellers should be aware of the potential harm caused by the products they sell. This includes drugs that can lead to addiction and other serious health issues, weapons that can be used for criminal purposes, and cybercrime tools that enable malicious activities. Ethical sellers should prioritize the well-being and safety of their customers and society as a whole.

Overall, becoming a Dark Web market seller requires navigating a complex landscape of anonymity, security, legality, and ethics. It is essential for individuals to understand the risks and challenges involved and make informed decisions about their involvement in Dark Web activities.

Types of goods and services sold on Dark Web markets

Dark Web markets have gained notoriety for providing a platform where a wide range of illegal goods and services can be bought and sold anonymously. These marketplaces operate on encrypted networks, making it difficult for law enforcement agencies to track their activities. In this section, we will explore the different types of goods and services that are commonly sold on Dark Web markets and the associated risks and challenges.

Drugs and Pharmaceuticals

One of the primary categories of goods sold on Dark Web markets is drugs and pharmaceuticals. These markets offer a vast selection of illicit substances, including cocaine, heroin, marijuana, MDMA (Ecstasy), prescription medications, and designer drugs. The anonymity provided by the Dark Web makes it an attractive platform for drug dealers and buyers who want to evade law enforcement. The convenience, wide variety, and competitive pricing of drugs on Dark Web markets contribute to their popularity among drug users.

Example: The Silk Road was one of the most infamous Dark Web marketplaces, which primarily facilitated the sale of drugs. It was known for its user-friendly interface and escrow system, providing a level of trust for buyers and sellers.

Digital Goods and Services

Dark Web markets are not limited to physical goods; they also serve as a platform for selling various digital goods and services that may be illegal or unethical. These include hacking tools, stolen data, compromised accounts, counterfeit documents, and fake identification cards.

Example: A cybercriminal selling access to a botnet on a Dark Web marketplace, allowing buyers to launch large-scale distributed denial-of-service (DDoS) attacks on targeted websites.

Weapons and Firearms

Another troubling category of goods available on Dark Web markets is weapons and firearms. These marketplaces offer a range of firearms, ammunition, explosives, and other related accessories. The anonymous nature of these transactions poses a serious risk, as it allows individuals with criminal intent or prohibited backgrounds to acquire dangerous weapons.

Example: In 2016, law enforcement agencies shut down the AlphaBay marketplace, which was known for its extensive selection of firearms. The site facilitated the illegal sale of handguns, rifles, and even fully automatic weapons.

Hacking and Cybercrime Services

Dark Web markets also host a plethora of services related to hacking and cybercrime. These services include hacking tutorials, botnets for rent, distributed denial-of-service (DDoS) attacks, malware development, phishing campaigns, and personal data hacking.

Example: A hacker offering their services on a Dark Web marketplace to launch a phishing campaign on behalf of a buyer, aiming to steal sensitive information like credit card details or login credentials.

Fraud and Financial Services

Dark Web markets are notorious for facilitating various types of fraud and financial services. These include stolen credit card details, bank account credentials, counterfeit currency, passports, driver's licenses, and social security numbers. Fraudsters utilize these services to carry out identity theft, money laundering, and other illicit financial activities.

Example: A vendor selling pre-embossed credit cards on a Dark Web marketplace, allowing buyers to make fraudulent transactions using stolen credit card information.

Counterfeit Goods

Dark Web markets are also a hub for the sale of counterfeit goods, including luxury brands, electronics, pharmaceuticals, and documents. These goods are often indistinguishable from genuine products, making it difficult for buyers to identify fakes.

Example: A seller offering counterfeit passports on a Dark Web marketplace, along with supporting documents, to facilitate illegal immigration or identity theft.

Human Trafficking and Exploitation

Disturbingly, Dark Web markets are involved in facilitating human trafficking and exploitation. These markets provide a platform for the sale of personal information, including compromising photos or videos. Additionally, they may enable the recruitment of individuals for forced labor, sex trafficking, or other forms of exploitation.

Example: A trafficker advertising the services of a person on a Dark Web marketplace, promoting them as a victim available for forced labor or sexual exploitation.

Other Illegal and Illicit Goods

Apart from the categories mentioned above, Dark Web markets also host a range of other illegal and illicit goods and services. These may include stolen artworks, counterfeit currencies, hacked accounts, counterfeit documents, confidential databases, and even contracted violence.

Example: A vendor offering a paid assassination service on a Dark Web marketplace, allowing buyers to hire hitmen anonymously.

Risks and Precautions

It is important to note that engaging in any activity on Dark Web markets is illegal and potentially dangerous. Participants face risks such as identity theft, scams, and exposure to criminal elements. Moreover, law enforcement agencies actively monitor these marketplaces, making the risk of prosecution a significant concern. Users are strongly advised to avoid interacting with Dark Web markets altogether.

Precautions for Dark Web market users:

- Use secure and anonymous communication tools, such as Tor, to access Dark Web marketplaces.
- Beware of scams and fake vendors. Conduct thorough research and read user reviews before engaging in any transaction.
- Utilize cryptocurrency, such as Bitcoin, for transactions as it provides an additional layer of anonymity.
- Minimize personal information exposure. Use pseudonyms and avoid providing any identifiable information.
- Regularly update and secure devices to prevent malware infections and reduce the risk of being targeted by hackers.

In conclusion, Dark Web markets offer a wide range of illegal goods and services, including drugs, weapons, hacking services, fraud, counterfeit goods, and even human exploitation. The anonymous nature of these marketplaces poses considerable risks to both buyers and sellers. Law enforcement agencies are actively working to combat these marketplaces, but users must exercise caution and avoid involvement in illegal activities on the Dark Web.

Pricing strategies on Dark Web markets

One of the key aspects of Dark Web markets is the pricing strategies employed by sellers to attract buyers and maximize their profits. The anonymity provided by the Dark Web creates a unique pricing environment where sellers can take advantage of the relative lack of regulation and law enforcement. In this section, we will explore the various pricing strategies utilized on Dark Web markets and discuss their implications.

Price Differentiation

Price differentiation is a common pricing strategy used by Dark Web market sellers to cater to different segments of buyers. This strategy involves offering different prices for the same product or service based on factors such as quality, quantity, or timing. The goal is to extract maximum profits from buyers who are willing to pay more while still attracting price-sensitive buyers.

For example, a seller of illegal drugs may offer different prices for varying quantities of the same substance. Buyers looking to purchase smaller amounts may be charged a higher price per gram, while those buying in bulk may receive a discounted rate. This approach allows sellers to target a wide range of buyers with different budgets and preferences.

Dynamic Pricing

Dynamic pricing is another commonly employed strategy on Dark Web markets. This strategy involves adjusting prices based on various factors, such as market demand, product availability, or the reputation of the seller. Dark Web marketplaces are known for their volatility, and dynamic pricing allows sellers to adapt to changing market conditions and maximize their profits.

For instance, in a highly competitive market with a large supply of a specific drug, sellers might lower their prices to attract buyers and gain a competitive edge. On the other hand, if a rare and in-demand commodity becomes available, sellers may increase their prices to take advantage of the scarcity.

Bundling and Upselling

Bundling and upselling are techniques commonly used not only in traditional retail but also on Dark Web markets. Sellers often offer bundled packages or additional services to entice buyers and increase their average order value.

For example, a seller specializing in stolen credit card information may offer a bundled package that includes not only the card details but also additional personal information such as social security numbers or addresses. By offering these extras, the seller can charge a higher price while providing perceived value to the buyer.

Upselling involves persuading buyers to purchase more expensive or higher-quality goods or services. Dark Web sellers may use various tactics, such as offering premium versions of a product or suggesting related and complementary items to buyers to increase their total spend.

Auctions and Negotiation

Some Dark Web marketplaces facilitate auctions and negotiation between buyers and sellers. This pricing strategy allows buyers to bid on products or negotiate prices directly with sellers, creating a dynamic pricing environment.

Auctions can be particularly useful for sellers of unique or rare items, such as zero-day exploits or exclusive hacking tools. By allowing buyers to bid on these items, sellers can create bidding wars that often result in higher prices and increased profits.

Negotiation, on the other hand, enables buyers and sellers to reach mutually agreed upon prices for goods and services. This strategy is more common for high-value items where individual negotiation can lead to a better outcome for both parties involved.

Cryptocurrency Pricing

Due to the nature of the Dark Web, where anonymity is paramount, sellers often only accept cryptocurrencies as a form of payment. Cryptocurrencies like Bitcoin, Ethereum, or Monero are decentralized and offer a high level of privacy, making them the preferred choice for Dark Web transactions.

When it comes to pricing, sellers may adjust their rates to account for the volatility and fluctuations in cryptocurrency values. For example, if the price of Bitcoin goes up significantly, sellers might increase their prices in terms of Bitcoin to ensure they receive the desired fiat value.

Additionally, the use of cryptocurrencies allows sellers to avoid traditional financial institutions and payment processors, reducing the risk of detection and seizure of funds by law enforcement.

Implications and Risks

While these pricing strategies can be effective for sellers on Dark Web markets, they also carry significant risks. The anonymity and characteristics of the Dark Web attract both buyers and sellers seeking illegal goods and services. However, the lack of regulation and accountability exposes participants to scams, fraud, and security threats.

Buyers face risks such as receiving counterfeit or substandard goods after making a payment, or getting caught by law enforcement. Sellers, on the other hand, might encounter payment disputes, scams from buyers, or become victims of law enforcement operations targeting Dark Web marketplaces.

It is crucial for buyers and sellers to exercise caution and perform due diligence when engaging in transactions on Dark Web markets. Understanding pricing strategies, verifying the credibility of sellers, and adopting proper safety measures are paramount to mitigate risks inherent in this illicit environment.

Summary

In this section, we explored the pricing strategies employed by sellers on Dark Web markets. We discussed various techniques such as price differentiation, dynamic pricing, bundling and upselling, auctions and negotiation, and cryptocurrency pricing. We highlighted the implications and risks associated with these strategies, emphasizing the need for caution and diligent research when participating in the Dark Web market ecosystem. By being aware of the pricing dynamics on the Dark Web, buyers and sellers can navigate this underground market more effectively and minimize their exposure to potential risks.

How Dark Web market sellers ensure anonymity and security

Ensuring anonymity and security is crucial for Dark Web market sellers who want to protect themselves from law enforcement and maintain the trust of their buyers. In this section, we will explore the various methods and techniques employed by Dark Web market sellers to achieve these goals.

Technological Tools for Anonymity

Dark Web market sellers heavily rely on technology to maintain their anonymity. The following are some of the key technological tools used:

1. **Tor Network:** The Tor network plays a vital role in facilitating anonymous communication on the Dark Web. It routes internet traffic through a series of encrypted relays, making it difficult to trace the origin of the data. Market sellers leverage the Tor network to access Dark Web marketplaces without revealing their real IP addresses.

2. **Virtual Private Networks (VPNs):** VPNs are commonly used by Dark Web market sellers to hide their real IP addresses and encrypt their internet connections. By connecting to a VPN server, sellers can route their traffic through a remote location, further obscuring their online activities and making it challenging for anyone to trace their actions back to their physical location.

3. **Encryption Tools:** Dark Web market sellers use encryption tools to secure their communications and transactions. Public-key encryption, such as Pretty Good Privacy (PGP), allows sellers to encrypt messages and verify their identity using digital signatures. Encryption ensures that only the

intended recipients can access the information, providing an additional layer of security.

Multiple Layers of Pseudonyms

To enhance their anonymity, Dark Web market sellers adopt a strategy of using multiple pseudonyms or handles. This practice is known as "sockpuppeting" and aims to create confusion and make it harder for law enforcement to attribute illegal activities to a specific individual.

By using different pseudonyms across various platforms and marketplaces, sellers minimize the risk of linking all their activities. They also rotate their pseudonyms regularly to prevent patterns or habits from emerging that could aid in their identification.

Bitcoin and Cryptocurrencies

Cryptocurrencies, especially Bitcoin, are the primary medium of exchange on Dark Web markets. Bitcoin transactions offer a certain level of pseudo-anonymity, as they do not require the disclosure of personal information. Dark Web market sellers use Bitcoin for various reasons:

- **Anonymity:** Bitcoin allows sellers to receive payments without revealing their real identities. Each transaction is recorded on the blockchain, but the information attached to the transaction does not necessarily link back to the seller's real-world identity.

- **Irreversibility:** Bitcoin transactions are irreversible, providing an advantage to sellers who want to avoid scams or fraudulent chargebacks. Once a transaction is confirmed, it cannot be reversed without the buyer's cooperation, minimizing the risk for the seller.

- **Decentralization:** Bitcoin operates on a decentralized network, which means there is no central authority controlling the currency. This aspect makes it difficult for law enforcement to seize or regulate funds held in Bitcoin.

Sellers may also employ additional privacy-focused cryptocurrencies like Monero or Zcash, which offer enhanced privacy features such as transaction obfuscation and the concealment of transaction amounts.

Operational Security Practices

Dark Web market sellers are constantly mindful of operational security (OPSEC) practices to minimize the risk of detection. Here are some common operational security measures employed by sellers:

- **Secure Communication Channels:** Sellers utilize encrypted messaging platforms, such as Wickr or Signal, to communicate with buyers. These platforms provide end-to-end encryption and self-destructing messages, ensuring that sensitive conversations are kept private.
- **Stealth Shipping:** To maintain security during the delivery of physical goods, sellers employ techniques such as deceptive packaging, false return addresses, and alternative shipping methods. These measures help prevent detection during the shipping process.
- **Discretionary Posting Behavior:** Dark Web market sellers avoid discussing personal details or revealing information that could potentially identify them. They take care not to reveal any identifying patterns in their posting behavior, such as specific writing styles or habits that could be linked to their real-world identities.

Challenges and Caveats

While Dark Web market sellers employ various methods to ensure anonymity and security, it is important to note that these measures are not foolproof. There are several challenges and caveats to consider:

- **Technological Vulnerabilities:** Despite using sophisticated technologies, sellers are not immune to vulnerabilities. Exploits or zero-day vulnerabilities in the tools they use, such as Tor or encryption software, can potentially compromise their anonymity and security.
- **Law Enforcement Infiltration:** Dark Web marketplaces are not immune to infiltration by law enforcement agencies. Sellers must be cautious about potential law enforcement operations or honey traps set up to expose their activities.
- **Exit Scams and Trust:** Trust is essential on Dark Web markets. However, sellers must navigate the fine line between maintaining anonymity and building trust with buyers. Exit scams, where sellers abruptly shut down

their operations and disappear with the funds, pose a significant risk to both buyers and the reputation of sellers.

Overall, Dark Web market sellers employ a combination of technological tools, operational security practices, and anonymous payment methods to ensure their anonymity and protect themselves from law enforcement. While not infallible, these measures significantly increase the difficulty of identifying and apprehending sellers on the Dark Web.

Law enforcement and Cybersecurity Professionals

Role of law enforcement in combating Dark Web markets

Law enforcement plays a crucial role in combating Dark Web markets, which are notorious for facilitating illegal activities. The presence of these markets poses significant challenges in terms of law enforcement's ability to detect and apprehend criminals operating in the shadows of the internet. In this section, we will explore the strategies and initiatives employed by law enforcement agencies to combat Dark Web markets and disrupt illicit activities.

1. Investigation and Intelligence Gathering: Law enforcement agencies employ various techniques to gather intelligence and investigate Dark Web marketplaces. These strategies involve:

1.1 Infiltration and Undercover Operations: Law enforcement agents may create undercover accounts on Dark Web platforms to gather information, identify criminals, and build cases against them. By acting as buyers or sellers, they can engage with criminal actors and gain insights into their operations. These operations require specialized skills, such as maintaining anonymity, understanding encryption techniques, and assessing risk.

1.2 Cooperation with International Agencies: Given the transnational nature of Dark Web markets, collaboration between different law enforcement agencies is crucial. Joint investigations, information sharing, and coordinated efforts can enhance the effectiveness of combating these illicit activities. Interpol, Europol, and other international organizations play a vital role in facilitating such collaborations.

2. Cyber Forensics and Data Analysis: Law enforcement agencies leverage advanced digital forensics and data analysis techniques to trace illicit activities back to their source. This includes:

2.1 Monitoring and Takedown of Dark Web Marketplaces: Law enforcement agencies continuously monitor Dark Web marketplaces to identify and analyze emerging trends, patterns, and criminal activities. They leverage sophisticated tools and technologies to track online transactions and trace the flow of illicit funds. When necessary, they take decisive action to dismantle these marketplaces, often requiring cooperation with hosting providers and other stakeholders.

2.2 Blockchain Analysis: Cryptocurrencies, such as Bitcoin, are commonly used for transactions on Dark Web markets due to their pseudonymous nature. Law enforcement agencies employ blockchain analysis techniques to link transactions to individuals and build evidence against criminals. By analyzing transaction patterns, they can unravel networks and identify key players involved in illicit activities.

3. Legislation and Policy Development: Law enforcement agencies work closely with lawmakers and policymakers to develop and update legislation that addresses the challenges posed by Dark Web markets. This includes:

3.1 Strengthening Cybercrime Laws: Law enforcement agencies advocate for the enhancement of cybercrime laws to encompass the specific offenses associated with Dark Web activities. By providing a comprehensive legal framework, authorities can take appropriate legal action against criminals involved in various illegal activities, such as drug trafficking, weapon sales, and cybercrime-as-a-service.

3.2 International Cooperation in Legislation: Given the global nature of Dark Web markets, international cooperation in developing consistent legislation is crucial. Standardized laws can enable effective collaboration among different jurisdictions and streamline the extradition process for offenders.

4. Public Awareness and Education: Law enforcement agencies recognize the significance of educating the public about the dangers of participating in Dark Web markets. Strategies to raise awareness include:

4.1 Information Campaigns: Law enforcement agencies conduct public awareness campaigns through various channels, such as social media, educational institutions, and community outreach programs. These campaigns aim to inform the public about the risks associated with engaging in illegal activities on Dark Web platforms, the legal consequences, and the potential harm to individuals and society as a whole.

4.2 Collaboration with Schools and Communities: Law enforcement agencies collaborate with schools and community organizations to educate young people about the dangers of the Dark Web. By promoting digital literacy, cybersecurity awareness, and responsible online behavior, they aim to prevent individuals from being drawn into illegal activities on the Dark Web.

In conclusion, law enforcement agencies play a critical role in combating Dark Web markets. Through intelligence gathering, cyber forensics, legislation, and public awareness campaigns, they strive to disrupt illicit activities, bring criminals to justice, and protect individuals and society from the harms associated with these hidden corners of the internet. Collaboration, technological advancements, and continuous adaptation are key to staying one step ahead of criminals operating on the Dark Web.

Challenges faced by law enforcement agencies

Law enforcement agencies face numerous challenges in combating Dark Web markets. The nature of these underground marketplaces, characterized by anonymity, encryption, and global reach, presents unique obstacles that traditional law enforcement methods are often ill-equipped to handle. In this section, we will explore some of the key challenges faced by law enforcement agencies.

Anonymity and Encryption

One of the primary challenges for law enforcement agencies is the anonymity provided by the Dark Web. Dark Web marketplaces operate on encrypted networks, such as the Tor network, which make it difficult to trace the physical location of the servers hosting these marketplaces. Additionally, users on the Dark Web often employ encryption techniques to protect their identities, making it challenging for law enforcement to identify and track individuals involved in illegal activities.

The use of cryptocurrencies, such as Bitcoin, further complicates the issue. These digital currencies enable anonymous transactions, making it difficult for law enforcement to follow the money trail and identify the individuals behind the financial transactions on Dark Web markets.

Jurisdictional Issues

Dark Web markets operate on a global scale, transcending traditional jurisdictional boundaries. This poses a significant challenge for law enforcement agencies, as different countries have varying laws and regulations regarding cybercrimes and the Dark Web. Coordinating efforts across multiple jurisdictions can be time-consuming and complex, often requiring mutual legal assistance treaties and cooperation between law enforcement agencies from different countries.

Technological Advancements

Dark Web marketplaces constantly evolve, incorporating new technologies and techniques to stay one step ahead of law enforcement. Law enforcement agencies must keep up with these technological advancements to effectively combat Dark Web markets. This requires investing in advanced monitoring and surveillance tools, as well as training law enforcement officials in the latest techniques for investigating and infiltrating Dark Web marketplaces.

Encryption Backdoors

The debate surrounding encryption backdoors poses a significant challenge for law enforcement agencies. While encryption is crucial for protecting sensitive information and maintaining cybersecurity, it also hinders law enforcement's ability to access encrypted communications on the Dark Web. Some argue for the implementation of encryption backdoors to enable law enforcement agencies to access encrypted data, while others emphasize the importance of maintaining strong encryption to safeguard privacy and security.

Resource Allocation

The fight against Dark Web markets requires significant resources, including skilled personnel, advanced technological tools, and dedicated funding. Yet, law enforcement agencies often face resource constraints, making it challenging to allocate sufficient resources to combat the complex and ever-evolving landscape of Dark Web markets. Prioritizing efforts and effectively allocating resources is crucial for law enforcement agencies to tackle the challenges posed by Dark Web markets.

Cooperation and Information Sharing

Collaboration and information sharing are essential for effective law enforcement efforts against Dark Web markets. However, achieving cooperation between different law enforcement agencies, both national and international, can be challenging due to differing priorities, legal frameworks, and information-sharing protocols. Establishing efficient mechanisms for sharing intelligence and coordinating operations is imperative to overcome these challenges.

Human Intelligence Gathering

While technological solutions play a crucial role, human intelligence gathering remains vital in combating Dark Web markets. Law enforcement agencies need skilled personnel with expertise in conducting undercover operations, infiltrating criminal networks, and developing informants. Building trust and cultivating sources of information within the Dark Web community is crucial but challenging, as the veiled nature of the Dark Web makes it difficult to verify the credibility of sources.

In summary, law enforcement agencies face a myriad of challenges in their efforts to combat Dark Web markets. These challenges include anonymity and encryption, jurisdictional issues, technological advancements, encryption backdoors, resource allocation, cooperation and information sharing, as well as the need for effective human intelligence gathering. Overcoming these challenges requires a multi-faceted approach, combining advanced technologies, international collaboration, regulatory frameworks, and specialized skills, to stay one step ahead in the ongoing battle against Dark Web markets.

Techniques used by law enforcement to infiltrate Dark Web marketplaces

Law enforcement agencies around the world are constantly working towards combating illegal activities conducted on Dark Web marketplaces. In order to effectively infiltrate these marketplaces and gather evidence to prosecute offenders, law enforcement utilizes a variety of techniques. In this section, we will explore some of the key techniques used by law enforcement to infiltrate Dark Web marketplaces.

Undercover Operations

Undercover operations play a crucial role in law enforcement's efforts to infiltrate Dark Web marketplaces. Trained officers, posing as regular users or potential buyers, create fake identities and engage with sellers and other participants on the platforms. These undercover operations allow law enforcement to gather intelligence, identify key criminals, and monitor illegal activities taking place on these platforms.

To maintain authenticity, law enforcement officers must carefully craft their undercover personas, ensuring that they align with the expectations and norms of the Dark Web marketplaces they are targeting. This requires a deep understanding of the specific marketplace's culture, terminology, and overall modus operandi. By assimilating into the ecosystem, undercover officers can gain the trust of sellers and buyers, enabling them to extract valuable information for subsequent investigations.

Blockchain Analysis

Cryptocurrencies, such as Bitcoin, are commonly used for transactions on Dark Web marketplaces due to their perceived anonymity. However, law enforcement agencies are increasingly employing blockchain analysis techniques to trace these transactions and identify the individuals involved.

Blockchain analysis involves examining the publicly available transaction history of a cryptocurrency and mapping the flow of funds from one account to another. By linking known addresses associated with Dark Web marketplaces to real-world identities, law enforcement can uncover the individuals behind the illicit transactions. Various tools and software are available to assist in this process, allowing investigators to analyze complex transaction patterns and visualize the movement of funds.

While blockchain analysis can provide valuable evidence, it is essential for law enforcement to adhere to legal and ethical guidelines, ensuring that the privacy rights of individuals not involved in illegal activities are respected.

Exploiting Vulnerabilities

Dark Web marketplaces heavily rely on digital platforms and technologies to facilitate their operations. Law enforcement agencies work to identify and exploit vulnerabilities in these platforms to gain access to illicit activities and gather evidence.

One common method is the exploitation of software vulnerabilities. Law enforcement may identify and exploit vulnerabilities in the marketplace's infrastructure, including the website, servers, or communication channels, to gain insight into ongoing criminal activities. By leveraging these vulnerabilities, investigators can intercept communications between buyers and sellers, monitor transactions, and track the movement of illegal goods.

However, it is important to note that the exploitation of vulnerabilities by law enforcement raises ethical concerns. Balancing the need for public safety with the potential impact on privacy is crucial to ensure that such techniques are used responsibly and within the boundaries of the law.

Collaboration with International Partners

Combating Dark Web marketplaces requires international cooperation and collaboration between law enforcement agencies across different jurisdictions. Many criminal activities on the Dark Web have a global reach, with participants and servers located in multiple countries. Hence, law enforcement agencies work together to share information, coordinate investigations, and dismantle illicit networks.

International partnerships enable law enforcement to access expertise, resources, and jurisdictional support that may not be available in their own country. By pooling their efforts, agencies can successfully infiltrate Dark Web marketplaces, arrest offenders, and disrupt the operations of these illegal platforms.

Proactive Monitoring

In addition to reactive investigative techniques, law enforcement agencies employ proactive monitoring strategies to identify and prevent criminal activities on Dark Web marketplaces. This involves the use of sophisticated monitoring tools and technologies designed to detect suspicious behavior, illegal listings, or discussions related to illicit activities.

By continuously monitoring the Dark Web, law enforcement can gather intelligence, identify emerging threats, and proactively disrupt criminal operations. Automated systems, machine learning algorithms, and natural language processing are employed to analyze large volumes of data and flag potentially illegal activities. These tools enable law enforcement to stay one step ahead of criminals and take preventive action.

It is important to strike a balance between proactive monitoring for public safety and respecting individual privacy. Strict adherence to legal frameworks and oversight mechanisms is crucial to ensure that these monitoring activities are conducted in a lawful and responsible manner.

Examples and Real-World Application

One prominent example of law enforcement successfully infiltrating a Dark Web marketplace is the case of "Operation Bayonet", which led to the takedown of the infamous AlphaBay marketplace in 2017. AlphaBay was one of the largest Dark Web marketplaces, known for its vast inventory of illegal drugs, weapons, and stolen data.

Law enforcement agencies from several countries collaborated to bring down AlphaBay. Through undercover operations and sophisticated tracking techniques, investigators were able to trace the administrator of the marketplace, gather evidence, and subsequently shut it down. The operation resulted in the arrest of the marketplace's founder and the seizure of significant amounts of cryptocurrency and other assets.

This operation demonstrated the effectiveness of international cooperation, undercover work, and technological expertise in infiltrating and disrupting Dark Web marketplaces. It served as a major blow to the illegal activities conducted on AlphaBay and sent a strong message to Dark Web market operators worldwide.

Conclusion

Infiltrating Dark Web marketplaces requires a combination of undercover operations, technological expertise, collaborative efforts, and proactive monitoring. Law enforcement agencies must constantly evolve their techniques to keep pace with the ever-changing landscape of Dark Web activities.

By leveraging these techniques effectively and responsibly, law enforcement agencies can dismantle illicit networks, bring offenders to justice, and enhance public safety. However, it is essential to strike a balance between investigative powers and the protection of individual privacy rights. The fight against Dark Web markets demands an ethical and lawful approach to ensure the preservation of democratic values while addressing the challenges posed by the digital underground.

Collaboration between global law enforcement agencies

In the fight against Dark Web markets, collaboration between global law enforcement agencies is crucial. Dark Web activities transcend national borders, making it necessary for agencies from different countries to work together to effectively dismantle these illicit marketplaces. This section will explore the importance of collaboration, the challenges faced, and the strategies employed by global law enforcement agencies to combat Dark Web markets.

Importance of Collaboration

Collaboration between global law enforcement agencies is vital due to the transnational nature of Dark Web activities. Dark Web marketplaces can be accessed from anywhere in the world, and their operations are not confined to a single jurisdiction. Criminals operating on the Dark Web often exploit differences in laws and regulations across countries to evade detection and prosecution.

By working together, law enforcement agencies can share intelligence, resources, and expertise, thereby strengthening their investigative capabilities. Cooperation between agencies can help identify and apprehend key individuals involved in operating Dark Web marketplaces, disrupting their activities and dismantling the infrastructure supporting them.

Challenges in Collaboration

Collaboration between global law enforcement agencies is not without challenges. One of the primary challenges is the differences in legal frameworks and jurisdictions. Each country has its own laws and procedures, which can complicate joint investigations. Legal barriers, such as extradition processes and differing standards of evidence, can hinder timely and effective collaboration.

Another challenge is the language and cultural barriers that may exist between law enforcement agencies from different countries. Effective communication is essential for successful collaboration, and overcoming language and cultural differences is crucial in sharing information and coordinating operations.

Moreover, sharing sensitive information across borders can raise concerns about the protection of privacy and national security. Law enforcement agencies must strike a balance between information sharing and safeguarding national interests.

Strategies for Collaboration

To address the challenges mentioned above, global law enforcement agencies employ various strategies to enhance collaboration in combating Dark Web markets.

One strategy is the establishment of international task forces or joint investigative teams. These teams bring together law enforcement officials from different countries to work collectively on challenging cases related to Dark Web marketplaces. By pooling their resources and expertise, these teams can tackle complex investigations more effectively.

Interpol, the International Criminal Police Organization, plays a critical role in promoting international collaboration. It acts as a platform for law enforcement agencies from different countries to share information, coordinate operations, and provide training on combating cybercrime, including Dark Web activities. Interpol's Global Complex for Innovation (IGCI) focuses specifically on issues associated with cyberspace, providing a hub for cooperation and exchanging best practices.

Furthermore, bilateral and multilateral agreements between countries facilitate collaboration by establishing mechanisms for sharing information and evidence. Mutual legal assistance treaties (MLATs) enable law enforcement agencies to request assistance from their counterparts in other countries, including gathering evidence and extraditing suspects.

Case Study: Operation Bayonet

One notable example of successful collaboration between global law enforcement agencies is Operation Bayonet, a joint effort by the United States FBI, the DEA, and the Dutch National Police. Initiated in 2017, this operation targeted and dismantled the infamous AlphaBay and Hansa Market, two prominent Dark Web marketplaces.

The operation involved extensive collaboration between the involved agencies, including sharing of intelligence and coordinating simultaneous takedowns. By working together, the agencies were able to not only shut down the marketplaces but also apprehend key individuals responsible for their operations.

Operation Bayonet demonstrated the effectiveness of collaboration in combating Dark Web markets. It highlighted the importance of information sharing, mutual support, and coordinated action.

Exercises

1. Research and discuss another notable case of collaboration between global law enforcement agencies in tackling Dark Web marketplaces.

2. Imagine you are a law enforcement officer involved in the fight against Dark Web markets. What challenges do you anticipate in collaborating with international counterparts? How would you overcome these challenges?

3. What are some ethical considerations that need to be taken into account when collaborating between global law enforcement agencies in the context of Dark Web investigations? Discuss potential conflicts, concerns, and ways to address them.

4. As a cybersecurity professional, what role can you play in supporting collaboration between global law enforcement agencies? How can you contribute to the fight against Dark Web markets?

Resources

1. "DarkMarket: Cyberspace Culture and the Market for Illegal Commodities" by M. Levi and M. A. Moustaki (2015).

2. Interpol's website: `https://www.interpol.int/`

The need for cybersecurity professionals in the fight against Dark Web markets

The existence and proliferation of Dark Web markets pose significant challenges to law enforcement agencies and society as a whole. The illicit activities conducted on these platforms, such as the sale of illegal goods, cybercrime services, and the distribution of sensitive information, call for proactive measures to counter and mitigate the risks. This is where cybersecurity professionals play a crucial role in the fight against Dark Web markets.

Cybersecurity professionals are skilled individuals who possess knowledge and expertise in safeguarding digital systems, networks, and data from unauthorized access, exploitation, and attacks. Their specialized skills are invaluable in tackling the complex and ever-evolving threats posed by Dark Web markets.

Understanding the Role of Cybersecurity Professionals

In the context of Dark Web markets, cybersecurity professionals are needed to address the following key aspects:

1. **Threat Intelligence and Analysis:** Cybersecurity professionals contribute to the identification, analysis, and understanding of the various threats prevalent on the Dark Web. By monitoring Dark Web activities, they gather intelligence and assess the risks associated with different marketplaces, cybercrime services, and emerging trends. This information helps in formulating effective strategies and countermeasures.

2. **Dark Web Monitoring and Investigations:** Cybersecurity professionals are responsible for monitoring Dark Web activities to detect and track illicit transactions, cybercriminal activities, and potential threats. They employ advanced tools, techniques, and forensic methodologies to gather evidence, build cases, and provide support to law enforcement agencies during investigations. Their expertise in analyzing Dark Web marketplaces allows them to identify patterns, illegal vendors, and criminal networks.

3. **Cybercrime Prevention and Mitigation:** One of the primary roles of cybersecurity professionals is to develop and implement preventive measures to mitigate the risks posed by Dark Web markets. They collaborate with organizations, government agencies, and law enforcement to establish robust cybersecurity frameworks, secure digital infrastructure, and deploy advanced security technologies. By conducting vulnerability assessments, penetration testing, and security audits, they identify weak points and recommend suitable security measures.

4. **Cryptocurrency and Blockchain Analysis:** Cryptocurrencies like Bitcoin are commonly used as a medium of exchange on Dark Web markets due to

their pseudonymous nature. Cybersecurity professionals play a critical role in analyzing blockchain transactions, tracing the flow of funds, and identifying the individuals involved in illicit activities. They employ advanced analytics tools, data mining techniques, and blockchain analysis platforms to uncover financial trails and enable law enforcement agencies to follow the money.

5. **Collaboration and Information Sharing:** Cybersecurity professionals facilitate collaboration between law enforcement agencies, government entities, cybersecurity firms, and other stakeholders in the fight against Dark Web markets. They participate in information sharing initiatives, intelligence forums, and joint investigations to exchange knowledge, tactics, and best practices. Their ability to foster these collaborations strengthens the overall response and increases the effectiveness of efforts to combat Dark Web activities.

Skills and Expertise Required

Cybersecurity professionals involved in countering Dark Web markets need to possess a diverse range of skills and expertise. Some key areas include:

- **Digital Forensics:** Proficiency in digital forensics is crucial for analyzing and extracting evidence from various digital media. Cybersecurity professionals must have a solid understanding of forensic techniques, tools, and methodologies to uncover critical information from seized devices, network traffic, and communication logs.

- **Incident Response:** Cybersecurity professionals need to be skilled in incident response, enabling them to react swiftly and effectively when security breaches or cyber-attacks occur. Their ability to triage incidents, contain threats, and analyze the impact of security breaches is essential for mitigating risks and minimizing the damage caused by Dark Web-related activities.

- **Cyber Threat Intelligence:** In-depth knowledge of threat intelligence is essential for cybersecurity professionals in the Dark Web landscape. They need to comprehend the latest cyber threats, emerging attack vectors, and trends in criminal methodologies to develop proactive strategies and countermeasures.

- **Network Security:** Competence in network security is fundamental for detecting and preventing unauthorized access, data breaches, and other cyber-attacks. Cybersecurity professionals must possess strong knowledge of network architecture, encryption protocols, and intrusion detection systems to secure digital infrastructures against Dark Web threats.

- **Cryptocurrency and Blockchain Analysis:** Understanding the technical aspects of cryptocurrencies and blockchain technology is essential for investigating Dark Web transactions. Cybersecurity professionals need to be adept at analyzing blockchain transactions, tracing cryptocurrency flows, and working with financial authorities to disrupt illicit activities facilitated by cryptocurrencies.

- **Legal and Ethical Compliance:** Cybersecurity professionals should have a solid grasp of legal frameworks, regulations, and ethical considerations surrounding cybersecurity and Dark Web investigations. They need to operate within legal boundaries, ensuring that their actions comply with relevant laws, regulations, and guidelines.

Resources for Cybersecurity Professionals

Procuring and sharpening the necessary skills for combating Dark Web markets requires continuous learning and staying updated with the evolving threat landscape. Cybersecurity professionals can turn to various resources, including:

- Professional certifications such as Certified Information Systems Security Professional (CISSP), Certified Ethical Hacker (CEH), and Certified Cyber Threat Intelligence Professional (CCTIP) provide comprehensive training and validation of cybersecurity skills.

- Cybersecurity conferences, webinars, and seminars offer opportunities to network with experts, attend workshops, and gain insights into the latest trends and technologies in the field.

- Online communities and forums dedicated to cybersecurity allow professionals to engage in discussions, seek advice, and share knowledge.

- Academic courses and programs in cybersecurity, digital forensics, and network security equip individuals with a strong foundation and theoretical understanding of cybersecurity principles.

- Open-source tools and platforms, such as TheHive and MISP, provide cybersecurity professionals with resources for threat intelligence sharing, incident response, and collaboration.

- Collaboration with law enforcement agencies, government organizations, and private industry groups enables cybersecurity professionals to access specialized knowledge, intelligence, and shared resources.

Ethical Challenges for Cybersecurity Professionals

Engaging in the fight against Dark Web markets can present cybersecurity professionals with a range of ethical considerations. Some of the significant challenges they might encounter include:

- Balancing Privacy and Security: Ensuring the privacy and security of individuals and organizations while combating Dark Web activities is a delicate balance. Cybersecurity professionals must navigate the ethical implications of surveillance, data collection, and the potential impact on innocent users.

- Minimizing Collateral Damage: The actions taken in response to Dark Web activities should be precise to avoid unintended consequences and collateral damage. Cybersecurity professionals need to uphold ethical standards and minimize any harm caused to legitimate users or systems during investigations.

- Transparency and Accountability: Maintaining transparency and accountability is crucial for cybersecurity professionals involved in Dark Web operations. They must document their actions, justify their methodologies, and ensure that all procedures align with legal and ethical guidelines.

- Respecting Legal Boundaries: Cybersecurity professionals must operate within legal frameworks and respect the due process of law. They need to understand the limitations of their authority and collaborate closely with law enforcement agencies to avoid overstepping boundaries.

- Safeguarding Anonymity and Privacy: Protecting the identities and privacy of cybersecurity professionals involved in Dark Web investigations is crucial. Ensuring the safety of individuals working undercover or collecting sensitive intelligence is necessary to avoid compromising their effectiveness and personal safety.

Exercises

To further engage students and enhance their understanding of the role of cybersecurity professionals in the fight against Dark Web markets, consider the following exercises:

1. Research and discuss a real-world case where cybersecurity professionals played a significant role in countering Dark Web market activities. Analyze the methods and techniques employed by these professionals and examine the impact of their actions on disrupting criminal networks.

2. Form a group and carry out a simulated investigation of Dark Web activities. Assign roles to different group members, such as threat intelligence analyst, digital forensics expert, and network security specialist. Develop a plan of action, identify key areas to monitor, and analyze any findings to present a comprehensive report on the simulated investigation.

3. Organize a panel discussion or invite a guest speaker who is a cybersecurity professional involved in combating Dark Web markets. Explore their experiences, challenges faced, and ethical considerations encountered during their work. Engage in an interactive Q&A session to gain further insights into the fight against Dark Web activities.

By equipping students with knowledge about the role of cybersecurity professionals in countering Dark Web markets, they can develop a deeper understanding of the importance of cybersecurity in the digital landscape. Additionally, this knowledge can inspire and guide students who are considering a career in cybersecurity or related fields.

The Dark Web Market Ecosystem

Dark Web Market Infrastructure

The role of hosting services in Dark Web marketplaces

In Dark Web marketplaces, hosting services play a crucial role in providing the infrastructure necessary for the operation of these illicit online platforms. These services enable the creation and maintenance of websites on the Dark Web, facilitating the exchange of illegal goods and services. Understanding the role of hosting services is essential in comprehending the functioning and dynamics of Dark Web marketplaces.

The need for hosting services

Dark Web marketplaces require hosting services to ensure the availability and accessibility of their platforms. Unlike traditional websites on the Surface Web, Dark Web marketplaces operate within a decentralized network known as the Tor network. This network provides anonymity and privacy to users, making it increasingly attractive for illicit activities. Hosting services within the Tor network are designed to protect the identity and location of Dark Web marketplaces, allowing them to evade detection by law enforcement agencies.

Challenges faced by Dark Web market infrastructure providers

Hosting services on the Dark Web face unique challenges due to the illegal nature of the activities they are supporting. These challenges include:

1. Evading law enforcement: Hosting services need to develop robust mechanisms to hide the physical locations of their servers. This involves utilizing

various techniques, such as routing data through numerous relays within the Tor network or employing other anonymization strategies.

2. Handling high traffic and bandwidth: Dark Web marketplaces often experience heavy traffic due to the large number of buyers and sellers using their platforms. Hosting services need to manage this load efficiently to ensure continuous access and prevent service disruptions.

3. Preventing cyber attacks: The nature of Dark Web marketplaces makes them attractive targets for cybercriminals and hackers. Hosting services must employ robust security measures to safeguard their infrastructure from potential attacks, ensuring that the anonymity and privacy of users are not compromised.

The use of encryption and anonymous communication tools

To enhance security and protect user identities, hosting services in Dark Web marketplaces employ encryption and anonymous communication tools. These tools help in encrypting the communications between users and the marketplace servers, making it harder for outsiders to intercept and decipher the data.

The Onion Routing protocol, implemented by the Tor network, plays a significant role in providing encryption and anonymization. It ensures that communication between users and the marketplace servers is routed through multiple relays, making it difficult to trace the origin and destination of the data. The use of encryption and anonymous communication tools enhances the security and privacy of Dark Web marketplaces, allowing users to transact with increased confidence.

Future trends and challenges

As law enforcement agencies and cybersecurity professionals continue to develop more advanced techniques for combating Dark Web marketplaces, hosting services face increasing challenges. They must adapt to evolving security measures and find innovative ways to ensure the continued operation and anonymity of Dark Web marketplaces.

Additionally, with the emergence of new technologies such as blockchain and decentralized hosting services, the landscape of Dark Web market infrastructures may undergo significant changes. These technologies have the potential to provide enhanced privacy and security while also making it more difficult for law enforcement to target hosting services.

It is crucial for hosting services to stay ahead of these advancements and remain proactive in addressing the challenges posed by law enforcement and cybercriminals. Collaborating and sharing information within the hosting services community can help develop better strategies for ensuring the long-term viability of Dark Web marketplaces.

In conclusion, hosting services are indispensable in enabling the operation of Dark Web marketplaces. They provide the necessary infrastructure and security measures to ensure the anonymity, accessibility, and continuous functioning of these illicit online platforms. However, hosting services must navigate numerous challenges to maintain their operations in the face of increasing scrutiny and advancements in law enforcement techniques. Staying at the forefront of technological advancements and adopting innovative practices will be crucial for the survival and evolution of Dark Web market infrastructures.

Challenges faced by Dark Web market infrastructure providers

Dark Web market infrastructure providers play a crucial role in enabling the operation of Dark Web marketplaces. These providers offer hosting services and other technical solutions that allow Dark Web markets to exist and function. However, they face various challenges that pose significant risks to their operations and overall security. This section will explore some of the major challenges faced by Dark Web market infrastructure providers and their implications.

One of the primary challenges faced by infrastructure providers is the constant threat of law enforcement intervention. Due to the illegal activities taking place on Dark Web markets, law enforcement agencies worldwide are actively working to dismantle these marketplaces and bring the individuals involved to justice. As a result, infrastructure providers are at risk of being targeted by law enforcement, as their services directly support the functioning of these illicit marketplaces.

To mitigate this risk, infrastructure providers need to employ robust security measures to protect their infrastructure from law enforcement infiltration. They often have to carefully monitor their networks, proactively detect any suspicious activities, and quickly respond to any security breaches. Moreover, infrastructure providers may need to invest in advanced encryption technologies and other defensive mechanisms to ensure the confidentiality and integrity of their systems.

Another significant challenge for Dark Web market infrastructure providers is maintaining anonymity and evading detection. The Dark Web relies on anonymizing software, such as the Tor network, to conceal the identities and locations of its users. The infrastructure providers must ensure that their services effectively safeguard the anonymity of Dark Web market operators and participants. Any breach in anonymity could compromise the security of the entire marketplace and lead to the identification and arrest of individuals involved in illegal activities.

Ensuring the availability and reliability of the infrastructure is also a critical challenge. Dark Web marketplaces can experience significant fluctuations in traffic due to various factors such as law enforcement actions, market closures, or periods of high demand for certain illicit products or services. Infrastructure providers must have scalable and resilient systems in place to handle these fluctuations and maintain a seamless user experience. This may involve utilizing load balancing techniques, redundant servers, and other infrastructure management strategies.

Furthermore, Dark Web market infrastructure providers must contend with the ever-evolving techniques employed by cybercriminals. Threat actors are continuously attempting to exploit vulnerabilities in the infrastructure to gain unauthorized access or disrupt the market's operations. Infrastructure providers must regularly update and patch their systems, implement strong access controls, and stay abreast of emerging security threats and defensive mechanisms.

One unconventional challenge that infrastructure providers face is the ethical dilemma of supporting illegal activities. While infrastructure providers may not directly engage in illegal activities themselves, their provision of services to Dark Web markets can be seen as enabling these activities. This raises ethical concerns about their complicity in facilitating criminal behavior. Infrastructure providers must carefully consider the social and legal implications of their actions and strike a balance between providing services and preventing harm.

Overall, the challenges faced by Dark Web market infrastructure providers require a comprehensive approach to security and risk management. These providers must navigate the complex landscape of law enforcement interventions, anonymity protection, scalability, cyber threats, and ethical considerations to maintain the operation of Dark Web marketplaces. By addressing these challenges, infrastructure providers contribute to shaping the future of the Dark Web markets and their impact on society.

The use of encryption and anonymous communication tools

The Dark Web is often associated with illegal activities and illicit trade. To ensure the privacy and security of their activities, users on the Dark Web employ encryption and anonymous communication tools. These tools provide a layer of protection against surveillance and tracing by law enforcement agencies. In this section, we will explore the various encryption techniques and communication tools used on the Dark Web.

Encryption Techniques

Encryption plays a vital role in securing communications and data on the Dark Web. It involves the process of converting plain text into ciphertext using algorithms and keys. Let's explore some of the commonly used encryption techniques on the Dark Web:

1. **Symmetric Encryption:** This encryption method uses a single key for both encryption and decryption. The same key is shared by both the sender and the recipient. It is fast and efficient but requires a secure way to exchange the key.

2. **Asymmetric Encryption:** Also known as public-key encryption, this technique uses a pair of keys - a public key and a private key. The sender uses the recipient's public key to encrypt the message, while the recipient uses their private key to decrypt it. Asymmetric encryption ensures secure communication between parties without the need to exchange secret keys.

3. **End-to-End Encryption:** This method ensures that only the intended recipient can read the message. The message is encrypted on the sender's device and decrypted on the recipient's device, with no intermediate party having access to the plaintext. End-to-end encryption is commonly used in messaging applications on the Dark Web.

4. **PGP Encryption:** Pretty Good Privacy (PGP) is a widely used encryption protocol on the Dark Web. It provides a strong level of security by combining symmetric and asymmetric encryption. PGP incorporates digital signatures to verify the identity of the sender and ensures the integrity of the message.

Anonymous Communication Tools

Securing communication and maintaining anonymity are crucial factors on the Dark Web. Here are some commonly used tools for anonymous communication:

1. **Tor (The Onion Router):** Tor is a widely used open-source software that enables anonymous communication by routing internet traffic through a network of volunteer-operated servers called nodes. Tor encrypts the traffic in multiple layers, making it difficult to track the user's identity and location.

2. **Virtual Private Networks (VPNs):** VPNs create a secure and encrypted connection between the user's device and a remote server. They hide the user's IP address and encrypt the internet traffic, providing an additional layer of privacy.

3. **I2P (Invisible Internet Project):** I2P is an anonymous overlay network that allows users to access websites and services anonymously. It encrypts the traffic and routes it through multiple nodes, similar to Tor.

4. **Secure Messaging Applications:** These applications provide end-to-end encrypted communication between users. Signal and Telegram are among the popular messaging apps used on the Dark Web, known for their strong encryption and privacy features.

It is important to note that while encryption and anonymous communication tools provide a level of security, they are not foolproof. Law enforcement agencies and cybersecurity professionals continuously strive to develop techniques to trace and track users on the Dark Web. The use of multiple tools in combination with careful operational security practices is crucial for maintaining anonymity and privacy on the Dark Web.

Caveats and Risks

While encryption and anonymous communication tools provide a layer of protection, there are still potential risks and caveats to consider:

1. **Exit Node Vulnerability:** When using Tor or similar networks, the exit node poses a potential risk. It is the final node through which the encrypted traffic exits the network and reaches the destination. If the exit node is compromised or operated maliciously, it can intercept the communication and compromise the user's anonymity.

2. **Cryptocurrency Tracing:** Although encryption secures financial transactions on the Dark Web, tracing cryptocurrency transactions remains a challenge. Law enforcement agencies use blockchain analysis and other techniques to trace the flow of funds, linking transactions to individuals.

3. **Social Engineering Attacks:** While encryption tools protect against data interception, users can still fall prey to social engineering attacks. Phishing emails, fake login pages, and other techniques can deceive users into revealing sensitive information or compromising their anonymity.

4. **Operational Security Mistakes:** Users can inadvertently compromise their anonymity by making operational security mistakes. Reusing pseudonyms, revealing personal information, or accessing the Dark Web from an insecure device or network can jeopardize their anonymity and expose their activities.

Real-World Example: Silk Road

One of the most infamous examples of Dark Web marketplaces is Silk Road. Ross Ulbricht, the creator of Silk Road, heavily relied on encryption and anonymous communication tools to maintain the marketplace's operations secret. However, despite his efforts, law enforcement agencies eventually traced and arrested

Ulbricht through a combination of traditional investigative techniques and technology.

The Silk Road case highlights the cat-and-mouse game between law enforcement and Dark Web operators. It emphasizes the need to continually enhance encryption and communication tools to ensure the privacy and security of individuals on the Dark Web.

Exercises

1. Research and compare different encryption algorithms used on the Dark Web. Discuss their strengths and weaknesses.

2. Investigate the impact of encryption and anonymous communication tools on the fight against cybercrime. How do they hinder or aid law enforcement efforts?

3. Explore recent advancements in blockchain analysis techniques and their implications for tracing cryptocurrency transactions on the Dark Web.

4. Conduct a risk assessment of using anonymous communication tools. Identify the potential risks and propose mitigation strategies.

Additional Resources

1. Greenberg, A. (2017). *This Machine Kills Secrets: How Wikileaks, Cypherpunks, and Hacktivists Aim to Free the World's Information.* Penguin Books.

2. Dingledine, R., Mathewson, N., & Syverson, P. (2004). *Tor: The Second-Generation Onion Router.* In *USENIX Security Symposium* (Vol. 13, pp. 21-21).

3. Bonneau, J., Anderson, J., Danezis, G., Davidson, T., Crane, S., Schneier, B., ... & Kroll, J. A. (2015). *Mixing secrets: Escrowing darkweb trust with secret sharing.* In *Proceedings of the 24th USENIX security symposium* (Vol. 14, pp. 109-126).

Dark Web Market Security and Trust

Escrow systems on Dark Web markets

In the world of Dark Web markets, where illegal goods and services are bought and sold anonymously, trust is a scarce commodity. Buyers and sellers cannot rely on the usual mechanisms of trust, such as reputation or legal recourse, to ensure fair transactions. This is where escrow systems come into play.

Definition and Function of Escrow Systems

Escrow systems act as trusted intermediaries between buyers and sellers in Dark Web markets. When a buyer wants to purchase goods or services, they initiate a transaction through the escrow system. The system holds the buyer's payment in escrow until the buyer receives the goods or services and confirms their satisfaction. Once the buyer is satisfied, the escrow system releases the payment to the seller. If the buyer is not satisfied, they can dispute the transaction, and the escrow system acts as a mediator to resolve the issue.

The primary function of an escrow system is to provide a secure mechanism for buyers and sellers to engage in transactions without the risk of fraud or non-delivery. It helps build trust between the parties involved and reduces the likelihood of scams or disputes.

Design and Operation of Escrow Systems

Escrow systems on Dark Web markets are designed with a focus on anonymity and security. The key components of these systems include:

1. **Multi-signature wallets:** Escrow systems utilize multi-signature wallets to hold funds in escrow. A multi-signature wallet requires multiple signatures (e.g., from the buyer, seller, and escrow system) to authorize any transactions. This adds an extra layer of security and ensures that no single party has control over the funds.

2. **Smart contracts:** Smart contracts, implemented using blockchain technology, are utilized to automate the release of funds once the predefined conditions are met. These contracts contain the rules and conditions agreed upon by the buyer and seller, ensuring fair and transparent transactions.

3. **Dispute resolution mechanism:** Escrow systems provide a dispute resolution mechanism to handle conflicts between buyers and sellers. This can include an arbitration process where a neutral third party assesses the evidence and makes a decision. In some cases, reputation-based systems may be used to determine the credibility of the parties involved in the dispute.

Challenges and Limitations of Escrow Systems

While escrow systems play a crucial role in ensuring trust and security on Dark Web markets, they are not without challenges and limitations. Some of these include:

1. **Scamming by the escrow system:** In some cases, the escrow system itself may be fraudulent or biased towards one party. This can result in unfair dispute resolution or theft of funds. To mitigate this risk, reputable Dark Web markets employ independent and trusted escrow services with a proven track record.

2. **Dispute resolution complexities:** Resolving disputes in an anonymous environment can be challenging. Without knowing the identity of the parties involved, it becomes difficult to validate claims or gather evidence. Escrow systems must employ sophisticated techniques and mechanisms to ensure a fair resolution process.

3. **Trustworthiness of sellers:** While escrow systems provide a level of protection for buyers, sellers still have the opportunity to engage in fraudulent activities. Escrow systems often rely on reputation-based systems to establish the credibility of sellers, but these systems can be manipulated or biased.

Example: The Evolution of Silk Road's Escrow System

One notable example of an escrow system in the Dark Web market is the one used by Silk Road, one of the first and most infamous online drug marketplaces. Silk Road's escrow system worked as follows:

1. The buyer would deposit funds into the Silk Road's escrow account.

2. The seller would ship the product to the buyer and provide a tracking number as proof of shipment.

3. Once the buyer received the product and confirmed their satisfaction, they would release the funds from escrow, and the seller would receive payment.

4. In case of disputes, the Silk Road administrators would act as arbitrators to resolve the issues and make a decision based on the evidence presented.

Silk Road's escrow system played a crucial role in maintaining trust among buyers and sellers, and it became a model for subsequent Dark Web marketplaces. However, its operation was not without flaws, as the administrators could potentially act dishonestly or exhibit bias in dispute resolution.

Conclusion

Escrow systems are vital tools that enable secure and trustworthy transactions on Dark Web markets. They provide a layer of protection for buyers and sellers in an environment where anonymity and trust are critical. However, the design and operation of escrow systems must address the challenges and limitations to ensure fairness and mitigate risks. As Dark Web markets continue to evolve, advancements in escrow systems and dispute resolution mechanisms will be necessary to maintain trust and security.

Reputation and Feedback Systems

Reputation and feedback systems play a crucial role in Dark Web markets by providing a means for buyers and sellers to establish trust and make informed decisions. These systems allow participants to rate and review their transaction partners based on their experience, thereby creating a reputation for each user.

Importance of Reputation

In the anonymous and unregulated environment of the Dark Web, trust is a scarce and valuable commodity. Buyers and sellers have no way to rely on traditional mechanisms, such as personal referrals or legal protections, to assess the trustworthiness of their counterparts. Reputation systems fill this void by enabling participants to make informed judgments based on the experiences of others.

A positive reputation not only increases the chances of successful transactions but also attracts more potential customers. Sellers with a good reputation are likely to command higher prices and have a larger customer base, while buyers with a good reputation are more likely to receive quality goods and services.

Feedback Mechanisms

Feedback mechanisms in Dark Web markets allow users to provide ratings and reviews for their transaction partners. These feedback mechanisms are usually based on a five-star rating system, where users can rate their experience on a scale from one to five stars. In addition to the numerical rating, users can also leave written comments elaborating on their experience.

The feedback left by users serves multiple purposes. Firstly, it provides a public record of a user's past transactions, allowing others to assess their reputation. Secondly, it serves as a mechanism for users to provide feedback to each other, offering insights into the quality of goods or services, timeliness of delivery, and overall transaction experience. Lastly, feedback allows the marketplace itself to identify and take action against fraudulent or unethical sellers.

Trustworthiness and Manipulation

While reputation and feedback systems are essential for establishing trust, they are not foolproof. Like any system, they can be manipulated to create false or misleading reputations. Dark Web market participants may engage in various tactics to artificially inflate their reputation, such as creating fake accounts and providing positive feedback for themselves.

To combat these manipulations, Dark Web marketplaces employ various techniques to ensure the trustworthiness of feedback. Firstly, many marketplaces require users to have a minimum number of transactions or a certain amount of time on the platform before they can leave feedback. This helps prevent new users from immediately gaining a high reputation without demonstrating their reliability.

Secondly, some marketplaces use advanced algorithms to analyze patterns in feedback and detect suspicious activity. These algorithms can identify unusual patterns, such as a high number of positive reviews from newly created accounts or a large number of negative reviews targeting a specific seller.

Lastly, market moderators play a crucial role in maintaining trust. They review feedback and can remove or flag suspicious reviews or accounts. Additionally, they may engage in undercover operations to identify fraudulent sellers and protect users.

The Impact of Reputation and Feedback Systems

Reputation and feedback systems have a profound impact on Dark Web markets. They not only help establish trust but also contribute to market dynamics and competition. Sellers with a strong reputation have a competitive advantage and can charge higher prices, while buyers with a good reputation have more negotiating power.

These systems also provide a mechanism for quality control. Sellers with a history of poor feedback are less likely to receive new customers, leading to market forces incentivizing sellers to provide quality products and services. Similarly, buyers with a reputation for dishonesty or unfairness may find it more challenging to make successful transactions.

Furthermore, reputation and feedback systems contribute to the overall security and stability of Dark Web markets. By identifying and flagging fraudulent or untrustworthy participants, these systems help protect users from scams and reduce the prevalence of illicit activities.

Ethical Considerations

While reputation and feedback systems are crucial for trust-building, they also raise ethical considerations. The anonymity of the Dark Web can sometimes lead to false accusations or unjust negative feedback. Innocent users may be targeted by malicious individuals, damaging their reputation and affecting their ability to transact.

Therefore, it is essential for marketplaces to strike a balance between transparency and privacy. They must ensure that users have the means to report and address unjust feedback, while also safeguarding the overall integrity of the system.

Additionally, marketplaces need to consider the ethical implications of allowing users to rate illegal goods and services. While feedback can help other users make informed decisions, it may indirectly condone or support illegal activities. Marketplaces must navigate this ethical dilemma by implementing policies that prioritize user safety while complying with legal standards.

Summary

Reputation and feedback systems are instrumental in establishing trust and facilitating transactions in Dark Web markets. These systems allow participants to assess each other's trustworthiness based on past experiences and provide a mechanism for quality control. While not foolproof, reputation systems help promote honesty and transparency in an anonymous and unregulated environment. However, ethical considerations regarding privacy, false accusations, and the rating of illegal activities need to be carefully addressed to ensure the integrity of these systems.

Trust and Security Challenges on Dark Web Markets

Trust and security are significant concerns for both buyers and sellers on Dark Web markets. The anonymity provided by the Dark Web creates unique challenges in establishing trust between participants, while the illicit nature of the transactions raises numerous security risks. In this section, we will explore the trust and security challenges that exist on Dark Web markets and the strategies employed by participants to mitigate these risks.

Trust Challenges on Dark Web Markets

Establishing trust is crucial for both buyers and sellers on Dark Web markets, as they engage in illicit transactions with strangers. The lack of face-to-face interaction and anonymous nature of the Dark Web make it difficult for participants to trust each other. Some of the key trust challenges on Dark Web markets include:

1. **Identity Verification:** The anonymity provided by the Dark Web makes it challenging to verify the true identity of buyers and sellers. In traditional online marketplaces, participants can rely on various identity verification methods, such as user profiles, ratings, and reviews. However, on the Dark Web, participants must rely on alternative trust indicators.

2. **Scams and Fraudulent Activities:** Dark Web markets are notorious for scams and fraudulent activities. Sellers sometimes deceive buyers by misrepresenting their products or failing to deliver goods and services as promised. Buyers may also engage in fraudulent activities, such as making false claims for refunds or charging back transactions after receiving the purchased items.

3. **Fake Reviews and Ratings:** Reviews and ratings play a crucial role in building trust on online marketplaces. However, on Dark Web markets, fake reviews and ratings are prevalent. Sellers may create fake accounts to post positive reviews for their products, while competitors may leave negative reviews to tarnish their rivals' reputations.

4. **Infiltration by Law Enforcement:** Dark Web markets often attract the attention of law enforcement agencies. Buyers and sellers must be cautious to avoid getting caught in law enforcement operations. The fear of infiltration by law enforcement creates mistrust among participants and increases the risks associated with conducting transactions.

5. **Lack of Legal Recourse:** Due to the illicit nature of Dark Web markets, participants face significant challenges in seeking legal recourse in case of fraud or scams. The absence of a legal framework and the anonymous nature of transactions make it difficult for victims to identify and hold the perpetrators accountable.

Mitigating these trust challenges requires participants on Dark Web markets to adopt various strategies and safeguards.

Security Challenges on Dark Web Markets

In addition to trust challenges, Dark Web markets also face significant security risks. Due to the sensitive nature of the transactions and the illegal activities involved, participants need to address the following security challenges:

1. **Risk of Law Enforcement Surveillance:** Dark Web marketplaces attract the attention of law enforcement agencies globally. Participants are at risk of being monitored and tracked by authorities, which can lead to arrests and prosecutions. Sellers must ensure their activities remain anonymous and take precautionary measures to avoid detection.

2. **Data Breaches and Hacking Attempts:** Dark Web markets are attractive targets for hackers and cybercriminals. These illicit marketplaces often store sensitive user information, including personal details and cryptocurrency wallets. The risk of data breaches and hacking attempts is a constant threat, and participants must take steps to protect themselves and their information.

3. **Cryptocurrency Theft:** Dark Web transactions rely heavily on cryptocurrencies, primarily Bitcoin. However, the use of cryptocurrencies comes with its own security challenges. Participants must be vigilant to protect their cryptocurrency wallets from theft and hacking attempts. Additionally, the use of cryptocurrency can expose participants to potential money laundering and legal repercussions.

4. **Escrow System Vulnerabilities:** Dark Web markets rely on escrow systems to facilitate transactions and protect both buyers and sellers. However, these escrow systems are not immune to vulnerabilities. Participants must be cautious of potential weaknesses in the escrow systems and employ additional security measures to mitigate risks.

5. **Malicious Software and Phishing Attacks:** Dark Web markets are breeding grounds for malicious software and phishing attacks. Participants must be wary of fake websites and links that attempt to steal credentials or spread malware. Using reputable platforms and employing robust cybersecurity measures is essential to protect against such threats.

Addressing these security challenges requires participants to adopt a proactive approach and implement various security measures.

Strategies to Mitigate Trust and Security Challenges

Participants on Dark Web markets employ several strategies to mitigate trust and security challenges. These strategies include:

- **Reputation-based Trust:** Participants rely on the reputation of buyers and sellers to establish trust. Positive reviews and ratings from previous transactions can indicate the reliability of a participant. However, caution must be exercised, as fake reviews and ratings are common. Participants should thoroughly analyze the reputation of a buyer or seller before engaging in a transaction.

- **Use of Escrow Services:** Escrow services act as trusted intermediaries between buyers and sellers. They hold the funds until the buyer confirms the receipt of goods or services. Escrow services help mitigate the risk of fraud, providing a level of assurance to both parties involved in the transaction. However, participants should verify the authenticity and reliability of the chosen escrow service.

- **Pseudonymous Identities:** To maintain anonymity and protect against law enforcement surveillance, participants use pseudonymous identities. These identities help to conceal the real-world identities of buyers and sellers, reducing the risk of detection. However, participants must acknowledge that pseudonymous identities do not guarantee complete anonymity, as sophisticated techniques can potentially de-anonymize users.

- **Secure Communication Channels:** Participants on Dark Web markets must prioritize secure communication channels to protect their conversations from eavesdropping. Encrypted messaging platforms, secure email services, and other privacy-enhancing technologies ensure that sensitive information remains encrypted and inaccessible to unauthorized individuals.

- **Multi-Signature Wallets:** To protect against cryptocurrency theft, participants often use multi-signature wallets. These wallets require multiple signatures to authorize transactions, reducing the risk of a single point of failure. Multi-signature wallets provide an additional layer of security, ensuring that stolen credentials or compromised accounts cannot result in unauthorized transactions.

While these strategies can help mitigate trust and security challenges, participants must remain vigilant, as new vulnerabilities and risks continue to emerge on Dark Web markets.

Ethical Considerations

While discussing trust and security on Dark Web markets, it is essential to consider the ethical implications of participating in or combating illicit activities. Both buyers and sellers must recognize the harm caused by their involvement in illegal transactions, such as drug trade, weapons sales, or cybercrime. Law enforcement agencies and cybersecurity professionals face ethical dilemmas in balancing privacy and security concerns while investigating Dark Web market activities.

Ethical considerations in combating Dark Web markets include:

- **Respecting Privacy:** Participants' right to privacy should be respected, even in the context of illicit activities. Law enforcement agencies must ensure that their surveillance efforts are targeted, proportionate, and comply with legal frameworks. Balancing the need to combat crime with individual privacy rights is a delicate ethical challenge.

- **Fairness and Due Process:** Law enforcement agencies should uphold the principles of fairness and due process in their actions against Dark Web market participants. Ensuring that investigations are comprehensive, evidence-based, and free from prejudice is crucial to avoid undue harm to innocent individuals. Fairness in prosecuting alleged offenders is paramount for a just legal system.

- **Minimizing Collateral Damage:** Efforts to combat Dark Web markets should aim to minimize collateral damage inflicted upon innocent individuals. Raising awareness about the risks of illegal activities on the Dark Web and fostering prevention measures can help individuals avoid involvement in illicit transactions altogether.

- **Staying Updated:** Law enforcement agencies and cybersecurity professionals must stay updated with emerging technologies and evolving trends on Dark Web markets. Ethically navigating this landscape requires continuous learning and adaptation to effectively combat illicit activities while respecting privacy and avoiding unnecessary harm.

In conclusion, trust and security challenges on Dark Web markets are unique and multifaceted. Participants must navigate these challenges while employing strategies to establish trust and mitigate security risks. Ethical considerations are crucial in maintaining a balance between combating illegal activities and respecting privacy and due process. The ongoing battle against Dark Web markets necessitates collaboration, innovation, and effective law enforcement strategies to ensure a safer digital landscape.

Techniques used by buyers and sellers to establish trust

Establishing trust is crucial in Dark Web markets, as both buyers and sellers operate in a highly anonymous and often illegal environment. Buyers and sellers need to have confidence in each other's credibility, reliability, and honesty in order to engage in successful transactions. In this section, we will explore some of the techniques used by buyers and sellers to establish trust in Dark Web markets.

Reputation and Feedback Systems

One of the primary ways trust is built and maintained on Dark Web markets is through the use of reputation and feedback systems. These systems allow buyers and sellers to rate and review each other based on their experiences during transactions.

Buyers can leave feedback and ratings for the sellers they have interacted with, providing information about the quality, accuracy, and timeliness of the products or services they received. These ratings are often accompanied by written reviews that provide further details about the transaction, such as the seller's responsiveness, communication, and packaging. In this way, sellers are incentivized to provide excellent products and customer service in order to maintain a positive reputation.

Similarly, sellers can leave feedback for buyers based on their reliability, prompt payment, and adherence to any rules or agreements. This allows sellers to identify trustworthy buyers and avoid those who may engage in fraudulent activities or cause disruptions in the marketplace.

Reputation and feedback systems play a significant role in building trust on Dark Web markets as they provide valuable information about the reliability and legitimacy of buyers and sellers. However, it's important to note that these systems are not foolproof. Some unscrupulous actors may engage in manipulative tactics, such as creating fake accounts or leaving false feedback to boost their reputation or sabotage their competitors. Therefore, buyers and sellers need to exercise caution and critically evaluate the feedback they receive.

Establishing Communication Channels

Another technique used by buyers and sellers to establish trust on Dark Web markets is the establishment of secure and encrypted communication channels. Communication is essential for negotiating prices, discussing product details, and addressing any concerns or questions both parties may have.

Buyers and sellers often utilize encrypted messaging platforms, such as PGP (Pretty Good Privacy) or secure chat services, which allow for the exchange of messages without the risk of interception or surveillance. These platforms ensure that sensitive information, such as delivery addresses and payment details, remains confidential.

Furthermore, buyers and sellers may establish a trusted and consistent mode of communication, such as a dedicated messaging channel or email address. This allows for a more personalized and ongoing interaction, fostering a sense of trust and reliability between the parties involved.

Use of Escrow Systems

Escrow systems are commonly used in Dark Web markets to enhance trust between buyers and sellers. In this system, an independent third party holds the buyer's payment until the goods or services are received and confirmed to be satisfactory. Once the buyer acknowledges the successful transaction, the payment is released to the seller.

Escrow systems provide a level of assurance for buyers that they will not be scammed or receive subpar products. If a seller fails to fulfill their end of the transaction, buyers have the option to dispute the transaction and request a refund. This gives buyers confidence that their funds are protected until they receive what they paid for.

Sellers also benefit from escrow systems as they know that the buyer's payment is secure and will only be released once the buyer is satisfied. This minimizes the risk of fraudulent buyers who may attempt to exploit sellers by claiming non-receipt of goods or services.

Utilizing Trusted Vendors and Middlemen

Buyers and sellers on Dark Web markets often rely on trusted vendors and middlemen to establish trust in their transactions. Trusted vendors are sellers who have built a strong reputation over time and have consistently delivered high-quality products or services. Buyers are more likely to trust these vendors due to their established track record.

Similarly, middlemen can play a crucial role in facilitating transactions and mitigating trust-related risks. Middlemen act as intermediaries between buyers and sellers, ensuring that both parties fulfill their obligations. They can offer dispute resolution services, additional security measures, and even act as guarantors for the transaction. The involvement of a trusted middleman provides an extra layer of assurance and can help establish trust between the buyer and seller.

It's important to note that while these techniques can help establish trust, they are not foolproof. Risks still exist, and buyers and sellers must exercise caution and take additional precautions to protect their anonymity, security, and financial well-being. Trust is a delicate balance in Dark Web markets, and both parties must navigate the landscape carefully to ensure successful and secure transactions.

Overall, the techniques discussed in this section contribute to the establishment of trust between buyers and sellers on Dark Web markets. Reputation and feedback systems, secure communication channels, escrow systems, and the utilization of trusted vendors and middlemen all play a significant role in building trust and reducing the risks associated with anonymous transactions. However, it is important to approach these techniques with caution and awareness of the potential limitations and vulnerabilities present on the Dark Web.

The role of Dark Web market moderators in maintaining trust

Trust is a vital component of any marketplace, whether it operates in the physical world or on the Dark Web. However, establishing and maintaining trust on Dark Web markets presents unique challenges due to the anonymous and illicit nature of the platform. To address this, Dark Web marketplaces employ moderators who play a crucial role in ensuring trust among buyers and sellers. In this section, we will explore the responsibilities and strategies employed by Dark Web market moderators to maintain trust within the ecosystem.

Responsibilities of Dark Web market moderators

Dark Web market moderators act as intermediaries between buyers and sellers, enforcing rules and ensuring the smooth operation of the marketplace. Their primary responsibilities include:

- **Enforcing marketplace rules:** Moderators enforce a set of rules that governs the conduct of buyers and sellers on the Dark Web market. These rules pertain to prohibited activities, such as the sale of certain illegal goods or engaging in scams, ensuring compliance among marketplace participants.

- **Monitoring transactions:** Moderators constantly monitor transactions to identify any suspicious or fraudulent activities. They review product listings, messages, and feedback to maintain the integrity of the marketplace and protect users from potential scams.

- **Resolving disputes:** In the event of a dispute between buyers and sellers, moderators act as mediators to find a fair resolution. They carefully evaluate the evidence and testimonies provided by both parties to make an informed decision.

- **Maintaining communication channels:** Moderators facilitate communication between buyers and sellers, ensuring that messages are delivered securely and efficiently. They ensure that the lines of communication remain open and any issues or concerns are addressed promptly.

- **Monitoring feedback and reviews:** Moderators monitor the feedback and reviews left by buyers for sellers, ensuring that they are authentic and reflect the actual buying experience. They take action against fake reviews and manipulate feedback to maintain the credibility of the marketplace.

- **Detecting and preventing scams:** Moderators actively scan the marketplace for any signs of fraudulent activity or scams. They work closely with law enforcement agencies to identify potential threats and take immediate action to prevent harm.

Strategies employed by Dark Web market moderators

Maintaining trust on Dark Web markets requires a combination of technological tools and human intervention. Here are some strategies commonly employed by Dark Web market moderators:

- **Strict verification process:** Moderators ensure that sellers undergo a rigorous verification process before they can join the marketplace. This process may include verifying their identity, reputation, and trading history, allowing only trusted sellers to participate in the marketplace.

- **Escrow systems:** Escrow systems are commonly used on Dark Web markets to provide an additional layer of trust. Moderators act as intermediaries, holding the buyer's funds until the product or service has been delivered satisfactorily. This protects both buyers and sellers from potential scams.

- **Establishing reputation systems:** Moderators implement reputation systems that allow buyers and sellers to provide feedback and ratings for each transaction. This helps to identify trustworthy sellers and encourages transparency within the marketplace.

- **Active surveillance:** Moderators employ advanced monitoring techniques to detect and prevent fraudulent activities. They analyze patterns of behavior, transaction history, and communication to identify potential scams or suspicious activities.

- **Collaboration with law enforcement:** Moderators collaborate with law enforcement agencies to report illegal activities, share information, and assist in investigations. This partnership strengthens the overall security of the Dark Web market ecosystem.

- **Continuous improvement:** Moderators continually adapt and improve their strategies to keep up with emerging threats and new methods employed by malicious actors. They actively gather feedback from users and incorporate user suggestions into their processes.

Example: Evolution of AlphaBay moderators

AlphaBay, one of the largest Dark Web marketplaces that operated until its takedown in 2017, had an extensive network of moderators who played a pivotal role in maintaining trust within the marketplace. These moderators were responsible for ensuring the smooth operation of the marketplace and preventing scams. They actively monitored product listings, resolved disputes between buyers and sellers, and continuously improved the marketplace's security.

One notable feature of AlphaBay was their strict verification process for sellers. Moderators conducted thorough background checks to verify the authenticity and reliability of sellers before allowing them to offer their products or services on the marketplace. This ensured that buyers could trust the sellers they were dealing with, leading to a more secure and trustworthy environment.

AlphaBay moderators also implemented an escrow system, holding funds in a secure account until buyers confirmed the receipt and satisfaction of their purchases.

This system provided an additional layer of trust, mitigating the risk of scammers disappearing with buyers' funds.

Furthermore, the moderators on AlphaBay actively collaborated with law enforcement agencies and shared information about potential illegal activities occurring within the marketplace. This partnership between moderators and law enforcement played a vital role in identifying and prosecuting individuals involved in illicit trade on the platform.

The example of AlphaBay demonstrates the critical role that Dark Web market moderators play in maintaining trust within the marketplace. By implementing strict verification processes, utilizing escrow systems, actively surveilling the marketplace, and collaborating with law enforcement, they ensure a safer and more reliable environment for buyers and sellers.

Caveats and challenges

While Dark Web market moderators play a crucial role, their effectiveness is not without challenges. Some of the key challenges faced by moderators include:

- **Maintaining anonymity:** Moderators must ensure their own anonymity while interacting with buyers and sellers. This requires sophisticated privacy-enhancing technologies and strict adherence to operational security practices.

- **Dealing with emerging threats:** As new techniques and technologies emerge, moderators must stay ahead of malicious actors. This requires continuous monitoring, updating processes to counter new threats, and leveraging innovative technological solutions.

- **Balancing trust and privacy:** Moderators must strike a delicate balance between trust and privacy. While maintaining trust is crucial, they must respect the fundamental need for privacy among Dark Web market participants.

- **Handling large volumes of data:** Dark Web marketplaces generate massive amounts of data. Moderators must develop effective systems to handle and analyze this data to detect fraudulent activities and ensure the smooth functioning of the marketplace.

- **Limited legal recourse:** Due to the anonymous nature of the Dark Web, moderators face challenges in pursuing legal actions against malicious actors.

They must rely on collaboration with law enforcement agencies to address illegal activities effectively.

Addressing these challenges requires a combination of technological advancements, collaboration with law enforcement, and continuous improvement of processes and strategies.

Conclusion

In the world of Dark Web markets, trust is critical to the functioning of the ecosystem. Dark Web market moderators play a vital role in establishing and maintaining trust among buyers and sellers. By enforcing marketplace rules, monitoring transactions, resolving disputes, and utilizing various strategies, moderators create a safer and more secure environment for marketplace participants.

However, the role of moderators is not without challenges. They must continuously adapt to emerging threats, balance trust and privacy, and handle large volumes of data. Collaboration with law enforcement agencies and the use of advanced technologies are essential in overcoming these challenges.

As Dark Web markets continue to evolve, the role of moderators will remain crucial in ensuring trust and security within the ecosystem. The ongoing battle against Dark Web markets necessitates collaboration, innovation, and a deep understanding of the dynamics of this hidden part of the internet. Through collective efforts, we can strive to mitigate the risks associated with Dark Web markets and protect individuals from the potential harm they pose.

Tools and Technologies Used on Dark Web Markets

Cryptocurrencies and their role in Dark Web transactions

Cryptocurrencies have played a pivotal role in the growth and operation of Dark Web markets. These digital currencies provide a means of conducting anonymous and secure transactions, making them the preferred medium of exchange in this illicit online ecosystem.

The Basics of Cryptocurrencies

Before diving into their role in Dark Web transactions, let's briefly revisit the basics of cryptocurrencies. Cryptocurrencies are decentralized digital currencies that use cryptography for secure financial transactions. They operate on a technology called blockchain, which is a decentralized and distributed ledger that records all transactions across a network of computers.

Bitcoin, the first and most well-known cryptocurrency, revolutionized the digital currency landscape. It introduced the concept of a peer-to-peer electronic cash system without the need for intermediaries like banks. Since its inception, numerous other cryptocurrencies, known as altcoins, have emerged.

The Appeal of Cryptocurrencies on the Dark Web

The Dark Web, being an anonymous and hidden online space, requires a form of currency that allows for discrete transactions. Cryptocurrencies offer several key advantages that make them a preferred choice for Dark Web transactions:

1. **Anonymity:** Cryptocurrencies provide a level of anonymity that traditional payment methods cannot match. While blockchain records all transactions, the identities of the transacting parties remain pseudonymous. Users can conduct transactions without sharing personal information, such as names or addresses.

2. **Decentralization:** Cryptocurrencies are decentralized, meaning they are not controlled by any central authority or government. This decentralization ensures that transactions cannot be easily traced or censored by governing bodies.

3. **Security:** The cryptographic nature of cryptocurrencies makes them highly secure. Transactions are protected by complex algorithms and protocols, making it extremely difficult for unauthorized parties to tamper with or counterfeit the currency.

4. **Global Accessibility:** Cryptocurrencies transcend geographical boundaries and can be accessed by anyone with an internet connection. This global accessibility enables Dark Web market participants from around the world to engage in transactions without currency exchange concerns or regulatory restrictions.

5. **Ease of Use:** Cryptocurrencies provide a convenient and user-friendly alternative to traditional payment methods. With digital wallets and an increasing number of user-friendly platforms, individuals with little technical expertise can easily participate in Dark Web transactions.

Bitcoin's Dominance on the Dark Web

While several cryptocurrencies are accepted on Dark Web markets, Bitcoin remains the dominant and most widely used currency. There are several reasons why Bitcoin has become the de facto standard on the Dark Web:

1. **First-Mover Advantage:** Bitcoin's early adoption and recognition established it as a trusted and widely accepted cryptocurrency. Dark Web markets, being among the earliest adopters of cryptocurrencies, predominantly embraced Bitcoin.

2. **Marketplace Acceptance:** Dark Web marketplaces have built infrastructure and payment systems that primarily support Bitcoin transactions. Vendors and buyers on these platforms have become accustomed to using Bitcoin as the main currency for their illicit activities.

3. **Liquidity and Exchange Support:** Bitcoin's widespread use has led to high liquidity, meaning it can be easily converted into other cryptocurrencies or traditional fiat currencies. Dark Web participants value this liquidity and rely on it for their financial operations.

4. **Perceived Anonymity:** While Bitcoin transactions are pseudonymous, they can be traced back to real-world identities through analysis and blockchain forensic techniques. However, many Dark Web users are under the misconception that Bitcoin transactions are fully anonymous. This perception, coupled with Bitcoin's popularity, has contributed to its continued dominance.

Challenges and Innovations in Dark Web Cryptocurrencies

Cryptocurrencies on the Dark Web face unique challenges and ongoing efforts to address these challenges are shaping the landscape. Some of the notable challenges include:

1. **Regulatory Pressure:** Governments worldwide have recognized the use of cryptocurrencies in illegal activities and have implemented regulations to combat them. This increased scrutiny has led to crackdowns on Dark Web marketplaces and exchanges, urging participants to adopt more privacy-focused cryptocurrencies.

2. **Privacy-focused Cryptocurrencies:** To address the privacy concerns associated with Bitcoin and other widely used cryptocurrencies, privacy-focused cryptocurrencies have emerged. Examples include Monero, Zcash, and Dash, which prioritize user anonymity and obfuscate transaction details.

3. **Tumbling Services:** Tumbling services, also known as mixers or tumblers, have been developed to enhance the anonymity of cryptocurrency transactions. These services shuffle and mix transactions, making it challenging to trace the flow of funds, thereby increasing privacy for Dark Web users.

4. **Law Enforcement Efforts:** Law enforcement agencies have stepped up their efforts to track illicit activities on the Dark Web. Through the use of blockchain analysis tools and collaboration with cryptocurrency exchanges, they aim to disrupt criminal operations and identify individuals involved in illegal transactions.

5. **Emerging Technologies:** Innovations such as zero-knowledge proofs and secure multi-party computation hold promise in further enhancing the privacy and security of Dark Web transactions. These technologies aim to provide stronger anonymity guarantees and protect user identities.

Ethical Considerations

The use of cryptocurrencies on the Dark Web raises several ethical considerations. While some argue that privacy is a fundamental right and cryptocurrencies enable that, others highlight the negative impact of illicit activities enabled by this technology. It is crucial to strike a balance between privacy and security, ensuring that efforts to combat illegal activities do not infringe upon legitimate users' rights.

Moreover, the environmental impact of cryptocurrency mining, which is energy-intensive, is another ethical concern. Efforts are being made to develop more sustainable mining practices and explore alternative consensus algorithms that consume less energy.

Conclusion

Cryptocurrencies have become an integral part of Dark Web markets, enabling anonymous and secure transactions. Bitcoin, with its first-mover advantage and market acceptance, remains the dominant currency in this underground ecosystem.

However, regulatory pressures and technological advancements are shaping the future of Dark Web cryptocurrencies, seeking to enhance privacy and address the challenges posed by illicit activities. It is essential to continue the dialogue around ethical considerations to strike a balance between privacy, security, and accountability.

Privacy-enhancing technologies on the Dark Web

Privacy is a fundamental concern for users of the Dark Web. In an environment where anonymity is highly valued, privacy-enhancing technologies play a crucial role in safeguarding the identities and activities of individuals on Dark Web markets. These technologies provide a layer of protection against surveillance, tracking, and potential exposure by law enforcement or malicious actors. In this section, we will explore some of the privacy-enhancing technologies commonly used on the Dark Web.

Virtual Private Networks (VPNs)

One of the most popular privacy-enhancing technologies on the Dark Web is the use of Virtual Private Networks (VPNs). VPNs create a secure and encrypted connection between a user's device and a server, effectively masking the user's IP address and location. By routing internet traffic through the VPN server, users can hide their identity and make it difficult for anyone monitoring the network to trace their online activities.

On the Dark Web, VPNs are widely used to protect against network surveillance and to access Dark Web marketplaces securely. They provide an additional layer of privacy by encrypting data transmitted over the network, making it harder for eavesdroppers to intercept and decipher sensitive information.

It is important to note, however, that while VPNs provide anonymity on the surface, they are not foolproof. Users must choose a reliable and trustworthy VPN provider, as some VPNs have been known to log user data or cooperate with law enforcement agencies. Additionally, VPN users may still be vulnerable to certain types of attacks or tracking methods that can compromise their privacy.

The Onion Router (Tor)

The Onion Router, commonly known as Tor, is a widely used privacy-enhancing technology on the Dark Web. Tor allows users to browse the internet anonymously by directing their internet traffic through a network of volunteer-operated servers called "relays." These relays are distributed worldwide and encrypt and route the traffic through multiple layers, making it incredibly difficult to trace back to the user.

Tor ensures privacy by encapsulating data in multiple layers of encryption, hence the term "onion." Each relay in the network only knows the identity of the previous relay and the next relay, effectively obscuring the origin of the traffic. This multi-layered encryption and routing system make it extremely challenging for anyone to identify the actual source or destination of the data.

Tor's decentralized nature and the encryption it employs make it a powerful tool for preserving privacy on the Dark Web. Users can access Dark Web marketplaces and communicate with others without revealing their real IP addresses and physical locations. However, it is important to note that while Tor provides anonymity, it may not guarantee complete security. Users must still exercise caution and follow best practices to protect their identities and data.

Cryptocurrencies

Cryptocurrencies, such as Bitcoin, are widely used on Dark Web markets for their privacy-enhancing properties. Unlike traditional financial transactions, cryptocurrencies operate on a decentralized network, and the identities of the parties involved are pseudonymous rather than linking directly to real-world identities.

Cryptocurrency transactions on the Dark Web provide a level of privacy and anonymity that is difficult to achieve with traditional payment methods. The use of cryptocurrencies allows buyers and sellers to conduct transactions without exposing their real identities, making it challenging for law enforcement agencies or other actors to trace the flow of funds.

While cryptocurrencies provide a degree of privacy, it is essential to note that they are not entirely anonymous. Transactions recorded on the blockchain are publicly visible, and with appropriate analysis and investigation, it is possible to link transactions to individuals. To enhance privacy, users can employ mixing services or use privacy-focused cryptocurrencies that offer additional anonymity features.

Anonymous Messaging Platforms

Communication is a critical aspect of Dark Web marketplaces, and maintaining privacy during exchanges is crucial. Anonymous messaging platforms, such as Off-the-Record Messaging (OTR) and Bitmessage, play a vital role in ensuring secure and private communication between buyers and sellers.

OTR is an encryption protocol that offers end-to-end encryption for instant messaging conversations. It guarantees that only the intended recipient can decipher the message, keeping the content confidential. OTR also provides a mechanism for deniable authentication, which allows users to deny participating in a conversation even if the contents can be decrypted.

Bitmessage, on the other hand, is a decentralized messaging system that uses public-key cryptography to provide privacy and anonymity. It offers encrypted messaging that is resistant to surveillance and is designed to prevent traffic analysis and message tampering.

These anonymous messaging platforms are widely used on the Dark Web to protect the confidentiality and privacy of conversations between parties involved in Dark Web market transactions. By encrypting messages and obfuscating their origin and content, these technologies make it difficult for third parties to intercept or decipher sensitive information.

Proxies and Tunnelling Techniques

Proxies and tunnelling techniques are additional privacy-enhancing technologies commonly employed on the Dark Web. Proxies act as intermediary servers between users and the websites they visit, effectively masking the users' IP addresses and allowing them to access resources anonymously.

Tunnelling techniques, such as Secure Shell (SSH) tunnelling or virtual private networks (VPNs), create an encrypted tunnel that encapsulates network traffic, making it difficult for anyone monitoring the network to decipher the information traversing the tunnel. These technologies provide an additional layer of privacy and security for users on the Dark Web.

Proxies and tunnelling techniques can help protect users' identities and conceal their activities from surveillance. However, it is important to note that using proxies or tunnelling techniques may introduce additional latency and can be susceptible to certain types of attacks if not properly configured or secured.

In conclusion, privacy-enhancing technologies play a crucial role in maintaining anonymity and protecting the privacy of individuals on the Dark Web. Virtual Private Networks (VPNs), The Onion Router (Tor), cryptocurrencies, anonymous messaging platforms, proxies, and tunnelling techniques all contribute to creating a secure and private environment on the Dark Web. However, it is important to remember that no technology can offer absolute privacy and security, and users must employ proper operational security practices to mitigate risks and safeguard their identities and activities.

Stealth addresses and encrypted messaging platforms

Stealth addresses and encrypted messaging platforms play a crucial role in ensuring privacy and security on Dark Web markets. In this section, we will explore the concept of stealth addresses, how they work, and their importance in protecting the identities of buyers and sellers. We will also discuss encrypted messaging platforms and their role in facilitating secure communication between market participants.

Stealth addresses

In the context of Dark Web markets, a stealth address is a cryptographic technique used to create a temporary, one-time address for receiving payments. Unlike traditional Bitcoin addresses, which are permanently associated with a user's identity, stealth addresses provide an additional layer of privacy by hiding the recipient's true address.

The process of generating a stealth address involves the use of a sender's public key and a recipient's private key. When a buyer wants to make a payment to a seller, they generate a new stealth address using the seller's public key and their own private key. This stealth address is included in the payment request, ensuring that only the intended recipient can decipher and access the funds.

From an observer's perspective, it is virtually impossible to link the sender's identity to the stealth address. This means that even if the transaction is recorded on the blockchain, the true identities of the parties involved are protected, enhancing the anonymity of Dark Web market participants.

Example:

Let's say Alice wants to buy illegal drugs from Bob on a Dark Web market. Instead of sending funds directly to Bob's Bitcoin address, Alice generates a stealth address using Bob's public key and her own private key. She sends the payment request with the stealth address to Bob. Bob can then use his private key to derive the actual Bitcoin address and access the funds.

By using a stealth address, Alice ensures that her identity is not linked to the transaction, providing an additional layer of anonymity and privacy.

Encrypted messaging platforms

Communication between buyers and sellers on Dark Web markets is a critical aspect of conducting business. To maintain privacy and security, encrypted messaging platforms are widely used to facilitate secure communication.

These platforms use end-to-end encryption, where messages are encrypted on the sender's device and can only be decrypted by the intended recipient. This means that even if the messages are intercepted, they appear as unreadable gibberish, protecting the content from unauthorized access.

Encrypted messaging platforms on Dark Web markets often employ techniques such as the Signal Protocol, which ensures the confidentiality, integrity, and authenticity of communications. The Signal Protocol is an open-source encryption protocol that provides strong encryption for instant messaging.

The use of encrypted messaging platforms not only protects the privacy of conversations but also enables buyers and sellers to discuss transaction details and negotiate terms securely. It minimizes the risk of interception by law enforcement agencies, making it more challenging for them to gather evidence and track illegal activities on Dark Web markets.

Example:

Suppose Charlie, a buyer, wants to inquire about the quality and price of a particular drug listed on a Dark Web market. Charlie initiates a conversation with the seller, Dave, using an encrypted messaging platform. The messages sent between Charlie and Dave are encrypted using end-to-end encryption, ensuring that only they can access and read the content.

Through the encrypted messaging platform, Charlie and Dave can discuss the transaction details, arrange delivery methods, and address any concerns or questions they may have. The use of encryption provides the necessary security and confidentiality for their communication, protecting both parties' identities and sensitive information.

Importance of stealth addresses and encrypted messaging platforms

Stealth addresses and encrypted messaging platforms are fundamental tools that enhance privacy and security on Dark Web markets. They help protect the identities of buyers and sellers, safeguard the content of their conversations, and maintain the overall integrity of transactions.

By using stealth addresses, Dark Web market participants can ensure that their real Bitcoin addresses are not associated with their activities, making it difficult for outside observers to trace transactions back to them. This level of privacy is essential in maintaining the anonymity required for conducting illicit activities on the Dark Web.

Similarly, encrypted messaging platforms enable secure communication, preventing unauthorized parties from intercepting and deciphering messages. This enhanced security allows buyers and sellers to exchange sensitive information and discuss transaction details without fear of detection, ultimately enabling the smooth operation of Dark Web markets.

It is important to note that while stealth addresses and encrypted messaging platforms offer significant privacy benefits, they are not foolproof. Law enforcement agencies and cybersecurity professionals continue to develop technologies to track and monitor Dark Web activities. Therefore, market participants must stay vigilant, follow best practices, and adapt to evolving privacy and security measures to mitigate risks.

Summary

In this section, we explored the concept of stealth addresses and encrypted messaging platforms in the context of Dark Web markets. Stealth addresses provide an additional layer of privacy by hiding the recipient's true address, while encrypted messaging platforms enable secure communication between market participants. These tools are essential in ensuring the privacy and security of transactions on Dark Web markets, helping to protect the identities of buyers and sellers and maintain the integrity of the marketplace. However, it is important to remember that privacy technologies on the Dark Web are constantly evolving, and market participants must remain informed and adaptive to navigate the dynamic landscape of Dark Web marketplaces.

Tools for obfuscating online identities on Dark Web markets

In the realm of Dark Web markets, maintaining anonymity is of utmost importance for both buyers and sellers. To achieve this, several tools and techniques are employed to obfuscate online identities and activities. This section will explore some of the key tools used on Dark Web markets to enhance privacy and security.

Virtual Private Networks (VPNs)

One of the primary tools used for obfuscating online identities on Dark Web markets is the Virtual Private Network (VPN). A VPN creates a secure and encrypted connection between the user's device and the VPN server, effectively masking their IP address and encrypting their internet traffic. By routing their connection through a VPN server located in a different geographical location, users can hide their true location and make it difficult for anyone to trace their online activities.

VPNs have become increasingly popular due to their ability to provide privacy, security, and anonymity. They offer a high level of encryption, making it challenging for third parties to intercept or monitor online communications. Additionally, many VPN providers do not keep logs of user activity, further ensuring privacy.

However, it is crucial to choose a reliable and trustworthy VPN provider, as some may keep logs or even collaborate with law enforcement agencies. Users should opt for VPNs that have a no-logs policy and are located in jurisdictions that prioritize user privacy.

Tor (The Onion Router)

Tor, also known as The Onion Router, is another widely used tool on Dark Web markets for obfuscating online identities. It is a network of volunteer-operated servers that allows users to browse the internet anonymously. Tor routes internet traffic through multiple layers of encryption, making it nearly impossible to trace back to the original user.

By using Tor, users can access websites hosted on the Dark Web while maintaining their anonymity. Tor's architecture ensures that no single server knows both the source and destination of internet traffic, providing users with enhanced privacy and security.

To browse Dark Web marketplaces through Tor, users typically need to use the Tor Browser, a modified version of the Mozilla Firefox browser that has been configured to work with the Tor network. The Tor Browser automatically routes all internet traffic through the Tor network, ensuring anonymity and circumventing censorship.

While Tor is an effective tool for anonymity, it is not without its limitations. The network can be slow due to the multiple layers of encryption, and it may be susceptible to certain attacks if used improperly. Users must also exercise caution when accessing websites on the Dark Web, as not all sites are trustworthy, and malicious actors may be present.

Proxy Servers

Proxy servers act as intermediaries between users and the websites they visit. They can be used to obfuscate online identities by making it appear as though the user is accessing the internet from a different IP address. By connecting to a proxy server before accessing Dark Web marketplaces, users can hide their true IP addresses and maintain their anonymity.

Proxy servers work by forwarding users' requests for web content and relaying the responses back to the users. This effectively masks the user's IP address from the website they are accessing, making it difficult to trace their online activities.

There are various types of proxy servers, including HTTP proxies, SOCKS proxies, and reverse proxies. The choice of proxy server depends on the specific requirements and level of anonymity desired by the user. Proxy servers can be either free or paid, with paid services often providing higher levels of security and privacy.

However, it is important to note that proxy servers can introduce certain risks. Users should choose reputable proxy services, as some may log user activity or even inject malicious code into web pages. Additionally, relying solely on a single proxy server may not provide complete anonymity, as it is still possible for determined adversaries to trace the user's online activities.

Disposable Email Services

Maintaining anonymity on Dark Web markets also involves using anonymized email addresses to communicate with buyers and sellers. Disposable email services provide temporary email addresses that can be used for a specific duration or until the user decides to close the email account. These services allow users to maintain their privacy and avoid associating their true identities with their online activities.

Disposable email services work by creating a unique email address for the user, which forwards incoming messages to their actual email account. Any replies or subsequent communications can be conducted through the disposable email address, ensuring that the user's true email address remains private.

While disposable email services offer an additional layer of anonymity, it is important to consider the trustworthiness and security practices of the service provider. Some providers may log user activity or breach user privacy, so users should research and choose reputable services that prioritize user anonymity.

Cryptocurrencies

Dark Web markets heavily rely on cryptocurrencies such as Bitcoin for conducting transactions. Cryptocurrencies offer a level of anonymity that traditional payment methods cannot provide. By using cryptocurrencies as a medium of exchange, buyers and sellers can obfuscate financial transactions and avoid the traceability associated with traditional banking systems.

The decentralized nature of cryptocurrencies ensures that transactions are not tied to real-world identities. Each transaction is recorded on a public ledger called the blockchain, but the identity of the parties involved remains pseudonymous. While cryptocurrency transactions can be traced, it is challenging to tie them back to specific individuals without additional identifying information.

Cryptocurrencies offer several advantages for anonymity on Dark Web markets, but they also pose risks. The volatility of cryptocurrency prices can affect the value of transactions, and the lack of regulation may present challenges in resolving disputes. Additionally, law enforcement agencies have developed techniques to track and analyze cryptocurrency transactions, making it important for Dark Web market participants to use additional obfuscation techniques in combination with cryptocurrencies.

Conclusion

Tools for obfuscating online identities play a vital role in ensuring privacy and security on Dark Web markets. Virtual Private Networks (VPNs), Tor, proxy servers, disposable email services, and cryptocurrencies all contribute to maintaining anonymity for buyers and sellers. However, it is essential to select reputable tools and understand their limitations to effectively protect online identities on Dark Web markets. As technology continues to advance, new tools and techniques for preserving privacy and security will continue to shape the landscape of Dark Web markets. It is crucial for users to stay informed about the latest developments and best practices to navigate this complex ecosystem.

Law enforcement tools for tracking Dark Web activities

Law enforcement agencies face significant challenges in tracking and investigating illegal activities on the Dark Web. The anonymization techniques and encryption tools used by Dark Web users make it difficult to identify and locate individuals engaged in illicit activities. However, law enforcement agencies have developed specialized tools and techniques to aid in their efforts to track Dark Web activities. In this section, we will explore some of the tools used by law enforcement to combat criminal activities on the Dark Web.

Traffic analysis and network monitoring

One of the key tools used by law enforcement agencies is traffic analysis and network monitoring. By collecting and analyzing network traffic data, law enforcement can identify patterns and connections between Dark Web users. They can track the flow of data packets and monitor suspicious activities that may indicate illegal operations.

Law enforcement agencies also collaborate with cybersecurity experts to set up dedicated monitoring nodes within the Tor network. These nodes capture and analyze network traffic to uncover hidden services and monitor user activities. By identifying the entry and exit nodes used by Dark Web users, law enforcement can trace the origin and destination of data traffic, providing valuable leads in investigations.

Blockchain analysis

Cryptocurrencies, such as Bitcoin, are commonly used on Dark Web markets for conducting anonymous transactions. However, blockchain analysis has become a powerful tool for law enforcement agencies to trace and identify individuals involved in illicit activities.

Blockchain analysis involves examining public blockchain records to identify the flow of funds and track transactions. Every Bitcoin transaction is recorded on the blockchain, and by analyzing these records, law enforcement can identify patterns and connections between Dark Web users and their cryptocurrency wallets. This information can be used to trace the movement of illegal proceeds and identify individuals involved in criminal activities.

To enhance their capabilities in blockchain analysis, law enforcement agencies collaborate with experts in cryptocurrency forensics and use specialized software tools. These tools allow investigators to visualize the flow of funds, identify suspicious transactions, and link them to individuals or groups engaged in Dark Web activities.

Covert operations and undercover agents

Infiltration of Dark Web marketplaces and online communities through covert operations and undercover agents has proven to be an effective strategy for law enforcement agencies. By posing as buyers or sellers, undercover agents can gather valuable intelligence, identify key individuals, and collect evidence to support criminal investigations.

Covert operations involve the creation of fake personas and accounts to gain the trust of Dark Web users. These operations require careful planning and coordination with other law enforcement agencies to ensure the safety of the undercover agents and the success of the operation.

Law enforcement agencies also employ advanced techniques, such as steganography, to embed hidden information within images or files, allowing them to monitor conversations and track illegal activities on the Dark Web. This enables investigators to gather evidence without alerting suspects or compromising ongoing operations.

Collaboration and information sharing

The fight against Dark Web activities requires extensive collaboration and information sharing between law enforcement agencies at the national and international levels. Due to the global nature of the Dark Web, criminals can operate from anywhere in the world, making international cooperation essential.

Law enforcement agencies establish cross-border partnerships, such as Europol's European Cybercrime Centre (EC3) or the FBI's Cyber Division, to share intelligence, coordinate efforts, and jointly investigate Dark Web cases. These partnerships enable agencies to pool their expertise, resources, and technological capabilities to combat criminal activities on the Dark Web effectively.

International collaboration also extends to public-private partnerships, where law enforcement agencies work with technology companies, financial institutions, and cybersecurity firms. These partnerships foster the exchange of information, expertise, and best practices, enabling law enforcement agencies to stay updated on the latest tools and techniques used on the Dark Web.

Legal frameworks and regulatory measures

In addition to technological tools and operational strategies, law enforcement agencies rely on legal frameworks and regulatory measures to combat Dark Web activities. Countries around the world have enacted laws to address cybercrime, illegal drug trade, money laundering, and other illicit activities associated with Dark Web markets.

Law enforcement agencies work closely with legislative bodies and policymakers to shape legal frameworks that address the challenges posed by the Dark Web effectively. They advocate for laws that empower investigators with the necessary tools and authority to combat online criminal activities while safeguarding individual privacy and civil liberties.

Additionally, law enforcement agencies collaborate with financial institutions and payment processors to monitor and regulate the flow of funds on Dark Web markets. By working together, they can detect suspicious financial transactions and disrupt the economic infrastructure supporting criminal activities.

Conclusion

Law enforcement agencies employ a wide range of tools and strategies to track and investigate Dark Web activities. Traffic analysis, network monitoring, blockchain analysis, covert operations, and information sharing all play crucial roles in the fight against cybercrime on the Dark Web.

However, the evolving nature of the Dark Web and the rapid advancement of technology present ongoing challenges for law enforcement agencies. To effectively combat Dark Web activities, continuous research, innovation, and collaboration are necessary. The future of law enforcement tools for tracking Dark Web activities lies in the development of advanced data analysis techniques, machine learning algorithms, and strong international partnerships.

As the Dark Web continues to evolve, law enforcement agencies must adapt their strategies and tools to stay one step ahead of cybercriminals. By combining cutting-edge technology with effective legal frameworks, collaboration, and public awareness, we can strive to create a safer online environment and protect individuals from the threats posed by Dark Web markets.

Cybercrime on Dark Web Markets

Illicit Drug Trade on Dark Web Markets

The rise of online drug markets

The emergence and rapid growth of online drug markets on the Dark Web have posed significant challenges for law enforcement agencies worldwide. These digital marketplaces provide a platform for the buying and selling of illicit drugs, allowing both buyers and sellers to operate with a level of anonymity and security previously unseen in the traditional drug trade. This section explores the factors that have contributed to the rise of online drug markets and examines the implications of this phenomenon.

Factors contributing to the rise of online drug markets

The rise of online drug markets can be attributed to several key factors, including:

1. **Anonymity and security:** Online drug markets leverage the anonymity and encryption provided by the Dark Web to protect the identities of both buyers and sellers. Transactions are conducted using cryptocurrencies, ensuring a high level of security and making it difficult for law enforcement to trace the flow of funds.

2. **Convenience and accessibility:** Online drug markets offer a convenient alternative to traditional street-level drug dealing. Buyers can browse through a wide selection of drugs, read reviews and ratings, and make purchases from the comfort of their homes. This accessibility has expanded the customer base and attracted new users who may have been reluctant to engage in traditional drug transactions.

3. **Global reach:** Unlike local drug markets that are limited to a specific geographic area, online drug markets have a global reach. Sellers can ship drugs internationally, allowing them to tap into new markets and expand their customer base. This has led to an increase in cross-border drug trafficking and challenges for law enforcement agencies in coordinating efforts across jurisdictions.

4. **Quality control and reputation systems:** Online drug markets often have reliable reputation systems that allow buyers to provide feedback and ratings based on their experiences with sellers. This enables buyers to make more informed decisions and promotes a level of quality control that is lacking in traditional drug markets.

5. **Avoidance of violence and physical risk:** The online nature of these drug markets removes the need for physical confrontations that are often associated with traditional drug transactions. This has led to a perception of reduced risk for both buyers and sellers, attracting individuals who are averse to violence or who live in areas with high levels of drug-related violence.

These factors have created an environment conducive to the growth of online drug markets, presenting unique challenges for law enforcement agencies and policymakers in combating this illicit activity.

Implications of online drug markets

The rise of online drug markets has significant implications for various stakeholders, including:

1. **Public health:** Online drug markets have the potential to exacerbate public health concerns related to drug abuse. The ease of access and wide variety of drugs available online may lead to increased drug consumption, especially among vulnerable populations. Additionally, the lack of quality control and regulation in these markets raises concerns about the safety and purity of the drugs being sold.

2. **Law enforcement:** Online drug markets present unique challenges for law enforcement agencies. The anonymity and encryption techniques used on the Dark Web make it difficult to identify and apprehend individuals involved in drug trafficking. The global nature of these markets further complicates investigations, requiring international cooperation and coordination.

3. **Traditional drug markets:** The growth of online drug markets has disrupted traditional drug markets, leading to a decline in street-level drug dealing in some areas. This has forced traditional drug dealers to adapt their business models or seek alternative sources of income, potentially leading to an increase in other criminal activities.

4. **Policy and regulation:** The existence of online drug markets has raised questions about the effectiveness of drug control policies and the need for regulatory measures to address this evolving threat. Policymakers face the challenge of striking a balance between safeguarding public health and maintaining law and order, while also considering the ethical and legal implications of surveillance and enforcement activities.

In summary, the rise of online drug markets on the Dark Web has been driven by factors such as anonymity, convenience, and global reach. These marketplaces have disrupted traditional drug markets and posed challenges for law enforcement agencies and policymakers. The implications of online drug markets extend beyond law enforcement and public health, requiring a comprehensive, multifaceted approach to address this complex issue effectively.

Popular drugs sold on Dark Web markets

The availability of illicit drugs on Dark Web markets has greatly expanded over the years, providing users with easy access to a wide range of substances. These online platforms have become a hotbed for drug trade, allowing buyers and sellers to connect anonymously and conduct transactions securely. In this section, we will explore some of the most popular drugs sold on Dark Web markets.

Cocaine

Cocaine is one of the most widely sold drugs on Dark Web markets. It is a powerful stimulant that produces euphoria, increased energy, and heightened focus. Due to its high demand, vendors on Dark Web markets offer a variety of cocaine products, including powder cocaine, crack cocaine, and even synthetic alternatives. Buyers can browse through different brands, purities, and quantities before making a purchase.

The anonymity provided by Dark Web markets attracts both casual users and bulk buyers looking to resell the drug. The pricing of cocaine on these platforms varies depending on factors such as purity, quantity, and location. Sellers often use stealth packaging techniques to ensure discreet delivery, minimizing the risk of interception by law enforcement.

Heroin

Heroin, an opioid drug derived from morphine, is also readily available on Dark Web markets. It is typically sold as a brown or white powder, or in a black, sticky form known as "black tar" heroin. Dark Web vendors offer different grades of heroin, ranging from low-purity street-level heroin to high-purity pharmaceutical-grade heroin.

The ease of access and potential for anonymous transactions makes Dark Web markets an attractive platform for both heroin users and distributors. However, the sale of such a highly addictive and dangerous substance poses significant risks to public health and safety.

MDMA

MDMA, commonly known as ecstasy or Molly, is a synthetic psychoactive drug that alters mood and perceptions. It produces feelings of increased energy, euphoria, and empathy. Dark Web markets feature numerous listings for MDMA, allowing buyers to choose from a range of brands, pill strengths, and quantities.

The popularity of MDMA on Dark Web markets can be attributed to the demand for recreational drugs in party and festival scenes. Buyers often rely on vendor ratings and reviews to ensure the quality and purity of the MDMA they purchase. Dark Web markets also serve as a platform for the sale of MDMA-related products, such as testing kits and accessories.

LSD

LSD (lysergic acid diethylamide) is a potent hallucinogenic drug that alters perception and cognition. It is commonly sold in the form of small blotter paper squares, known as tabs, which are placed on the tongue for ingestion. Dark Web markets offer a diverse selection of LSD products, including different dosages, designs, and brands.

Due to the popularity of LSD among recreational drug users and enthusiasts, Dark Web markets provide a convenient avenue for purchasing the drug. Buyers often rely on vendor reputation, customer reviews, and accurate dosing information to ensure a safe and enjoyable experience.

Marijuana

Although marijuana has seen increasing legalization in many parts of the world, its sale and consumption still remain illegal in numerous jurisdictions. Dark Web markets facilitate the sale of marijuana, offering a wide variety of strains, concentrates, edibles, and other cannabis products.

The availability of marijuana on Dark Web markets appeals to both medical and recreational users. Sellers often promote their products based on potency, aroma, flavor, and other desirable characteristics. Buyers can conveniently browse through different vendors to find the specific strain or product that suits their needs.

Other Drugs

In addition to the aforementioned drugs, Dark Web markets also feature a range of other substances, including but not limited to:

- Methamphetamine: a highly addictive stimulant that increases energy levels and enhances focus.

- Prescription Drugs: various pharmaceutical drugs, such as opioids (e.g., OxyContin, Vicodin), benzodiazepines (e.g., Xanax, Valium), and stimulants (e.g., Adderall, Ritalin).

- Synthetic Drugs: a diverse category of substances designed to mimic the effects of illegal drugs, such as synthetic cannabinoids (e.g., Spice, K2) and synthetic cathinones (e.g., bath salts).
- Research Chemicals: novel psychoactive substances that have emerged as alternatives to illicit drugs, often packaged as "legal highs" or "research chemicals."

It is important to note that the sale and consumption of these drugs pose significant risks to individuals' well-being and can have severe legal consequences. Dark Web markets have amplified the availability and accessibility of these substances, requiring extra vigilance from law enforcement agencies and healthcare providers in addressing the associated challenges.

In the next section, we will explore the challenges faced by law enforcement in combating the online drug trade and the impact of drug marketplaces on drug policies.

Challenges for law enforcement in combating online drug trade

The illegal drug trade on Dark Web markets poses significant challenges for law enforcement agencies worldwide. The anonymity and decentralized nature of these markets make it difficult to identify and apprehend those involved in drug trafficking. In this section, we will explore the key challenges faced by law enforcement in combating online drug trade and discuss potential strategies to address these challenges.

Anonymity and Geographical Obstacles

One of the primary challenges for law enforcement is the anonymity provided by Dark Web markets. Buyers and sellers can operate under pseudonyms and communicate through encrypted channels, making it difficult to establish their true identities or physical locations. Additionally, transactions are typically conducted using cryptocurrencies, such as Bitcoin, which further obscures the traceability of funds.

Addressing this challenge requires sophisticated investigative techniques and international cooperation. Law enforcement agencies must leverage advanced technologies and tools to trace the flow of cryptocurrencies and identify individuals involved in drug transactions. Collaboration between different jurisdictions is also crucial, as Dark Web markets operate across national boundaries. Mutual legal assistance treaties and information sharing among countries can help overcome the geographical obstacles faced by law enforcement agencies.

Encryption and Dark Web Market Infrastructure

Dark Web markets rely on encryption technologies to ensure the privacy and security of transactions. The use of Tor and other anonymity networks makes it challenging for law enforcement to gather intelligence and monitor illegal activities. Moreover, Dark Web market infrastructure is designed to resist takedown attempts, making it difficult to shut down these platforms.

To combat this challenge, law enforcement agencies need to invest in technologies capable of monitoring encrypted communications and identifying patterns of illicit activities. Advances in machine learning and artificial intelligence can play a crucial role in analyzing vast amounts of data to detect suspicious behavior and identify drug trafficking networks. Collaboration with cybersecurity experts is essential to develop tools for monitoring and disrupting Dark Web market infrastructure.

Adapting to Evolving Strategies

Criminal organizations involved in online drug trade constantly adapt their strategies to evade detection and prosecution. They may employ sophisticated methods to conceal their activities, such as using multiple layers of encryption or operating within closed groups on the Dark Web. This poses a significant challenge for law enforcement agencies, as they must stay ahead of these evolving tactics.

To address this challenge, law enforcement agencies need to foster close collaboration with academic institutions and cybersecurity experts who can continually analyze and understand new techniques used by drug traffickers. Proactive intelligence gathering, advanced surveillance methods, and undercover operations can help law enforcement agencies adapt their strategies to effectively combat online drug trade.

Jurisdictional Challenges

Dark Web markets transcend geographical boundaries, making it difficult to determine which jurisdiction has authority to investigate and prosecute drug traffickers. The decentralized nature of cryptocurrencies further complicates jurisdictional matters, as funds can be easily transferred internationally.

To overcome jurisdictional challenges, international cooperation is paramount. Interpol, Europol, and other international law enforcement agencies play a crucial role in coordinating investigations and sharing information among different jurisdictions. Mutual legal assistance treaties and extradition agreements should be strengthened to ensure effective prosecution of individuals involved in online drug trade.

Balancing Privacy and Surveillance

As law enforcement agencies seek to combat online drug trade, they face the challenge of balancing privacy concerns with the need for surveillance. The use of advanced surveillance technologies and monitoring of encrypted communications on the Dark Web raises ethical and legal considerations.

To navigate this challenge, law enforcement agencies must work closely with legal experts and policymakers to establish guidelines and regulations that strike a balance between privacy and surveillance. Transparency and public awareness campaigns can help address concerns related to privacy and ensure that law enforcement activities are conducted within the framework of the law.

Real-World Impact

The online drug trade facilitated by Dark Web markets has tangible real-world consequences, including drug addiction, violence, and organized crime. Law enforcement agencies must constantly adapt their strategies to address the evolving dynamics of the drug trade and its impact on society.

To tackle these challenges, multi-agency collaboration is essential. Law enforcement agencies need to work in partnership with healthcare providers, addiction treatment centers, and community organizations to address the underlying causes of drug addiction and provide support to affected individuals. Additionally, educational campaigns targeted at raising awareness about the dangers of online drug trade can help deter potential buyers and sellers from engaging in illicit activities.

Overall, the challenges faced by law enforcement in combating online drug trade require a multi-faceted approach that encompasses advanced technological solutions, international collaboration, and a balance between privacy concerns and surveillance. By addressing these challenges, law enforcement agencies can make significant strides in curbing the illegal drug trade on Dark Web markets and safeguarding public safety.

The Impact of Drug Marketplaces on Drug Policies

The existence and proliferation of drug marketplaces on the dark web have significantly influenced drug policies worldwide. These illicit online platforms have revolutionized the drug trade by creating a new channel for drug distribution and sales. As a result, policymakers and law enforcement agencies have had to adapt their strategies to address the challenges posed by these marketplaces.

Background on Drug Policies

Drug policies aim to regulate the production, distribution, and consumption of controlled substances. These policies are typically shaped by cultural, social, economic, and health factors. The primary goals of drug policies are to reduce drug-related harm, control drug production and trafficking, and address the underlying factors that contribute to drug abuse.

Traditionally, drug policies have focused on law enforcement efforts to disrupt the drug trade and punish drug offenders. However, the emergence of drug marketplaces on the dark web has presented unique challenges to these policies and has called for a more multi-faceted approach.

Challenges Posed by Dark Web Drug Marketplaces

Dark web drug marketplaces have disrupted traditional drug control strategies in several ways, posing challenges for drug policies:

1. Anonymity and Safety: Drug marketplaces on the dark web enable buyers and sellers to remain anonymous, making it difficult for law enforcement to track and intercept drug transactions. Moreover, the use of encryption technologies and decentralized marketplaces further complicates these efforts.

2. Global Reach: Dark web drug marketplaces have a global customer base, allowing drug dealers to reach customers worldwide. This international reach makes it challenging for law enforcement agencies to coordinate their efforts across jurisdictions.

3. Variety and Availability: These marketplaces offer a wide range of drugs, including illegal substances and prescription medications, making them easily accessible to individuals who may not have had access otherwise. This increased availability contributes to drug abuse and addiction issues.

4. Innovative Business Models: Dark web drug marketplaces often operate using innovative business models, such as vendor ratings and reviews, escrow systems, and customer support services. These features mimic legitimate e-commerce platforms, further blurring the lines between the legal and illegal drug trade.

Impact on Drug Policies

The presence of dark web drug marketplaces has had a profound impact on drug policies, influencing both the approach to drug control and the public perception of drug enforcement. Some key impacts include:

1. Shift in Focus: Drug policies have started to shift from a solely law enforcement approach to more comprehensive strategies that also focus on harm reduction, prevention, and treatment. Policymakers recognize the need to address the root causes of drug abuse and addiction, rather than focusing solely on supply-side measures.

2. Policy Innovation: The emergence of dark web drug marketplaces has prompted policymakers to explore innovative approaches to drug control. This includes efforts to increase education and awareness, develop evidence-based prevention and treatment programs, and adopt harm reduction measures such as needle exchanges and safe consumption sites.

3. International Cooperation: The global nature of dark web drug marketplaces has forced law enforcement agencies to collaborate and share information more effectively. International cooperation and information sharing platforms are now crucial in combating the transnational drug trade facilitated by these marketplaces.

4. Legislative Changes: The existence of dark web drug marketplaces has prompted policymakers to review and update drug laws to address the challenges posed by online drug sales. This includes strengthening legislation related to cybercrime, money laundering, and the regulation of cryptocurrencies used in dark web transactions.

Case Study: The Silk Road

One notable example of the impact of dark web drug marketplaces on drug policies is the Silk Road. The Silk Road, one of the first well-known dark web marketplaces, facilitated the sale of illegal drugs and other contraband between 2011 and 2013. Its operations and subsequent takedown had far-reaching consequences.

The Silk Road highlighted the need for international cooperation among law enforcement agencies to combat online drug trafficking. The case resulted in the arrest of the site's founder and the seizure of significant amounts of drugs and assets. It also brought attention to the shortcomings of traditional drug control strategies and forced policymakers to reevaluate their approach to drug policies.

In response to the Silk Road and other dark web drug marketplaces, efforts have been made to improve intelligence sharing, enhance cybercrime investigative capabilities, and raise public awareness about the risks associated with online drug purchases.

Conclusion

The influence of dark web drug marketplaces on drug policies cannot be underestimated. These marketplaces have presented unprecedented challenges to traditional drug control strategies, disrupting law enforcement efforts and shaping public perception. Policymakers and law enforcement agencies continue to evolve their approaches to address the impact of these marketplaces, utilizing innovative measures that focus on harm reduction, prevention, treatment, and international cooperation. The battle against dark web drug marketplaces remains ongoing, requiring collaboration, technological advancements, and a comprehensive understanding of the complex web of factors at play.

Weapons and Firearms Trade on Dark Web Markets

The availability of weapons on Dark Web markets

The availability of weapons on Dark Web markets is a growing concern for law enforcement agencies and governments worldwide. The clandestine nature of these online marketplaces makes it easier for individuals to acquire illegal firearms and other weapons with little to no oversight. In this section, we will explore the issue of weapon availability on Dark Web markets, the challenges in regulating online weapon sales, the connection between Dark Web markets and real-world violence, and efforts to combat illicit weapon trade on these platforms.

The rise of online weapon markets

Over the past decade, the internet has become a hub for a wide range of illegal activities, including the trade of weapons. Dark Web markets have emerged as a significant platform for individuals seeking to purchase firearms and other weapons anonymously. These markets provide a space where buyers and sellers can connect and conduct transactions without the fear of being identified or tracked by law enforcement.

The availability of weapons on Dark Web markets is of particular concern due to the potential for misuse and the potential for these arms to end up in the hands of criminals or individuals with malicious intent. The ease of access and anonymity provided by these platforms has attracted individuals who would otherwise not be able to acquire firearms legally.

Challenges in regulating online weapon sales

Regulating online weapon sales on Dark Web markets poses numerous challenges for law enforcement agencies and governments. One of the primary obstacles is the decentralized nature of these markets. Dark Web marketplaces operate on encrypted platforms, making it difficult to trace the origins of the weapons or identify the individuals involved in the transactions.

Additionally, Dark Web marketplaces primarily rely on cryptocurrency as a means of payment, further increasing the anonymity and difficulty of tracking transactions. The use of cryptocurrencies, such as Bitcoin, enables buyers and sellers to conduct transactions without leaving a clear digital trail.

Moreover, the international nature of Dark Web markets adds another layer of complexity to regulating online weapon sales. These markets transcend geographical boundaries, making it challenging for law enforcement agencies to coordinate and collaborate effectively in their efforts to combat illicit weapon trade.

The connection between Dark Web markets and real-world violence

There is a concerning connection between Dark Web markets and real-world violence. The availability of weapons on these platforms can contribute to an increase in gun-related crimes, acts of terrorism, and even mass shootings. The anonymity provided by Dark Web markets allows individuals with hostile intentions to procure arms without attracting attention or triggering the usual safeguards and background checks.

For example, the investigation into the 2016 Munich shooting revealed that the perpetrator had acquired the weapon used in the attack from a Dark Web marketplace. This incident highlighted the role of Dark Web markets in facilitating access to firearms for individuals who may have otherwise been unable to obtain them through legal means.

Efforts to combat illicit weapon trade on Dark Web markets

Law enforcement agencies and governments worldwide are actively engaged in combating the illicit weapon trade on Dark Web markets. These efforts involve a combination of traditional law enforcement tactics and the development of cutting-edge technologies.

One strategy employed by law enforcement agencies is the infiltration of Dark Web marketplaces by undercover agents. These agents pose as buyers or sellers to gather intelligence and identify key players involved in weapon trafficking. This approach has led to successful operations, resulting in the takedown of Dark Web weapon markets and the arrest of individuals involved in illegal weapon trade.

In addition to traditional methods, technological advancements play a crucial role in combating the illicit weapon trade on Dark Web markets. The development of sophisticated monitoring and data analysis tools allows law enforcement agencies to track and trace weapon transactions, identify patterns, and gather evidence for prosecution.

Furthermore, advancements in machine learning and artificial intelligence have the potential to enhance the detection and prevention of illegal weapon trade on Dark Web markets. These technologies can help law enforcement agencies identify suspicious activities, predict potential threats, and take proactive measures to prevent them.

Conclusion

The availability of weapons on Dark Web markets presents a significant challenge for law enforcement agencies and governments globally. The decentralized nature of these online platforms, along with the use of cryptocurrencies and encryption, makes it difficult to regulate and track weapon sales. The connection between Dark Web markets and real-world violence further emphasizes the need for proactive measures to combat illicit weapon trade.

While law enforcement agencies continue to deploy traditional investigative methods, the integration of advanced technologies such as data analysis, machine learning, and artificial intelligence holds promise in detecting and preventing illegal weapon trade on Dark Web markets. By combining these strategies, authorities can enhance their ability to dismantle online weapon networks, protect public safety, and reduce the risks associated with the availability of weapons on Dark Web markets.

Challenges in Regulating Online Weapon Sales

Regulating online weapon sales on dark web markets presents several challenges for law enforcement agencies worldwide. These challenges stem from the unique characteristics of the dark web, the anonymity of users, and the encryption techniques used to ensure secure transactions. In this section, we will explore the specific difficulties faced in regulating and controlling the online weapon trade.

Anonymity and Pseudonymity

One of the primary challenges in regulating online weapon sales is the anonymity and pseudonymity provided by the dark web. Buyers and sellers on these platforms often use encrypted communication channels, such as tor hidden services, to conceal their identities and locations. This makes it difficult for law enforcement agencies to identify and track down individuals involved in illegal weapon transactions.

Moreover, users can create multiple pseudonymous accounts, further complicating the process of tracing their activities. As a result, law enforcement faces significant hurdles in identifying the true identities and physical locations of those engaged in weapon sales on the dark web.

Global Jurisdictional Issues

Regulating online weapon sales is also complicated by jurisdictional challenges. The nature of the dark web allows users to conduct transactions from anywhere in the world, making it difficult for law enforcement agencies to establish jurisdiction over specific cases. The anonymity and encryption techniques used on the dark web make it tough to determine the physical location of individuals involved in weapon sales, further exacerbating the jurisdictional issue.

Additionally, different countries have varying laws and regulations regarding weapon sales, making it challenging to coordinate international efforts to control online weapon trade. Law enforcement agencies must navigate through complex legal frameworks and often depend on the cooperation of multiple countries to effectively regulate online weapon sales.

Use of Cryptocurrencies

Cryptocurrencies pose a significant challenge in regulating online weapon sales on dark web markets. These digital currencies, such as Bitcoin, are often the preferred mode of payment due to their decentralized nature and the difficulty in tracking transactions. Cryptocurrencies allow users to conduct transactions pseudonymously, adding an additional layer of complexity for law enforcement agencies.

Furthermore, the use of cryptocurrencies enables sellers to avoid traditional financial systems, making it challenging to detect and seize funds associated with illegal weapon sales. The lack of financial intermediaries and the absence of a centralized authority make it difficult for law enforcement to trace the flow of funds and ultimately disrupt the weapon trade.

Availability and Accessibility of Weapons

The availability and accessibility of weapons on dark web markets present significant challenges. These platforms provide access to a wide range of weapons, including firearms, explosives, and deadly weapons. The easy accessibility of such weapons attracts criminal elements who seek to acquire arms for illicit purposes.

Regulating the sale and distribution of physical weapons poses logistical challenges as they can be shipped worldwide. Law enforcement agencies face difficulties in intercepting and preventing the transportation of weapons procured from dark web markets.

Encryption and Secure Communication

The use of encryption and secure communication tools on the dark web hampers regulation efforts. Sellers and buyers rely on encrypted communication channels to exchange information about weapon sales, making it challenging for law enforcement to gather evidence or intercept communications.

The encryption techniques used on the dark web protect the privacy and security of users, but it also poses a challenge for law enforcement agencies attempting to monitor and regulate online weapon sales. Breaking encryption protocols and intercepting communications require sophisticated technical capabilities and extensive resources.

Collaboration and Information Sharing

Regulating online weapon sales on dark web markets necessitates collaboration and information sharing between law enforcement agencies at local, national, and international levels. However, sharing information across borders and jurisdictions can be a challenge due to different legal frameworks, data protection laws, and concerns about national security.

Efforts to combat online weapon trade require cooperation between law enforcement agencies, financial institutions, and technology companies. Bridging the gap between these entities and fostering effective collaboration is crucial to enhancing regulation and control of weapon sales on the dark web.

Addressing the Challenges

Addressing the challenges in regulating online weapon sales on dark web markets requires a multi-faceted approach that encompasses legal, technological, and collaborative efforts.

Law enforcement agencies need to enhance their technical capabilities to identify and track individuals involved in illegal weapon sales, overcome encryption barriers, and effectively navigate jurisdictional issues. Investing in advanced forensic techniques, analytical tools, and cyber intelligence capabilities can aid in combating online weapon trade.

International collaboration and information sharing should be prioritized to dismantle global criminal networks operating on the dark web. Coordinated efforts between law enforcement agencies, financial institutions, and technology companies are vital to disrupting the financial infrastructure and supply chains that support illegal weapon trade.

Moreover, policymakers should consider implementing stricter regulations and international agreements to combat the online weapon trade. This may involve strengthening existing laws, creating new legislation specific to online weapon sales, and harmonizing legal frameworks among different jurisdictions.

Raising public awareness about the dangers of online weapon sales on the dark web is also crucial. Education campaigns targeting both potential buyers and sellers can help reduce the demand and supply of illegal weapons. Collaboration with community organizations, schools, and law enforcement can play a fundamental role in educating the public and empowering them to protect themselves from the influence of dark web markets.

In conclusion, regulating online weapon sales on dark web markets presents significant challenges due to anonymity, jurisdictional complexities, use of cryptocurrencies, weapon availability, and encryption. Addressing these challenges requires a comprehensive approach that combines legal measures, technological advancements, and international collaboration. By taking proactive and coordinated actions, law enforcement agencies and policymakers can disrupt the online weapon trade and protect public safety.

The connection between Dark Web markets and real-world violence

The existence of Dark Web markets has raised significant concerns regarding their potential connection to real-world violence. While the Dark Web provides a platform for anonymous transactions and facilitates the exchange of illegal goods and services, it is essential to explore the relationship between these online marketplaces and acts of violence in the physical world. In this section, we will analyze the various aspects that contribute to this connection, including the nature of the Dark Web, the availability of weapons, and the challenges in regulating online weapon sales.

The Dark Web: A Facilitator of Violence

The Dark Web, with its sophisticated encryption and anonymization techniques, has become a breeding ground for criminal activities. This includes the trade of illegal weapons, drugs, and other harmful goods or services. The anonymity and lack of regulation on Dark Web markets attract individuals involved in organized crime, terrorism, and other violent activities. These underground marketplaces provide a platform for criminals to connect with buyers, access illicit resources, and plan nefarious actions without detection.

Availability of Weapons on Dark Web Markets

One alarming aspect of the Dark Web markets is the availability of weapons for sale. These include firearms, explosives, and other dangerous instruments. The anonymity and privacy offered by the Dark Web allow potential buyers to browse through a vast selection of weapons without the fear of being tracked. This wide range of weapons accessible on Dark Web markets intensifies concerns about their potential misuse. Whether it is for personal protection or criminal intent, the ease of purchasing weapons online amplifies the risk of violence in society.

Challenges in Regulating Online Weapon Sales

Regulating online weapon sales on the Dark Web poses numerous challenges for law enforcement agencies and governments worldwide. Unlike legal firearms transactions that require background checks and licenses, purchases on Dark Web markets circumvent these regulations. The use of cryptocurrencies as a medium of exchange further complicates efforts to trace transactions and identify sellers and buyers. Additionally, the decentralized and global nature of the Dark Web makes it difficult for any single law enforcement agency to enforce regulations effectively.

The Connection between Dark Web Markets and Real-World Violence

The connection between Dark Web markets and real-world violence can be understood through various channels. First, the availability of weapons on these marketplaces increases the likelihood of individuals with malicious intent acquiring them. The ease of access, along with the anonymity provided by the Dark Web, lowers the barriers for engaging in violence. Second, the illicit drug trade facilitated by Dark Web markets can lead to increased criminal activities and violent confrontations, as turf wars and disputes arise over control of the drug market. Third, the anonymous communication channels provided by Dark Web markets enable the planning and coordination of violent acts, including terrorism, human trafficking, and extortion. These factors contribute to the convergence between the online realm and real-world violence.

Case Study: The Silk Road

The Silk Road is one of the most infamous Dark Web marketplaces, known for its association with both illegal drug trade and real-world violence. Operated by Ross Ulbricht, the Silk Road facilitated the sale of drugs, weapons, counterfeit documents, and hacking tools. The marketplace attracted thousands of buyers and sellers, leading to a multi-million dollar illegal enterprise. The Silk Road is also associated with instances of violence, including the notorious case of the Silk Road user "Dread Pirate Roberts" hiring a hitman to murder a former Silk Road employee. This case exemplifies the potential connection between Dark Web markets and real-world violence.

Ethical Concerns and Solutions

The connection between Dark Web markets and real-world violence raises important ethical questions. Balancing privacy and security in Dark Web investigations presents a challenge as law enforcement agencies strive to protect public safety without infringing upon individual privacy rights. Furthermore, the ethical implications of surveillance on the Dark Web require careful consideration, to avoid unjust targeting or violations of civil liberties.

Addressing the connection between Dark Web markets and real-world violence requires a multi-faceted approach. Enhanced collaboration between law enforcement agencies and international coordination can aid in monitoring and disrupting criminal activities. Technological advancements, such as improved Dark Web monitoring and data analysis using machine learning and artificial intelligence, can assist in identifying threats and potential acts of violence. Additionally, educating the public about the dangers of Dark Web involvement can empower individuals to make informed decisions and prevent them from engaging in criminal activities.

Conclusion

The connection between Dark Web markets and real-world violence cannot be ignored. The anonymity and lack of regulation on the Dark Web provide a fertile ground for criminal activities, including the availability of weapons and planning of violent acts. Regulating online weapon sales and monitoring Dark Web activities present significant challenges for law enforcement agencies. However, through enhanced collaboration, technological solutions, and increased awareness, it is possible to mitigate the risks associated with Dark Web involvement and combat the connection between these markets and real-world violence.

Efforts to combat illicit weapon trade on Dark Web markets

The illicit trade of weapons on Dark Web markets presents a major challenge for law enforcement agencies and governments worldwide. The anonymity and encryption technologies employed in these marketplaces make it difficult to track down sellers and buyers engaged in the illegal arms trade. However, various efforts are being made to combat this issue and disrupt the activities of these illicit weapon sellers. In this section, we will explore some of the strategies and initiatives being undertaken to combat the trade of weapons on Dark Web markets.

International Cooperation and Collaboration

Addressing the problem of illicit weapon trade on Dark Web markets requires close cooperation and collaboration among law enforcement agencies across borders. Given the global nature of the problem, intelligence sharing and joint operations are critical. International law enforcement agencies, such as Interpol and Europol, play a key role in coordinating efforts to combat the illegal arms trade on the Dark Web.

Through international cooperation, law enforcement agencies can combine their resources, expertise, and intelligence to identify and take down major weapon suppliers and disrupt their networks. This collaboration also enables the sharing of best practices, knowledge, and technological advancements in Dark Web investigation and surveillance techniques.

Infiltration and Undercover Operations

Law enforcement agencies often employ undercover agents or "cyber agents" to infiltrate Dark Web marketplaces and gather vital intelligence on weapon sellers and buyers. These agents pose as potential buyers to gain the trust of sellers, gather evidence, and track their activities.

Undercover operations require careful planning, implementation, and constant monitoring. The agents need to establish their credibility and maintain a covert identity while gathering evidence. In some cases, law enforcement agencies have successfully arrested weapon sellers or buyers during transactions arranged through undercover agents.

Blockchain Analysis and Cryptocurrency Tracing

Cryptocurrencies, such as Bitcoin, are commonly used on Dark Web markets for anonymous transactions, including the purchase of weapons. However, the decentralized nature of blockchain technology allows for forensic analysis to trace these cryptocurrency transactions.

Law enforcement agencies have been increasingly utilizing blockchain analysis tools and techniques to trace the flow of funds involved in illicit weapon trade. By monitoring and analyzing the blockchain, investigators can identify the wallets used in these transactions and potentially link them to individuals or entities involved in the trade. These investigations can help to identify patterns, track financial activity, and ultimately lead to the identification and prosecution of weapon sellers and buyers.

Covert Monitoring and Surveillance

Law enforcement agencies employ sophisticated techniques to monitor and surveil Dark Web marketplaces involved in the sale of weapons. This surveillance can involve the monitoring of communications between sellers and buyers, tracking their IP addresses, and gathering other evidence of their activities.

Advanced analytics tools and machine learning algorithms are used to identify suspicious patterns, detect potential threats, and enhance monitoring capabilities. These technologies allow for real-time analysis of large volumes of data to identify and flag transactions related to weapon trade, thereby enabling law enforcement agencies to take proactive action.

Legislative Measures and Policy Development

Governments and international organizations are continuously developing legislation and policies aimed at combating the illicit weapon trade on the Dark Web. These measures are designed to enhance law enforcement capabilities, strengthen cross-border cooperation, and increase penalties for those involved in the arms trade.

Legislation often targets both the sellers and buyers of illegal weapons, imposing severe penalties and liabilities. Governments also work with technology companies and industry associations to develop protocols and guidelines for combating the illicit weapon trade on the Dark Web.

Public Awareness and Education

Raising public awareness about the dangers and consequences of engaging in the illicit weapon trade on the Dark Web is an essential component of combating this issue. Government agencies, law enforcement, and cybersecurity professionals work together to educate the public about the risks associated with involvement in Dark Web markets.

Public awareness campaigns highlight the legal consequences, potential harm, and broader societal impacts of the illicit arms trade. Through education and awareness, individuals are encouraged to report any suspicious activity or information related to the trade of illegal weapons on the Dark Web. Additionally, educational programs are implemented to inform individuals about legal channels for obtaining and disposing of weapons safely and within the boundaries of the law.

Conclusion

Efforts to combat the illicit weapon trade on Dark Web markets require a multifaceted approach that combines international cooperation, technological advancements, legislative measures, and public awareness. Through collaboration between law enforcement agencies, the application of advanced analytics, the development of legislation, and education campaigns, progress is being made to disrupt the activities of weapon sellers and buyers on the Dark Web. However, this battle continues to evolve, and ongoing innovation and adaptation are essential to stay ahead of criminals operating within these illicit marketplaces.

Cybercrime-as-a-Service on Dark Web Markets

The underground economy of cybercrime services

In the dark corners of the internet, a thriving underground economy exists, fueled by the illicit activities and services offered by cybercriminals. This section delves into the fascinating world of the underground economy of cybercrime services, exploring the types of services available, the motivations behind them, and the impact they have on the digital landscape.

Understanding the underground economy

The underground economy of cybercrime services refers to the vast network of illegal activities offered by individuals or groups on the dark web. These activities encompass a wide range of cybercriminal operations, including hacking, phishing, malware distribution, identity theft, and the sale of stolen data or financial information.

Cybercriminals offer these services to facilitate various forms of illegal activities, such as financial fraud, information theft, or even launching large-scale cyber attacks. The underground economy thrives because it provides anonymity, convenience, and an infrastructure that enables cybercriminals to trade their skills and tools without detection.

Types of cybercrime services

The underground economy offers a wide array of cybercrime services, each catering to a different aspect of illegal activities. Some of the most common types of services include:

- **Hacking services:** These services involve gaining unauthorized access to computer systems or networks. Hackers may offer to breach social media accounts, corporate databases, or even government networks.
- **Phishing services:** Phishing is a technique used to trick individuals into sharing sensitive information, such as usernames, passwords, or credit card details. Cybercriminals offer phishing services to launch large-scale phishing campaigns or provide phishing tools to other attackers.
- **Malware creation and distribution:** Malware, such as viruses, worms, or ransomware, is a common tool used by cybercriminals. The underground economy offers services to create custom malware or distribute existing malware to a wide range of targets.
- **Stolen data trading:** The sale of stolen data is a lucrative business for cybercriminals. Underground marketplaces allow cybercriminals to trade stolen credit card information, login credentials, personal records, or even medical data.
- **Cryptojacking services:** Cryptojacking involves the unauthorized use of someone else's computer resources to mine cryptocurrencies. Cybercriminals offer services to infect systems with cryptojacking malware or provide tools to others to carry out such attacks.

These services not only provide cybercriminals with the means to commit illegal activities but also enable others to engage in cybercrime without possessing the necessary technical expertise.

Motivations behind cybercrime services

Understanding the motivations of cybercriminals is crucial to comprehending the dynamics of the underground economy. While financial gain remains a primary motivation, other factors contribute to the proliferation of cybercrime services:

- **Anonymity and reduced risk:** The dark web provides a certain level of anonymity for cybercriminals, making it harder for law enforcement agencies to track them down. The use of cryptocurrencies for transactions further adds a layer of anonymity, reducing the risk of detection and apprehension.
- **Profitability:** The underground economy of cybercrime services generates substantial profits. Cybercriminals can exploit vulnerabilities, sell stolen data, or offer services at a premium, attracting individuals seeking financial gain.
- **Access to advanced tools and resources:** The underground economy offers a treasure trove of tools, resources, and expertise that aid cybercriminals in their activities. These underground marketplaces enable the sharing and sale of cutting-edge hacking tools, exploit kits, or zero-day vulnerabilities.
- **Challenge and recognition:** For some cybercriminals, engaging in illegal activities provides a sense of adventure, challenge, or even recognition within their communities. These individuals may be driven by the desire to prove their technical skills or gain status among their peers.

By understanding the motivations behind cybercrime services, law enforcement agencies, cybersecurity professionals, and policymakers can develop effective strategies to combat these illicit activities.

Impact on the digital landscape

The proliferation of cybercrime services through the underground economy has far-reaching consequences for individuals, businesses, and society as a whole. The impact of these activities includes:

- **Financial losses:** Cybercrime costs individuals and organizations billions of dollars each year. Stolen funds, financial fraud, and the expenses associated with mitigating cyber attacks have a significant economic impact.

- **Compromised security:** Cybercriminals exploit vulnerabilities and weaknesses in systems and networks, jeopardizing the security of personal and sensitive information. This compromises individual privacy and can lead to identity theft, while also undermining trust in digital transactions.
- **Disruption of critical infrastructure:** Cybercriminals focused on large-scale attacks can disrupt critical infrastructure, such as power grids, telecommunications networks, or transportation systems. These attacks can have severe consequences on public safety and societal stability.
- **Negative social impact:** The underground economy supports the sale of illegal goods and services, including drugs, weapons, or counterfeit products. These activities contribute to criminal enterprises, addiction, violence, and a range of other social problems.

The presence of cybercrime services in the underground economy necessitates a coordinated effort from law enforcement, cybersecurity professionals, and society as a whole to mitigate the risks and combat these illicit activities.

Summary

The underground economy of cybercrime services is a complex and thriving network that fuels illegal activities in the digital realm. It encompasses various types of services, motivations, and impacts. Understanding this nefarious economy is essential to develop effective countermeasures and strategies to combat cybercrime. As we delve deeper into the fight against Dark Web markets, it is crucial to comprehend the inner workings of this underground economy and the role it plays in perpetuating cybercrime.

Types of cybercrime services available on Dark Web markets

The Dark Web serves as a platform for a wide range of illicit activities, including various types of cybercrime services. These services cater to the needs and demands of cybercriminals who are looking to exploit vulnerabilities, compromise systems, or engage in fraudulent activities. In this section, we will explore some of the common types of cybercrime services available on Dark Web markets.

1. Hacking Services: Dark Web markets provide a venue for individuals and groups offering hacking services. These services include hacking into email accounts, social media profiles, and websites, as well as exploiting software vulnerabilities and conducting Distributed Denial of Service (DDoS) attacks.

Cybercriminals can easily hire hackers to gain unauthorized access to systems or to orchestrate attacks on their behalf.

For example, a hacker offering their services on a Dark Web marketplace may advertise their ability to compromise a specific target's email account, providing the purchaser with login credentials and access to private correspondence. Such services pose a significant threat to individuals, businesses, and organizations concerned about the security of their digital assets.

2. Malware Development and Distribution: Dark Web markets also facilitate the development and distribution of malicious software, such as viruses, worms, Trojans, and ransomware. Malware developers offer their services to create custom-made malicious software targeting specific systems or organizations.

For instance, a cybercriminal might hire a malware developer to create a tailored ransomware strain that encrypts sensitive files on a victim's computer and demands a ransom in exchange for the decryption key. The Dark Web provides a marketplace for cybercriminals to collaborate and profit from the sale and distribution of such malicious software.

3. Stolen Data and Identity Theft: One of the most lucrative services available on Dark Web markets is the sale of stolen data and personal information. Cybercriminals can find a variety of data on offer, including credit card details, social security numbers, bank account credentials, and login credentials for various online platforms.

For example, a cybercriminal may purchase stolen credit card information to carry out fraudulent transactions or acquire login credentials for online banking to access and steal funds from individuals' accounts. With the vast amount of personal data available, the potential for identity theft and financial fraud is significant.

4. DDoS-for-Hire Services: Dark Web markets also host services that offer Distributed Denial of Service (DDoS) attacks on demand. These services allow individuals to target websites or online services by flooding them with a massive amount of traffic, rendering them inaccessible to legitimate users.

Cybercriminals can use DDoS-for-hire services to disrupt the operations of businesses, extort money from online platforms, or even settle personal grudges. The availability of these services on Dark Web markets increases the accessibility and prevalence of DDoS attacks.

5. Phishing and Fraudulent Services: Phishing is a popular technique used by cybercriminals to trick individuals into providing their personal information, such as login credentials or financial details, by impersonating legitimate entities. Dark Web markets offer phishing kits, tutorials, and services to assist cybercriminals in conducting successful phishing campaigns.

For instance, a cybercriminal might purchase a phishing kit that includes pre-built phishing websites designed to mimic popular online banking platforms. These kits typically come with instructions on how to deploy the websites and collect victims' data. Such services enable cybercriminals without extensive technical knowledge to engage in phishing activities.

6. Counterfeit Documents and IDs: Dark Web markets serve as marketplaces for counterfeit documents and forged identities. Cybercriminals can purchase counterfeit passports, driver's licenses, social security cards, and other official documents to facilitate identity theft or engage in other criminal activities.

For example, an individual involved in illegal activities might buy a counterfeit passport to evade law enforcement or gain access to restricted areas. The availability of counterfeit documents on Dark Web markets fuels identity fraud, making it more challenging to authenticate and verify individuals' identities.

It is important to note that engaging in any form of cybercrime is illegal and unethical. The purpose of highlighting these cybercrime services is to raise awareness of the ongoing issues surrounding Dark Web markets and the activities that take place within them. The fight against cybercrime requires collaboration between law enforcement agencies, cybersecurity professionals, and individuals alike.

Key Takeaways: - Dark Web markets offer a variety of cybercrime services, including hacking, malware development, and distribution, stolen data and identity theft, DDoS-for-hire, phishing and fraudulent services, and counterfeit documents. - These services pose significant threats to individuals, businesses, and organizations, leading to financial losses, data breaches, and identity theft. - Engaging in any form of cybercrime is illegal and unethical. - Combating cybercrime on Dark Web markets requires collaboration between law enforcement agencies, cybersecurity professionals, and individuals.

Further Reading: - Dhillon, G., & Backhouse, J. (2020). Cybercrime as a Service. Computer Fraud & Security, 2020(1), 6-8. - Goodman, J. (2018). Future Crimes: Inside the Digital Underground and the Battle for our Connected World. Anchor. - Sullivan, D., Beech, R., & Sullivan, I. (2018). Dark Web: Exploring and Data Mining the Dark Side of the Web (2nd ed.). Springer.

The impact of cybercrime-as-a-service on the digital landscape

Cybercrime-as-a-service (CaaS) refers to the provision of cybercrime activities, tools, and services through online platforms. It involves individuals or groups offering their expertise, tools, and infrastructure to facilitate various forms of cybercrime to be carried out by others. This section will delve into the impact of

CaaS on the digital landscape, examining the challenges it presents and its lasting effects on cybersecurity.

The proliferation of cybercrime

CaaS has significantly contributed to the proliferation of cybercrime. It has lowered the entry barriers for individuals with limited technical skills to engage in illicit activities such as hacking, phishing, and identity theft. Through the dark web and underground forums, cybercriminals can easily access services like malware development, distributed denial-of-service (DDoS) attacks, and stolen data marketplaces.

This easy accessibility coupled with the anonymity provided by cryptocurrency transactions has resulted in a surge in cybercrime activities. As a result, businesses, organizations, and individuals face an increased risk of falling victim to cyberattacks, leading to financial losses, reputational damage, and compromised sensitive information.

Amplification of threats

CaaS amplifies the scale and sophistication of cyber threats. Cybercriminals can now leverage the expertise and tools provided by CaaS platforms to carry out highly targeted attacks with minimal effort. For example, ransomware-as-a-service (RaaS) allows individuals with limited technical knowledge to deploy ransomware, which encrypts victims' files and demands a ransom in return.

Furthermore, the availability of specialized tools and services through CaaS platforms enables the rapid evolution of cyber threats. Malware developers can sell their creations on the dark web, allowing cybercriminals to constantly update and improve their attack techniques. This poses a significant challenge to cybersecurity professionals and requires constant adaptation and innovation to keep up with evolving threats.

Erosion of trust

The prevalence of CaaS has led to a significant erosion of trust in the digital landscape. The general public is increasingly concerned about the security of their personal information and the privacy of their online activities. The high-profile data breaches and cybersecurity incidents facilitated by CaaS platforms have heightened these concerns.

As a result, individuals and businesses may be hesitant to engage in online transactions or share sensitive information, fearing the potential repercussions of falling victim to cybercrime. This erosion of trust in the digital landscape can have far-reaching socioeconomic consequences, hindering the growth of e-commerce, hampering technological innovation, and impeding the adoption of emerging technologies.

Collaboration among cybercriminals

CaaS has fostered collaboration and cooperation among cybercriminals. Previously, cybercriminals typically operated independently or within small groups. However, CaaS platforms have created a marketplace where specialized services and tools can be easily accessed by anyone willing to pay for them. This has facilitated the formation of larger, more organized cybercrime networks.

The collaboration among cybercriminals allows for the sharing of resources, knowledge, and expertise, enabling them to launch more sophisticated and coordinated cyberattacks. By pooling their resources, cybercriminals can target larger and more lucrative victims. This collaborative environment also makes it difficult for law enforcement agencies to identify and apprehend individual cybercriminals, as they operate within a complex network of shared responsibilities and hierarchies.

The need for proactive defense

The impact of CaaS necessitates a shift in cybersecurity strategies from reactive to proactive defense. Traditional security measures focused primarily on detecting and mitigating cyber threats after they have occurred. However, with the widespread availability of advanced hacking tools and services through CaaS, it is crucial to adopt proactive defense measures that can identify and prevent cyberattacks before they happen.

Organizations must invest in comprehensive threat intelligence and monitoring systems that can detect early signs of cyber threats. These systems should leverage machine learning and artificial intelligence algorithms to identify patterns and anomalies in network traffic, enabling the timely detection of potential cyberattacks.

Additionally, cybersecurity professionals must collaborate with law enforcement agencies and industry partners to share intelligence, coordinate response efforts, and disrupt CaaS operations. By working together, they can identify and dismantle CaaS platforms, making it more challenging for cybercriminals to access the tools and services they rely on.

Conclusion

The impact of cybercrime-as-a-service on the digital landscape is profound. CaaS has fueled the growth of cybercrime, amplified the scale and sophistication of cyber threats, eroded trust in the digital environment, and facilitated collaboration among cybercriminals. To counter these challenges, a proactive defense approach is necessary, focused on early threat detection and prevention. Collaboration between cybersecurity professionals, law enforcement agencies, and industry partners is essential to disrupt CaaS operations and safeguard the digital ecosystem. Only through collective efforts can we mitigate the impact of CaaS and secure the future of the digital landscape.

Strategies for countering cybercrime-as-a-service offerings

The rise of cybercrime-as-a-service on Dark Web markets presents significant challenges for law enforcement agencies and cybersecurity professionals. These illicit online platforms offer a wide range of cybercrime services, including malware development, hacking tools, stolen data, and even hacker-for-hire services. To effectively combat this growing threat, a comprehensive set of strategies is required. In this section, we discuss various approaches that can be taken to counter cybercrime-as-a-service offerings.

Strengthening Law Enforcement Efforts

Law enforcement agencies play a crucial role in countering cybercrime-as-a-service. To effectively combat these activities, it is essential to enhance collaboration and coordination among national and international agencies. Some strategies that can be employed include:

- International cooperation: Establishing and strengthening partnerships between law enforcement agencies across different countries is crucial for sharing information, conducting joint operations, and exchanging best practices. International collaboration can help overcome jurisdictional challenges and ensure a coordinated response to cybercrime-as-a-service offerings.

- Capacity building: Investing in training and development programs for law enforcement personnel can enhance their skills in investigating cybercrime-as-a-service activities. Training should encompass technical knowledge, digital forensics, and legal frameworks related to cybercrime. By building specialized capabilities, law enforcement agencies can effectively tackle the evolving nature of cyber threats.

- Cyber task forces: Establishing specialized cybercrime task forces can aid in investigating and dismantling cybercrime-as-a-service operations. These task forces should bring together experts from various fields, including cybercrime investigation, digital forensics, and intelligence analysis. By pooling resources and expertise, agencies can enhance their effectiveness in combating cybercrime.

Improving Cybersecurity Measures

Effective cybersecurity measures are essential to prevent and detect cybercrime-as-a-service activities. Organizations and individuals must implement robust security practices to safeguard their systems and data. Some strategies to consider include:

- Threat intelligence sharing: Establishing mechanisms for sharing threat intelligence among organizations, industries, and cybersecurity vendors can enhance early detection and response to cyber threats. By sharing information on emerging cybercrime-as-a-service offerings, the community can collectively develop proactive defenses and countermeasures.
- Advanced analytics and AI: Leveraging advanced analytics and artificial intelligence (AI) technologies can enhance the detection and analysis of cybercrime-as-a-service activities. AI-powered systems can analyze large volumes of data to identify patterns, anomalies, and indicators of compromise. This can help in uncovering hidden connections, predicting future threats, and proactively countering cybercrime.
- Multi-factor authentication: Implementing multi-factor authentication mechanisms can significantly reduce the risk of unauthorized access to systems and sensitive information. By combining multiple layers of authentication, such as passwords, biometrics, and hardware tokens, organizations can mitigate the risk of unauthorized access by cybercriminals.
- Regular security assessments: Conducting regular security assessments, penetration testing, and vulnerability scans can help identify and address potential weaknesses and security gaps. By proactively assessing their systems and networks, organizations can identify vulnerabilities that could be exploited by cybercrime-as-a-service providers.

Legislative and Policy Initiatives

Legislation and policy frameworks play a vital role in deterring and punishing cybercriminals involved in cybercrime-as-a-service activities. Some strategies to consider include:

- Criminalizing cybercrime-as-a-service: Governments should enact specific legislation that explicitly criminalizes cybercrime-as-a-service activities. This will provide law enforcement agencies with the necessary legal tools to investigate and prosecute individuals or groups involved in offering cybercrime services.
- International cooperation on legislation: Countries should work together to develop harmonized frameworks and legislation to combat cybercrime-as-a-service effectively. This includes extradition treaties, mutual legal assistance agreements, and cooperation in enforcing cross-border laws related to cybercrime.
- Public-private partnerships: Collaboration between the public and private sectors is crucial in tackling cybercrime-as-a-service. Governments should foster partnerships with industry stakeholders to share knowledge, expertise, and resources in combating cyber threats. These partnerships can facilitate the exchange of information, implementation of best practices, and joint efforts in investigating and disrupting cybercrime-as-a-service operations.

Raising Public Awareness

Raising public awareness about the risks and consequences of engaging with cybercrime-as-a-service offerings is crucial in countering their popularity and impact. Some strategies to consider include:

- Educational campaigns: Launching public awareness campaigns that highlight the dangers of cybercrime-as-a-service can help individuals make informed decisions and avoid involvement in illegal activities. These campaigns can be targeted at different stakeholder groups, including students, businesses, and the general public, providing them with the knowledge and tools to protect themselves from cyber threats.
- Collaboration with educational institutions: Engaging educational institutions, such as schools, colleges, and universities, can facilitate the

inclusion of cybersecurity awareness programs in their curricula. By integrating cybersecurity education from an early age, individuals can develop a proactive mindset towards cyber threats and better understand the risks associated with cybercrime-as-a-service.

- Partnerships with technology companies: Collaborating with technology companies can help promote secure practices and raise awareness about the risks of cybercrime-as-a-service offerings. Technology companies can play a significant role in developing user-friendly security measures, providing security solutions, and educating their users about the importance of cybersecurity.

In summary, countering cybercrime-as-a-service requires a multi-faceted approach involving law enforcement efforts, improved cybersecurity measures, legislative initiatives, and public awareness campaigns. By employing these strategies collectively, we can better detect, prevent, and prosecute cybercriminals involved in cybercrime-as-a-service activities. It is essential to remain proactive and adaptive to stay ahead of evolving cyber threats and protect individuals, organizations, and society as a whole.

The Fight Against Dark Web Markets

Law Enforcement Strategies and Initiatives

Global efforts to dismantle Dark Web marketplaces

Dismantling Dark Web marketplaces is a complex and challenging task that requires coordinated efforts from law enforcement agencies, cybersecurity professionals, and international organizations. The rise of the Dark Web has fueled the growth of illegal activities, including the sale of drugs, weapons, and cybercrime-as-a-service. In response to this threat, various global initiatives have been launched to dismantle these illicit marketplaces and mitigate their impact on society. In this section, we will explore some of the major global efforts to combat Dark Web marketplaces.

One prominent global initiative is the collaboration between law enforcement agencies from different countries. Recognizing the transnational nature of Dark Web activities, law enforcement agencies have strengthened their cooperation and information sharing mechanisms. For example, the Joint Cybercrime Action Taskforce (J-CAT), established by the European Cybercrime Centre (EC3), facilitates collaboration among international law enforcement agencies to target Dark Web marketplaces. Through J-CAT, law enforcement agencies work jointly to identify, investigate, and dismantle illegal online marketplaces.

Another significant global effort is the Silk Road Task Force (SRTF), which was formed in 2012 to dismantle the notorious Silk Road marketplace, one of the first and most prominent Dark Web marketplaces. The SRTF consisted of members from the FBI, DEA, IRS, and other U.S. law enforcement agencies, as well as international partners. By leveraging sophisticated investigative techniques and international cooperation, the SRTF successfully arrested the founder of Silk Road and shut down the marketplace, sending a strong message to Dark Web actors.

The United Nations Office on Drugs and Crime (UNODC) also plays a crucial role in global efforts to combat Dark Web marketplaces. UNODC provides technical assistance and capacity-building support to member states, facilitating their efforts to investigate and prosecute Dark Web actors. Additionally, UNODC conducts research and analysis on emerging trends and threats related to the Dark Web, contributing to a better understanding of this complex ecosystem.

In addition to these collaborative initiatives, individual countries have implemented their strategies to dismantle Dark Web marketplaces. For example, the United States Department of Justice has established the Internet Crimes Against Children (ICAC) program, which focuses on investigating and prosecuting individuals involved in the online exploitation of children, including activities that take place on Dark Web marketplaces. The ICAC program combines law enforcement efforts, training, and public outreach to identify and apprehend perpetrators and protect children from harm.

Furthermore, Interpol, the International Criminal Police Organization, plays a crucial role in coordinating global efforts against Dark Web marketplaces. Interpol's Digital Crime Centre (IDCC) serves as a hub for information sharing, operational support, and capacity building in the fight against cybercrime, including Dark Web activities. It facilitates cross-border collaboration by providing a platform for law enforcement agencies to exchange intelligence, training, and expertise, leading to more effective investigations and dismantling of Dark Web marketplaces.

Despite these global efforts, dismantling Dark Web marketplaces remains a challenging task due to the inherent anonymity and encryption mechanisms employed by these platforms. The dynamic and evolving nature of the Dark Web ecosystem requires constant adaptation and innovative approaches from law enforcement and cybersecurity professionals. Furthermore, the international legal framework lags behind, making it difficult to prosecute Dark Web actors operating across different jurisdictions.

In conclusion, global efforts to dismantle Dark Web marketplaces are crucial to combating illicit activities and ensuring the safety and security of individuals and society. Collaboration between law enforcement agencies, the sharing of intelligence, and the development of technological solutions are key components of these efforts. However, it is essential to recognize that the fight against Dark Web marketplaces is an ongoing battle, requiring continuous adaptation and international cooperation.

Successful law enforcement operations against Dark Web markets

Law enforcement agencies around the world have been actively involved in combating Dark Web markets. Over the years, there have been several successful operations that have disrupted and dismantled these illicit platforms. In this section, we will explore some notable examples of law enforcement operations against Dark Web markets, highlighting their strategies, outcomes, and the challenges they faced.

One of the most significant law enforcement successes against Dark Web markets was the operation to take down the Silk Road in 2013. The Silk Road, founded by Ross Ulbricht, was one of the first and most notorious online marketplaces for illegal drugs and other illicit goods and services. The operation, led by the FBI, involved a combination of investigative techniques, technical expertise, and international cooperation.

The Silk Road operated on the Tor network, leveraging its anonymity features to facilitate transactions. However, law enforcement agencies were able to gather evidence and track down the individuals involved by employing a combination of traditional investigative methods and cutting-edge technology. The FBI managed to trace transactions on the Silk Road by cooperating with international partners, infiltrating the website through undercover agents, and making controlled purchases. These operations resulted in the arrest of Ross Ulbricht and the seizure of millions of dollars' worth of bitcoin.

Another notable operation against Dark Web markets was the takedown of AlphaBay in 2017. AlphaBay was one of the largest underground marketplaces, offering a wide range of illegal products and services, including drugs, hacking tools, stolen data, and counterfeit documents. The operation, a collaborative effort between law enforcement agencies from several countries, led to the arrest of AlphaBay's founder, Alexandre Cazes, and the shutdown of the marketplace.

Law enforcement agencies, including the FBI, Europol, and the Royal Canadian Mounted Police (RCMP), coordinated their efforts to gather intelligence, identify the server infrastructure, and gather evidence for prosecution. The operation involved the deployment of sophisticated cyber-investigative techniques, including the analysis of cryptocurrency transactions and the infiltration of undercover officers into AlphaBay's user base. The shutdown of AlphaBay had a significant impact on the Dark Web market ecosystem, disrupting the trade of illegal goods and services.

One of the challenges faced by law enforcement agencies in combating Dark Web markets is the continuous emergence of new marketplaces to replace those that have been taken down. These operations often involve a game of cat and mouse, as law enforcement forces work to shut down platforms while new ones spring up to take their place. Despite these challenges, successful operations against Dark Web markets demonstrate the commitment and effectiveness of law enforcement agencies in fighting cybercrime.

It is important to note that law enforcement operations against Dark Web markets are not without ethical considerations. The balance between privacy and security is a delicate one, as authorities must navigate the use of surveillance techniques while respecting individuals' rights. Ensuring fairness in prosecuting Dark Web market participants and protecting innocent users also poses ethical challenges. Law enforcement agencies need to strike the right balance in their efforts to combat Dark Web markets, promoting public safety while upholding the principles of justice.

In conclusion, successful law enforcement operations against Dark Web markets have played a crucial role in disrupting these illegal platforms. Operations such as the takedown of the Silk Road and AlphaBay have demonstrated the effectiveness of collaborative efforts, technological advancements, and international cooperation. However, challenges and ethical considerations persist, highlighting the need for ongoing innovation and collaboration in the fight against Dark Web markets.

Challenges faced by law enforcement in prosecuting Dark Web market participants

Prosecuting individuals involved in Dark Web markets presents various challenges for law enforcement agencies. The anonymous and decentralized nature of these markets makes it difficult to identify and apprehend the perpetrators. In this section, we will explore the key challenges faced by law enforcement in their pursuit of justice against Dark Web market participants.

Anonymity and Encryption

One of the primary challenges is the anonymity provided by the Dark Web. Participants can conceal their identities and locations through various means, such as using anonymous communication tools and encryption techniques. This makes it extremely challenging for law enforcement to trace the origin of illegal activities or link individuals to specific transactions.

Furthermore, the use of cryptocurrencies, like Bitcoin, adds another layer of complexity. These digital currencies enable anonymous transactions, making it difficult to track the flow of funds and identify the parties involved. Law enforcement agencies face an uphill battle in unmasking the true identities of Dark Web market participants, hindering their ability to gather evidence and build cases against them.

Jurisdictional Complexity

Dark Web markets transcend geographical boundaries, posing a significant challenge in terms of jurisdiction. The Tor network, which enables access to the Dark Web, routes internet traffic through multiple relays, often spanning different countries. This creates a jurisdictional maze for law enforcement, as they need to coordinate with international counterparts to investigate and prosecute offenders.

Coordination between law enforcement agencies becomes crucial in cases involving Dark Web market participants, as offenders and servers hosting illegal activities may be located in different jurisdictions. Discrepancies in legal frameworks and extradition processes add further complexities, potentially delaying or impeding the legal proceedings.

Limited Resources and Technical Expertise

Law enforcement agencies often face resource constraints when combating Dark Web markets. The ever-evolving nature of these markets demands specialized skills and expertise in areas such as digital forensics, cryptography, and Dark Web investigations. However, recruiting and training personnel with the necessary skills can be a challenging and time-consuming process.

Moreover, the sheer volume of illicit activities occurring on the Dark Web overwhelms law enforcement agencies' capacity to monitor and investigate effectively. The limited availability of resources, both in terms of funding and personnel, hampers their ability to keep up with the scale and complexity of Dark Web operations.

End-to-End Encryption and Privacy Concerns

The widespread use of end-to-end encryption on messaging platforms and other communication channels presents a significant challenge for law enforcement. While encryption is crucial for protecting privacy and sensitive information, it also hampers investigators' ability to access communications and gather evidence.

End-to-end encryption prevents third parties, including law enforcement agencies, from intercepting or deciphering the content of messages exchanged between Dark Web market participants. This encryption, combined with strict privacy policies and data protection regulations, makes it difficult for authorities to track criminal activities and build strong cases against offenders.

Evolution of Tactics and Technology

Dark Web market participants are not static; they constantly adapt to law enforcement actions and employ new tactics and technologies to evade detection and prosecution. As law enforcement agencies develop strategies to combat these markets, criminals find innovative ways to circumvent the countermeasures.

For example, there has been a rise in the use of decentralized marketplaces, peer-to-peer networks, and encryption techniques that further obfuscate the activities conducted on the Dark Web. Moreover, advancements in technologies like artificial intelligence and machine learning are leveraged by perpetrators to enhance their anonymity and secure their illicit operations.

Law enforcement agencies face the challenge of staying ahead of these evolving tactics and technologies, requiring continuous adaptation and investment in research and development.

Cooperation and Trust-building

Collaboration and information sharing between law enforcement agencies are essential in combating Dark Web markets. However, establishing trust and cooperation between different agencies, often from different jurisdictions, can be challenging due to differences in legal frameworks, operational protocols, and cultural barriers.

The dynamic nature of Dark Web markets necessitates real-time information sharing to disrupt illegal activities effectively. Developing and maintaining trust-based relationships between agencies at the regional, national, and international levels is crucial for successful investigations. Efforts to build these collaborations require ongoing dialogue, capacity-building initiatives, and the establishment of formal networks.

In conclusion, law enforcement agencies face several challenges in prosecuting Dark Web market participants. The anonymity and encryption techniques used, jurisdictional complexities, limited resources and technical expertise, end-to-end encryption, evolving tactics, and the need for cooperation present significant hurdles. Overcoming these challenges requires a multi-faceted approach, including international collaboration, technical advancements, policy reforms, and capacity-building efforts. Only through concerted efforts can law enforcement successfully disrupt and dismantle Dark Web markets, ensuring the safety and security of individuals and societies.

The role of international cooperation in combating Dark Web markets

International cooperation plays a crucial role in combating Dark Web markets, as these illicit activities often transcend national boundaries and require a collective effort to effectively address the challenges they pose. In this section, we will discuss the importance of collaboration among countries, law enforcement agencies, and cybersecurity professionals in tackling Dark Web markets and explore some strategies and initiatives that have been undertaken globally.

The need for international cooperation

Dark Web markets operate on a global scale, attracting participants from different countries and facilitating criminal activities that transcend national jurisdictions. As a result, tackling these markets requires the cooperation and coordination of law enforcement agencies, cybersecurity professionals, and governments across borders.

International cooperation is essential for several reasons:

- **Shared intelligence and resources:** Dark Web marketplaces often involve intricate networks of actors and complex encryption technologies. Collaborating internationally allows law enforcement agencies to pool their intelligence, expertise, and resources, enabling a more comprehensive understanding of the dynamics of these markets and facilitating more effective targeting of key actors.
- **Coordination of investigations:** Dark Web criminal operations frequently involve actors from multiple countries. Cooperation between law enforcement agencies in different jurisdictions helps ensure smoother coordination of investigations and the exchange of critical information. By working together, agencies can avoid duplication of efforts, streamline processes, and enhance the chances of successful prosecutions.
- **Global impact:** Dark Web markets have a global reach, and their activities can significantly impact societies worldwide. International cooperation ensures that the fight against these markets is not limited to individual countries but extends to a broader, coordinated effort to disrupt criminal networks, seize illicit assets, and protect the interests of countries and their citizens.

Strategies and initiatives

Several strategies and initiatives have been undertaken globally to enhance international cooperation in combating Dark Web markets. These efforts aim to strengthen collaboration, streamline information sharing, and leverage joint operations. Here are some notable examples:

1. **Europol's Dark Web Team:** Europol, the European Union's law enforcement agency, has established a dedicated Dark Web Team comprising experts from various member states. The team focuses on sharing intelligence, coordinating cross-border investigations, and providing operational support to member states in combating Dark Web markets. This collaborative approach has resulted in several successful operations, such as the takedown of AlphaBay and Hansa Market, two of the largest Dark Web marketplaces at the time.

2. **Joint Interagency Task Force:** The Joint Interagency Task Force (JIATF) is a collaborative effort between multiple U.S. government agencies, including the Federal Bureau of Investigation (FBI), the Drug Enforcement Administration (DEA), and the Department of Homeland Security (DHS). JIATF aims to disrupt Dark Web market activities by coordinating investigations, sharing intelligence, and conducting joint operations. The task force leverages its diverse expertise to target key actors involved in drug trafficking, cybercrime, and other illicit activities on the Dark Web.

3. **International Information Sharing:** Various platforms and initiatives have been established to facilitate the sharing of information and intelligence between countries and law enforcement agencies. For example, the Interpol Global Complex for Innovation (IGCI) hosts the DarkNet Working Group, which brings together experts from around the world to share insights, exchange best practices, and collaborate on investigations. These platforms enable real-time information sharing, which is crucial for combating the rapidly evolving landscape of Dark Web markets.

4. **International Legal Cooperation:** International legal cooperation plays a vital role in prosecuting individuals involved in Dark Web markets. Mutual legal assistance treaties (MLATs) and extradition agreements allow countries to request and provide legal assistance in gathering evidence, conducting investigations, and extraditing suspects. These legal frameworks enable countries to work together to hold accountable those involved in Dark Web market activities.

Challenges and considerations

While international cooperation is crucial in combating Dark Web markets, it is not without its challenges and considerations. Some of the key challenges include:

- **Jurisdictional complexities:** Dark Web markets operate in a borderless digital environment, making it challenging to determine jurisdiction and coordinate legal actions. Different legal systems, varying laws, and differing levels of law enforcement capabilities further complicate the collaborative efforts required to combat these markets effectively.
- **Information sharing constraints:** Sharing sensitive information across borders introduces legal and privacy concerns. Striking a balance between the need for information sharing and safeguarding national interests and privacy rights is an ongoing challenge that requires careful consideration and the establishment of robust frameworks and protocols.
- **Language and cultural barriers:** Collaboration across countries with different languages and cultures can pose communication challenges, hindering effective coordination and information sharing. Overcoming these barriers requires cultural sensitivity, language expertise, and targeted efforts to bridge communication gaps.

Case Study: Operation Bayonet

One notable example of international cooperation in combating Dark Web markets is Operation Bayonet, a joint operation by law enforcement agencies from the United States, Germany, and the Netherlands. The operation targeted and dismantled the Wall Street Market, one of the largest Dark Web marketplaces at the time.

Operation Bayonet demonstrated the effectiveness of international collaboration in tackling Dark Web markets. It involved the exchange of intelligence, simultaneous arrests in multiple countries, the seizure of servers, and the freezing of cryptocurrency accounts used in illegal transactions. By working together, the participating countries disrupted a significant hub of illegal activities, highlighting the importance of international cooperation in combating Dark Web markets.

Summary

International cooperation plays a vital role in combating Dark Web markets due to the transnational nature of these illicit activities. Collaborative efforts among countries, law enforcement agencies, and cybersecurity professionals enhance information sharing, streamline investigations, and increase the global impact of initiatives. However, challenges such as jurisdictional complexities, information sharing constraints, and language barriers need to be addressed to effectively combat Dark Web markets. Case studies like Operation Bayonet demonstrate that international collaboration can yield significant results and serve as a blueprint for future efforts.

In the next section, we will explore various technological solutions and advancements that aid in the surveillance and monitoring of Dark Web markets.

Technological Solutions for Dark Web Market Surveillance

Advances in Dark Web monitoring and data analysis

The fight against Dark Web markets requires constant adaptation and innovation in the field of monitoring and data analysis. As criminals become more sophisticated in their activities, law enforcement agencies and cybersecurity professionals must stay ahead of the game by developing advanced techniques and tools to track and analyze Dark Web activities. In this section, we will explore some of the recent advances in Dark Web monitoring and data analysis that have helped in combating illicit activities on the Dark Web.

Advanced Data Crawling and Scraping Techniques

One of the key challenges in monitoring the Dark Web is the vast amount of data that needs to be collected and analyzed. Traditional web crawling techniques used for the surface web are often not effective in accessing Dark Web content. However, recent advances in data crawling and scraping techniques have enabled law enforcement agencies and cybersecurity professionals to gather valuable information from Dark Web marketplaces.

Example: The development of specialized web crawlers that can navigate through the Tor network and access hidden services on the Dark Web has allowed investigators to collect data on illegal goods and services offered on Dark Web markets. These advanced crawlers can even bypass certain security measures implemented by Dark Web marketplaces, such as CAPTCHAs, to collect data more efficiently.

Machine Learning and Natural Language Processing

As the volume of Dark Web data continues to grow, manual analysis becomes increasingly challenging. To overcome this obstacle, machine learning algorithms and natural language processing techniques are being applied to analyze Dark Web content and identify potential criminal activities.

Example: Text classification models trained on labeled Dark Web data can automatically categorize listings based on their content, identifying those related to drugs, weapons, cybercrime services, and more. This automated approach allows investigators to quickly identify potentially illegal activities and prioritize their efforts.

Social Network Analysis

Dark Web marketplaces are not standalone platforms but rather interconnected communities. Understanding the relationships between buyers, sellers, and other actors on the Dark Web is crucial in dismantling criminal networks. Social network analysis techniques have proven invaluable in visualizing and analyzing these complex networks.

Example: By analyzing the connections between Dark Web market participants, investigators can identify key individuals and organizations involved in illegal activities. This knowledge enables them to target the most influential actors and disrupt criminal networks more effectively.

Big Data Analytics

The amount of data generated on the Dark Web is enormous and continues to increase rapidly. Analyzing this vast amount of information manually is impractical and time-consuming. Big data analytics techniques are being employed to process and extract valuable insights from Dark Web data.

Example: Through big data analytics, law enforcement agencies can identify patterns and trends in Dark Web activities. They can detect anomalies, such as sudden spikes in specific illegal goods or services, and use this information to focus their investigation efforts.

Dark Web Market Monitoring Tools

To keep up with the ever-changing landscape of Dark Web markets, monitoring tools specifically designed for this purpose have been developed. These tools continuously monitor Dark Web marketplaces for new listings, changes in existing listings, and other relevant information. They provide real-time updates on illicit activities and help law enforcement agencies track the movements of criminals operating on Dark Web platforms.

Example: Some Dark Web market monitoring tools use machine learning algorithms to detect suspicious behavior and categorize listings based on their risk level. These tools can alert investigators when illegal activities are identified and provide valuable intelligence for further investigation.

Ethical Considerations and Challenges

While the advances in Dark Web monitoring and data analysis have significantly enhanced the capabilities of law enforcement agencies and cybersecurity professionals, ethical considerations and challenges persist. The privacy of individuals who may innocently access the Dark Web, potential bias in automated analysis algorithms, and the responsible use of the gathered information are important aspects to be considered.

Example: A challenge in Dark Web monitoring is distinguishing between legitimate research activities and illegal actions. Law enforcement agencies and cybersecurity professionals must carefully balance the need to investigate criminal activities while respecting the privacy rights of individuals. Implementing strict policies and guidelines for data collection, storage, and analysis can help address these ethical challenges.

In conclusion, the development of advanced techniques and tools for Dark Web monitoring and data analysis has greatly improved the ability of law enforcement agencies and cybersecurity professionals to combat illicit activities on the Dark Web. These advancements enable the identification and tracking of criminals, the disruption of criminal networks, and the proactive prevention of cybercrime. However, it is important to continually reassess and adapt these techniques to address emerging challenges and ethical concerns in the fight against Dark Web markets.

Machine learning and artificial intelligence in the fight against Dark Web markets

Machine learning and artificial intelligence (AI) have emerged as powerful tools in the fight against Dark Web markets. By harnessing the capabilities of these technologies, law enforcement agencies and cybersecurity professionals have been able to enhance their surveillance, detection, and prevention efforts in targeting illicit activities and individuals operating within the Dark Web ecosystem.

Introduction to Machine Learning and AI

Machine learning is a subfield of AI that enables systems to learn and make predictions or decisions without being explicitly programmed. It involves the development of algorithms that process and analyze large volumes of data, identifying patterns and trends to create models for making accurate predictions or taking appropriate actions.

AI, on the other hand, refers to the broader concept of machines or systems exhibiting intelligence, including natural language processing, computer vision, and decision-making abilities. It encompasses machine learning as one of its core components.

In the context of Dark Web markets, machine learning and AI techniques can be employed to analyze vast amounts of data generated on these platforms, identify suspicious activities, and enhance law enforcement operations.

Data Analysis and Pattern Recognition

One of the key benefits of machine learning and AI in combating Dark Web markets is their ability to analyze and process large volumes of data. Law enforcement agencies can collect data from various sources, such as seized servers, online surveillance, and publicly available information, and use machine learning algorithms to uncover hidden patterns, connections, and trends.

For example, machine learning algorithms can be trained on historical data related to Dark Web market transactions, identifying common patterns associated with illicit activities such as drug trafficking or cybercrime. By building models based on these patterns, law enforcement agencies can proactively detect and prevent such activities in the future.

Furthermore, AI techniques can aid in the identification of potential Dark Web market sellers and buyers. By analyzing user behavior, communication patterns, and transactional data, AI algorithms can flag suspicious accounts or activities, allowing law enforcement agencies to focus their efforts on high-risk individuals.

Sentiment Analysis and Natural Language Processing

Another area where machine learning and AI can be utilized is in sentiment analysis and natural language processing. Dark Web marketplaces often rely on encrypted communication channels, making it challenging for law enforcement agencies to monitor conversations and gather intelligence.

However, by employing natural language processing techniques, AI systems can analyze textual data, decrypt messages, and identify keywords or phrases associated with illegal goods or services. Sentiment analysis can help determine the intent behind certain messages, distinguishing between casual discussions and potential criminal activities.

Law enforcement agencies can use this information to prioritize investigations, allocate resources effectively, and identify key individuals involved in illicit operations on the Dark Web.

Cybersecurity and Anomaly Detection

Machine learning and AI techniques can also be leveraged to enhance cybersecurity measures in the fight against Dark Web markets. Cybercriminals often employ sophisticated techniques to evade detection and maintain their anonymity. However, by employing anomaly detection algorithms, law enforcement agencies can identify unusual behavior or network traffic patterns that indicate potential malicious activities.

For instance, machine learning algorithms can learn from network traffic data and establish baselines for normal behavior. Any deviation from these baselines can be flagged as a potential security threat, enabling prompt intervention and investigation.

Moreover, AI systems can be trained to detect vulnerabilities in Dark Web infrastructure, identifying weak points that cybercriminals may exploit. By proactively addressing these vulnerabilities, law enforcement agencies and cybersecurity professionals can prevent illicit activities and protect individuals from falling victim to cybercrime.

Challenges and Limitations

Although machine learning and AI offer significant advantages in combating Dark Web markets, there are several challenges and limitations that need to be considered.

One critical challenge is the ever-evolving nature of Dark Web marketplaces. As new technologies and encryption methods emerge, cybercriminals adapt their strategies and techniques to evade detection. This constant cat-and-mouse game requires law enforcement agencies and cybersecurity professionals to continuously update and refine their machine learning models and AI systems.

Moreover, the ethical and privacy concerns associated with the use of AI in surveillance and monitoring activities must be carefully addressed. Balancing the need for security with individual privacy can be a delicate undertaking, requiring the development of transparent and accountable frameworks to ensure the responsible use of AI technologies in combating Dark Web markets.

Conclusion

Machine learning and AI have demonstrated their value in the fight against Dark Web markets. The ability to process and analyze large volumes of data, detect patterns and anomalies, and enhance cybersecurity measures has significantly bolstered law enforcement efforts in targeting illicit activities on the Dark Web.

However, it is essential to recognize that machine learning and AI are not standalone solutions and must be used in conjunction with other investigative techniques and collaborations between law enforcement agencies. By embracing the potential of these technologies while addressing the associated challenges, the fight against Dark Web markets can be strengthened, ultimately leading to a safer online environment for individuals and society as a whole.

The development of tools for proactive detection and prevention

As Dark Web markets continue to evolve and become more sophisticated, law enforcement agencies and cybersecurity professionals face the challenge of staying one step ahead. To effectively combat these illicit activities, proactive strategies are crucial. This section will explore the development of tools for proactive detection and prevention, focusing on advanced technologies and innovative approaches.

Machine Learning and Artificial Intelligence

One of the most promising areas of development in proactive detection and prevention is the use of machine learning and artificial intelligence (AI). These technologies have the potential to significantly enhance the capabilities of law enforcement agencies and cybersecurity professionals in identifying and combating Dark Web market activities.

Machine learning algorithms can analyze vast amounts of data to identify patterns and detect anomalies that may indicate illicit activities. By training these algorithms on large datasets, they can learn to recognize the behaviors and characteristics common among Dark Web market participants. This includes identifying the patterns of communication, transactional behavior, and even the use of specific keywords or phrases commonly used in illegal transactions.

Artificial intelligence systems can also analyze network traffic and monitor online forums and communities to identify potential threats and gather intelligence on Dark Web marketplaces. By analyzing the content and context of conversations, these AI systems can identify suspicious activities and alert law enforcement agencies or cybersecurity professionals.

Furthermore, natural language processing (NLP) techniques can be used to analyze textual data, such as product descriptions and user reviews, to identify keywords and phrases associated with illegal goods and services. This can help in automating the detection of illicit listings on Dark Web markets.

Proactive Dark Web Monitoring

In addition to machine learning and AI, proactive Dark Web monitoring plays a crucial role in detecting and preventing illicit activities. This involves continuously monitoring the Dark Web for any signs of illegal transactions, the emergence of new marketplaces, or changes in the tactics used by Dark Web market participants.

Technology solutions for Dark Web monitoring employ web crawlers and scrapers to collect data from Dark Web marketplaces and underground forums. These tools can extract information on product listings, sellers' profiles, and even capture conversations and private messages.

To keep pace with the ever-changing landscape of Dark Web markets, some technological solutions utilize automation and real-time data analysis. This allows for the rapid detection of new threats and the adjustment of detection algorithms accordingly.

Collaborative Intelligence Sharing

Another important aspect of proactive detection and prevention is the collaboration and sharing of intelligence among law enforcement agencies and cybersecurity professionals. This involves establishing networks and platforms for information exchange, allowing for the timely dissemination of threat intelligence and the coordination of actions.

Collaborative intelligence sharing can provide law enforcement agencies with access to a broader pool of knowledge and expertise. It enables them to identify emerging trends, share successful strategies, and learn from each other's experiences. This approach is particularly effective in countering the highly dynamic and transnational nature of Dark Web market activities.

Moreover, information sharing can be extended beyond law enforcement agencies to include private sector entities and academic institutions. This multi-stakeholder collaboration facilitates a holistic understanding of the evolving tactics and techniques employed by Dark Web market participants, leading to more effective detection and prevention strategies.

Ethical Considerations

While the development of tools for proactive detection and prevention is essential, it is important to address the ethical considerations associated with these technologies. Privacy concerns and potential misuse of AI and machine learning algorithms must be carefully evaluated and regulated.

Law enforcement agencies and cybersecurity professionals must strike a balance between privacy and security when monitoring Dark Web activities. Transparent and accountable practices should be adopted to ensure that personal information is protected and that the monitoring activities are focused solely on the detection and prevention of illegal activities.

Additionally, the use of AI and machine learning algorithms should be subject to rigorous testing and validation to prevent bias, false positives, or false negatives. The accuracy and reliability of these tools must be continuously evaluated and improved to avoid unwarranted intrusion or improper targeting.

Conclusion

The development of tools for proactive detection and prevention plays a vital role in the fight against Dark Web markets. By harnessing the power of machine learning and AI, law enforcement agencies and cybersecurity professionals can stay ahead of evolving threats and effectively combat illicit activities.

Proactive Dark Web monitoring, coupled with collaborative intelligence sharing, enhances the capabilities of detection and prevention efforts. These technological advancements, however, must be accompanied by the ethical considerations of privacy and responsible use to maintain public trust and ensure fairness in law enforcement actions.

As the battle against Dark Web markets continues, the development of tools for proactive detection and prevention will remain an ongoing process. By embracing innovative technologies and fostering collaboration, we can strive towards a safer digital landscape.

Emerging technologies for Dark Web market investigation

In the ongoing battle against Dark Web markets, law enforcement agencies and cybersecurity professionals are constantly exploring and developing new technologies to enhance their capabilities in investigating and combating illegal activities. These emerging technologies play a crucial role in gathering intelligence, tracking transactions, identifying individuals involved in Dark Web marketplaces, and preventing future crimes. In this section, we will discuss some of the most promising technologies that are being used or developed for Dark Web market investigation.

Machine Learning and Data Analytics

Machine learning algorithms and data analytics techniques have proven to be invaluable tools in uncovering patterns and extracting meaningful insights from vast amounts of data. In the context of Dark Web market investigation, these technologies can aid in the identification and profiling of cybercriminals, detection of suspicious activities, and prediction of emerging trends.

Law enforcement agencies are utilizing machine learning algorithms to analyze large volumes of data collected from various sources, such as seized marketplaces, social media, and forums. By monitoring and analyzing these data sets, patterns can be identified and used to link different individuals or groups involved in Dark Web market activities. Machine learning models can also assist in the classification of illicit goods and services, improving the efficiency of detection and investigation processes.

Furthermore, data analytics techniques provide law enforcement with the ability to process and make sense of the vast amount of data generated on the Dark Web. By employing advanced data mining and visualization tools, investigators can gain valuable insights into the operations of Dark Web marketplaces, including transaction patterns, pricing strategies, and seller reputation.

Blockchain Analysis

Blockchain technology, which underlies cryptocurrencies like Bitcoin, has become a critical area of focus in Dark Web market investigation. While cryptocurrencies offer a certain level of anonymity, they also leave a trail of transactions on the public blockchain ledger. Law enforcement agencies and cybersecurity professionals are utilizing blockchain analysis tools to trace and link these transactions to specific individuals and Dark Web marketplaces.

Through sophisticated blockchain analysis techniques, investigators can trace the flow of funds and identify the origin and destination of cryptocurrency transactions. By analyzing patterns and information embedded in the blockchain, such as addresses and transaction history, law enforcement can identify individuals involved in illegal activities on Dark Web markets. This information can then be used to build cases against the individuals and dismantle the marketplaces.

Dark Web Crawlers

Dark Web crawlers are specialized software tools used to systematically discover and index information on the Dark Web. These crawlers, also known as Dark Web search engines, navigate the anonymous networks and collect data from various underground websites and forums. By using advanced crawling algorithms, they can uncover hidden marketplaces, illicit goods, and services, and monitor the activities of potential criminals.

Law enforcement agencies employ Dark Web crawlers to gather intelligence, identify emerging threats, and gather evidence for criminal investigations. These tools help investigators stay updated with the dynamic nature of Dark Web marketplaces and aid in the identification of new trends and criminal activities. Dark Web crawlers can also assist in the monitoring of online forums and communication channels used by cybercriminals, allowing law enforcement to intervene and disrupt their operations.

Quantum Computing

Quantum computing, although still in the early stages of development, holds immense potential in the field of Dark Web market investigation. Unlike classical computers that rely on bits to store and process data, quantum computers use qubits, which can exist in multiple states simultaneously. This fundamental difference gives quantum computers the ability to perform complex calculations at an exponentially faster rate.

In the context of Dark Web market investigation, quantum computing could enable the decryption of encrypted information that is currently beyond the capabilities of conventional computers. The ability to decrypt messages and data obtained from Dark Web market activities could provide law enforcement agencies with unprecedented insights into the operations and infrastructure of illegal marketplaces.

However, it is important to note that quantum computing is still in its infancy and many technical challenges need to be overcome before it can be fully utilized in Dark Web investigations. Additionally, the development of quantum-resistant encryption methods will be necessary to ensure the security and privacy of legitimate users' data.

Ethical Considerations and Challenges

The use of emerging technologies in Dark Web market investigation raises several ethical considerations and challenges. It is crucial to strike a balance between privacy and security to prevent the overreach of law enforcement agencies and protect the rights of individuals. Ensuring transparency and accountability in the use of these technologies is essential to maintain public trust.

Furthermore, the rapid advancement of technology requires continuous training and upskilling of law enforcement and cybersecurity professionals. These individuals need to stay updated with the latest tools and techniques to effectively investigate Dark Web marketplaces and address the evolving tactics of cybercriminals.

It is also worth mentioning that the effectiveness of emerging technologies in Dark Web market investigation heavily relies on international cooperation and collaboration. Given the global nature of the Dark Web, it is imperative for law enforcement agencies and cybersecurity professionals to work together, share intelligence, and establish common standards and protocols for the use of these technologies.

Summary

Emerging technologies such as machine learning, blockchain analysis, Dark Web crawlers, and the potential of quantum computing hold great promise in the investigation and fight against Dark Web markets. These technologies provide law enforcement agencies and cybersecurity professionals with powerful tools to gather intelligence, track transactions, identify individuals involved in illegal activities, and prevent future crimes.

However, the ethical implications of using these technologies should be carefully considered, and measures should be in place to ensure transparency, accountability, and the protection of individuals' rights. Continuous training and collaboration between international agencies are also crucial to maximize the effectiveness of these technologies in combating Dark Web marketplaces.

As technology continues to evolve, it is essential to stay proactive in adapting and developing new tools and techniques to stay one step ahead of cybercriminals operating on the Dark Web. The ongoing battle against Dark Web markets requires collaboration, innovation, and a commitment to protecting individuals and society from the harms associated with illegal activities in the digital realm.

Education and Awareness Campaigns

The importance of educating the public about Dark Web markets

Education plays a crucial role in combating Dark Web markets. It is essential to educate the public about the nature, risks, and potential consequences of engaging with these illicit online platforms. By increasing awareness and knowledge, we can empower individuals to make informed decisions and protect themselves from the influence of Dark Web markets. This section will discuss the importance of educating the public about Dark Web markets and explore strategies for raising awareness about their dangers.

Understanding Dark Web markets

First and foremost, it is crucial to provide the public with a clear understanding of what Dark Web markets are. Many people are unaware of the existence of these hidden online platforms and the illegal activities that take place within them. By explaining the concept of the Dark Web and its distinct characteristics, individuals can grasp the magnitude and complexity of Dark Web markets.

Risks and dangers

One of the key objectives of public education is to highlight the risks and dangers associated with Dark Web markets. Individuals need to be aware that engaging with these platforms can expose them to various threats, including illegal activities, scams, identity theft, malware, and cyberattacks. By understanding the potential consequences, people are more likely to think twice before getting involved with Dark Web markets.

Impacts on society

Educating the public about the impacts of Dark Web markets on society is another crucial aspect. Dark Web marketplaces fuel the illicit drug trade, weapons trafficking, and cybercrime-as-a-service, leading to harmful consequences for individuals and communities. By showcasing real-world examples and explaining how these activities affect people's lives, we can emphasize the importance of taking action against Dark Web markets.

Recognizing warning signs

Public education should also focus on providing individuals with the ability to recognize the warning signs of Dark Web market involvement. By understanding the red flags and indicators, people can identify potential threats and avoid falling into illegal activities unknowingly. For example, recognizing unusual online behaviors, requests for cryptocurrency payments, or suspicious offers can help individuals stay away from Dark Web market entanglements.

Engaging the community

Engaging the community is a critical strategy in raising awareness about Dark Web markets. By organizing educational workshops, seminars, and public campaigns, we can directly reach a wider audience and facilitate discussions about the risks and impacts of Dark Web markets. Furthermore, involving community leaders, law enforcement agencies, and schools can reinforce the importance of combating Dark Web markets and promote a collective effort.

Collaboration with law enforcement

Collaboration with law enforcement agencies is vital in ensuring the effectiveness of public education campaigns. By working with law enforcement, we can provide accurate and up-to-date information about Dark Web market trends, emerging threats, and ongoing investigations. This collaboration not only enhances the credibility of the education initiatives but also creates a sense of trust and confidence among the public.

Resources and tools

To support public education efforts, it is essential to provide resources and tools that enable individuals to protect themselves from Dark Web market involvement. This can include online guides, informative websites, and interactive platforms that educate the public on how to identify, report, and mitigate potential risks associated with Dark Web markets. Additionally, providing resources for parents, educators, and guardians to educate younger generations about the dangers of the Dark Web is crucial in creating a safer digital environment.

Exercises and interactive learning

Incorporating exercises and interactive learning activities can make the education experience more engaging and effective. By simulating real-world scenarios and challenging individuals to make decisions related to Dark Web market involvement, we can enhance their comprehension and critical thinking skills. This approach encourages active participation and empowers individuals to apply their knowledge in practical situations.

Trickery-proofing

Given the sophisticated nature of Dark Web markets, it is crucial to educate the public about common tricks and scams employed by criminals. Providing examples and explanations of common deceptive practices can help individuals recognize and avoid falling victim to manipulation. By trickery-proofing the public through education, we can reduce the success rate of illicit activities on Dark Web markets.

In conclusion, public education plays a vital role in combating Dark Web markets. Through comprehensive and engaging educational initiatives, we can increase awareness, highlight the risks, and empower individuals to protect themselves and their communities. By educating the public about Dark Web markets, we can foster a safer digital environment and contribute to the ongoing fight against cybercrime.

Strategies for raising awareness about the dangers of Dark Web market involvement

Raising awareness about the dangers of Dark Web market involvement is crucial in the fight against cybercrime and the protection of individuals from potential harm. By educating the public about the risks associated with participating in Dark Web markets, we can empower them to make informed decisions and protect themselves from falling into illegal activities. This section will discuss strategies that can be adopted to effectively raise awareness about the dangers of Dark Web market involvement.

Education campaigns in schools and universities

One effective strategy for raising awareness is to conduct education campaigns in schools and universities. By integrating cybersecurity and online safety education into the curriculum, students can gain a better understanding of the risks associated with the Dark Web and the potential consequences of engaging in illegal activities. This can be done through the development of age-appropriate educational materials, workshops, and presentations delivered by cybersecurity experts. It is important to present the information in an engaging and relatable manner, using real-world examples and case studies to illustrate the dangers and impact of Dark Web market involvement.

Public awareness campaigns

To reach a wider audience, public awareness campaigns can be organized through various media channels, including television, radio, social media, and online platforms. These campaigns can provide information about the dangers of Dark Web market involvement, explain the potential consequences, and offer guidance on how to protect oneself from the influence of the Dark Web. Collaborating with law enforcement agencies, cybersecurity organizations, and community leaders can enhance the credibility and effectiveness of these campaigns. Engaging celebrities, influencers, and public figures in the promotion of awareness messages can also help increase the visibility and impact of the campaigns.

Community engagement and partnerships

Community engagement plays a vital role in spreading awareness about the dangers of Dark Web market involvement. By partnering with local communities, non-profit organizations, and community centers, awareness programs can be implemented at the grassroots level. These programs can include workshops, seminars, and panel discussions, where experts can provide insights and guidance on detecting and avoiding Dark Web activities. Creating a network of trusted individuals who can act as local resources for reporting suspicious activities and providing support can contribute to a safer online environment.

Collaboration with social media platforms

Given the widespread use of social media, collaborating with popular platforms can be an effective way to disseminate information and raise awareness about Dark Web market dangers. Social media companies can incorporate educational messages, relevant content, and warnings about the risks associated with Dark Web involvement into their platforms. Partnering with social media influencers and content creators who have a large following can help amplify the reach of the awareness messages. Additionally, social media platforms can also develop reporting mechanisms to allow users to report Dark Web-related content, ensuring a proactive approach in combating illegal activities.

Participation in industry conferences and events

Participating in industry conferences and events focused on cybersecurity and online safety can provide an opportunity to raise awareness about the dangers of Dark Web market involvement. Presentations, panels, and workshops can be organized to share insights, best practices, and case studies highlighting the impact of Dark Web activities. By engaging with professionals from different sectors, such as law enforcement, academia, and private organizations, collective efforts can be made to combat Dark Web markets and protect individuals from the associated risks.

Encouraging responsible online behavior

Promoting responsible online behavior is key to preventing individuals from being lured into Dark Web market activities. Encouraging individuals to practice good cybersecurity habits, such as using strong and unique passwords, regularly updating software, and being cautious while sharing personal information online, can help mitigate the risks. Providing resources, guidelines, and tools to enhance online safety and privacy can empower individuals to protect themselves and make informed choices in the digital landscape.

In conclusion, raising awareness about the dangers of Dark Web market involvement is essential in the ongoing battle against cybercrime. Through education campaigns, public awareness initiatives, community engagement, collaboration with social media platforms, participation in industry events, and promoting responsible online behavior, we can empower individuals to stay vigilant and protect themselves from the risks associated with the Dark Web. By combining these strategies, we can work towards creating a safer online environment and reducing the societal impact of Dark Web markets.

Engaging communities, schools, and law enforcement in prevention efforts

Preventing the proliferation and impact of Dark Web markets requires a holistic approach that involves engaging various stakeholders, including communities, schools, and law enforcement. In this section, we will explore the importance of engaging these entities and discuss strategies for their involvement in prevention efforts.

Raising awareness in communities

Engaging local communities is a crucial aspect of preventing individuals from participating in Dark Web markets. By raising awareness and educating community members about the risks and consequences associated with illegal online activities, we can empower them to take proactive measures to protect themselves and their loved ones.

To engage communities effectively, law enforcement agencies can organize informational sessions or workshops focused on highlighting the dangers of Dark Web markets. These sessions can cover topics such as the types of illegal goods and services available, the potential impact of involvement in online criminal activities, and strategies for recognizing and reporting suspicious online behavior.

Additionally, engaging community leaders and influencers, such as local business owners, religious leaders, or educators, can help spread the message further and encourage community members to support prevention initiatives. Collaboration with community organizations, such as neighborhood watch groups or youth clubs, can also be instrumental in reaching a broader audience.

Integration of prevention efforts in schools

Schools play a vital role in shaping young minds and instilling responsible digital citizenship. Integrating prevention efforts into school curricula can help educate students about the dangers of the Dark Web and emphasize the importance of ethical online behavior.

One effective approach is incorporating cybersecurity education into technology or computer science classes. This can include topics such as online privacy, safe browsing habits, and the risks associated with sharing personal information online. Bringing in guest speakers from law enforcement agencies or cybersecurity experts can provide valuable insights and real-world examples to help students understand the consequences of engaging with illegal online activities.

Furthermore, schools can organize awareness campaigns or workshops targeting both students and parents. These events can cover a range of topics, including the identification of Dark Web marketplaces, the potential impact on academic and professional futures, and strategies for safely reporting suspicious online activities to law enforcement.

Collaboration with law enforcement

Engaging law enforcement agencies is essential for effectively combating Dark Web markets. Collaboration between schools, communities, and law enforcement can help create a united front against illegal online activities.

One strategy is to establish partnerships between local law enforcement agencies and schools. This can involve dedicated liaisons or resource officers who can provide guidance and support to schools in prevention efforts. These officers can also serve as a point of contact for students and staff to report suspicious online activities.

Furthermore, law enforcement agencies can conduct joint workshops or seminars with schools and communities to share up-to-date information on emerging threats and prevention strategies. This collaboration can also help bridge the gap between law enforcement and the community, fostering trust and encouraging the reporting of illegal online activities.

Additionally, law enforcement agencies can leverage their expertise to provide training and assistance to community leaders, educators, and parents. This training can equip them with the necessary skills to identify signs of involvement in Dark Web markets and take appropriate action to protect their communities.

The role of technology in prevention efforts

Technology plays a vital role in prevention efforts against Dark Web markets. Law enforcement agencies can leverage advanced data analytics tools and machine learning algorithms to monitor online activities and identify potential Dark Web market participants. These technologies can help detect patterns, identify emerging trends, and provide early warning signs of illegal online activities.

Furthermore, collaboration between technology companies, law enforcement, and schools can lead to the development and implementation of innovative tools and solutions for preventing access to Dark Web markets. For instance, internet service providers can employ content filtering or blocking mechanisms to restrict access to known Dark Web marketplaces. Similarly, software developers can create educational applications or browser plug-ins that alert users when they are engaging with potentially dangerous online content.

It is important to note that while technology can enhance prevention efforts, it should be used ethically and responsibly, respecting privacy and civil liberties.

Summary

Engaging communities, schools, and law enforcement in prevention efforts is crucial for combating Dark Web markets. Raising awareness in communities, integrating prevention efforts in schools, and collaborating with law enforcement can help educate and empower individuals to protect themselves and their communities from the dangers of illegal online activities. Additionally, leveraging technology ethically can enhance prevention strategies and aid in the fight against Dark Web markets. By working together, we can create a safer digital landscape for all.

Empowering individuals to protect themselves from the influence of Dark Web markets

In order to effectively combat the influence of Dark Web markets, it is essential to empower individuals with the knowledge and tools to protect themselves from potential harm. Education and awareness campaigns play a crucial role in this regard, as they enable individuals to make informed decisions and take necessary precautions. This section will discuss strategies for empowering individuals to protect themselves from the influence of Dark Web markets.

The Importance of Education

Education is the foundation for protecting oneself from the dangers of Dark Web markets. Providing accurate and comprehensive information about the risks associated with illegal activities on the Dark Web is essential. Educational programs can be designed for different audiences, including students, parents, and community members.

One approach is to integrate cybersecurity education into school curricula. By teaching young students about the potential risks and consequences of engaging with Dark Web markets, we can create a culture of digital responsibility and vigilant online behavior. Schools can also invite cybersecurity professionals and law enforcement officers to conduct workshops on online safety, privacy protection, and responsible internet usage.

Furthermore, public awareness campaigns targeting adults can be conducted through various channels such as social media, TV, radio, and community events. These campaigns should focus on raising awareness about the dangers of Dark Web markets, the prevalence of cybercrime, and the potential impact on society as a whole.

Strategies for Raising Awareness

Raising awareness about Dark Web markets involves more than just providing information. It requires engaging and capturing the attention of the target audience. Here are some strategies to consider:

1. Personal testimonies: Sharing real-life stories or case studies of individuals who have been affected by the Dark Web can help create a sense of urgency and personal relevance.

2. Collaboration with influencers: Partnering with influential individuals, such as bloggers, vloggers, or social media influencers, can amplify the reach and impact of awareness campaigns. These individuals can create content that is relatable and appealing to their audiences, while also emphasizing the risks associated with Dark Web activities.

3. Utilizing interactive formats: Incorporating interactive elements, such as quizzes, games, and simulations, can make the learning experience more engaging and memorable. This approach can help individuals understand the potential

consequences of engaging with Dark Web markets in a practical and concrete manner.

4. Building strong partnerships: Collaborating with law enforcement agencies, educational institutions, community organizations, and businesses can enhance the credibility and effectiveness of awareness campaigns. By working together, these stakeholders can contribute their expertise, resources, and networks to reach a larger audience and deliver a consistent message.

Engaging Communities, Schools, and Law Enforcement

Preventing individuals from falling into the trap of Dark Web markets requires a comprehensive approach involving communities, schools, and law enforcement. Here are some strategies for engaging these key stakeholders:

1. Community-based interventions: Organizing workshops, seminars, or town hall meetings within local communities can help disseminate information about the dangers of Dark Web markets. Engaging community leaders, religious organizations, and grassroots initiatives can amplify the impact and effectiveness of these interventions.

2. School partnerships: Collaborating with schools is essential to reach students and parents. Schools can integrate cybersecurity education into the curriculum, organize awareness events, and establish partnerships with local law enforcement agencies to provide resources and expertise.

3. Law enforcement involvement: Law enforcement agencies should proactively engage with communities and schools to enhance awareness and prevention efforts. This can be achieved through guest lectures, participation in community events, and sharing information about emerging trends on the Dark Web.

4. Support systems: Establishing support systems for individuals who may have been exposed to the influence of Dark Web markets is crucial. This can include counseling services, support groups, and helpline numbers where individuals can seek assistance and guidance.

Empowering Individuals

Empowering individuals to protect themselves from the influence of Dark Web markets requires equipping them with the necessary knowledge, skills, and tools. Here are some ways to empower individuals:

1. Privacy protection and online security training: Providing individuals with guidance on enhancing their privacy and security online can significantly reduce their vulnerability to Dark Web market influence. This includes teaching them to

use strong passwords, enabling two-factor authentication, and avoiding suspicious websites or downloads.

2. Recognizing phishing attempts: Educating individuals about the techniques used by cybercriminals to deceive and trick them into engaging in illegal activities is essential. By recognizing phishing attempts, individuals can avoid falling for scams or becoming unknowingly involved in illegal transactions on the Dark Web.

3. Reporting suspicious activities: Encouraging individuals to report any suspicious activities they encounter online is crucial for maintaining a safe digital environment. This can include reporting suspicious websites, social media accounts, or individuals who are engaged in illegal activities on the Dark Web.

4. Promoting ethical digital behavior: Empowering individuals to make responsible choices online is essential. This includes promoting the ethical use of technology, respecting others' privacy, and understanding the potential consequences of their actions on the Dark Web.

By implementing these strategies and empowering individuals, we can create a stronger defense against the influence of Dark Web markets. Education, awareness, and collaboration are key in building a safer digital society. Remember, protecting oneself from the influence of Dark Web markets is not just about personal safety but also about contributing to the overall well-being of our communities.

Future Trends and Ethical Considerations

Emerging Trends in Dark Web Markets

Technological advancements shaping the future of Dark Web markets

In recent years, technological advancements have played a pivotal role in shaping the future of Dark Web markets. These advancements have not only facilitated the growth of these illicit marketplaces but have also posed new challenges for law enforcement and cybersecurity professionals. In this section, we will explore some of the key technological developments that are likely to have a lasting impact on the Dark Web market landscape.

Blockchain Technology and Cryptocurrencies

One of the most significant technological advancements that has fueled the growth of Dark Web markets is blockchain technology and the rise of cryptocurrencies. Cryptocurrencies like Bitcoin, Ethereum, and Monero have become the preferred medium of exchange on Dark Web marketplaces due to their inherent privacy and anonymity features.

The decentralized nature of blockchain ensures that transactions conducted using cryptocurrencies are secure and transparent, making it difficult for law enforcement agencies to trace the flow of funds. Additionally, cryptocurrencies allow for quick and seamless international transactions, eliminating the need for traditional banking systems.

As blockchain technology continues to evolve, we can expect to see further innovations that enhance the privacy and security of transactions on Dark Web markets. For instance, techniques like CoinJoin and Zero-Knowledge Proofs are being developed to improve the anonymity of cryptocurrency transactions, making it even more challenging for law enforcement to track illicit activities.

Advancements in Encryption Techniques

Encryption plays a critical role in securing communications and data on the Dark Web. As law enforcement agencies become increasingly adept at monitoring online activities, individuals and marketplaces operating within the Dark Web are adopting stronger encryption techniques to protect their identities and transactions.

End-to-end encryption, for example, has become a standard practice for secure communication on Dark Web marketplaces. With end-to-end encryption, messages are encrypted on the sender's device and can only be decrypted by the intended recipient, ensuring that even if intercepted, the content remains unreadable.

Moreover, advancements in encryption algorithms, such as the adoption of Elliptic Curve Cryptography (ECC), are making it possible to achieve higher levels of security with shorter key lengths. This allows for faster encryption and decryption processes, enabling Dark Web market participants to communicate more efficiently while maintaining robust security.

Emergence of Decentralized Market Platforms

Traditional Dark Web marketplaces, such as the infamous Silk Road, relied on a centralized architecture which made them vulnerable to law enforcement takedowns. However, recent technological advancements have led to the emergence of decentralized market platforms built on blockchain technology.

These decentralized marketplaces operate without a central authority, making it challenging for law enforcement agencies to target a single point of failure. Instead, transactions on these platforms are managed through smart contracts, which are automatically executed when predefined conditions are met, reducing the need for human intervention.

Decentralized market platforms not only increase the resilience of Dark Web marketplaces but also provide participants with increased privacy and security. These platforms leverage the immutable nature of blockchain to ensure transparency and trust in transactions while safeguarding the identities of buyers and sellers.

Artificial Intelligence and Machine Learning in Law Enforcement

While technological advancements have facilitated the growth of Dark Web markets, law enforcement agencies are also leveraging emerging technologies to combat illicit activities. Artificial Intelligence (AI) and Machine Learning (ML) are playing a crucial role in enhancing the capabilities of law enforcement agencies in monitoring and investigating Dark Web marketplaces.

AI and ML algorithms can analyze vast amounts of data collected from the Dark Web, including forum discussions, chat transcripts, and transaction records, to identify patterns and detect potential threats. These technologies can aid in profiling Dark Web market participants, predicting criminal activities, and prioritizing law enforcement actions.

Furthermore, AI-powered chatbots have been developed to mimic buyers and sellers on Dark Web marketplaces, allowing law enforcement agencies to monitor conversations and gather intelligence in real-time. These chatbots can identify keywords and suspicious behavior, enabling law enforcement to intervene when necessary.

Rise of Privacy-Enhancing Technologies

In response to increased scrutiny and surveillance, privacy-enhancing technologies are becoming more prevalent on the Dark Web. These technologies aim to ensure the anonymity of market participants and protect their operations from prying eyes.

Systems like Onion Routing, which is the backbone of the Tor network, are continuously evolving to provide enhanced privacy and security on the Dark Web. Additionally, anonymous communication tools like Invisible Internet Project (I2P) and Freenet offer alternative platforms for accessing Dark Web marketplaces while maintaining anonymity.

The development of innovative privacy-enhancing tools, such as decentralized mixnets, which mix and route network traffic to further obfuscate the source and destination of communications, are likely to become prominent features of the Dark Web market ecosystem in the future.

In conclusion, technological advancements are reshaping the future of Dark Web markets. The adoption of blockchain technology and cryptocurrencies, advancements in encryption techniques, the emergence of decentralized market platforms, the integration of AI and ML in law enforcement efforts, and the rise of privacy-enhancing technologies are all factors that will continue to impact the Dark Web market landscape. As these technologies evolve, so too will the challenges faced by law enforcement and cybersecurity professionals, necessitating ongoing innovation and collaboration to combat illicit activities on the Dark Web.

Changes in the types of goods and services offered on Dark Web markets

Dark Web markets have undergone significant changes over the years in terms of the types of goods and services that are offered. The evolution of technology and the growing sophistication of both buyers and sellers have contributed to these changes. In this section, we will explore the major shifts in the Dark Web market landscape and discuss the implications of these changes.

The Shift from Physical to Digital Goods

One notable change in Dark Web markets is the shift from predominantly physical goods to a greater emphasis on digital goods and services. In the early days of Dark Web markets, the majority of listings consisted of drugs, counterfeit documents, stolen credit card information, and weapons. However, with advancements in technology and the increasing demand for digital products, the market has expanded to include a wide range of digital goods and services.

Digital goods offered on Dark Web markets now include stolen personal information, such as credit card details, social security numbers, and login credentials. These items are in high demand by cybercriminals who use them for identity theft, financial fraud, or gaining unauthorized access to online accounts. The sale of hacking tools, exploit kits, and malware is also prevalent on these platforms, allowing potential cybercriminals to launch various attacks without much technical expertise.

Moreover, Dark Web markets have become hubs for the trade of copyrighted content, such as pirated software, movies, music, and e-books. These platforms provide a means for individuals to access copyrighted materials without paying for them, leading to substantial financial losses for content creators and copyright holders.

Emergence of Cybercrime Services

In addition to the shift towards digital goods, Dark Web markets have seen a rise in the availability of cybercrime services. Cybercriminals now offer a range of services including hacking services, ransomware-as-a-service, distributed denial-of-service (DDoS) attacks-for-hire, and botnet rentals. These services allow less technically skilled individuals to engage in cybercriminal activities, further expanding the reach of cybercrime.

The demand for these cybercrime services stems from various motivations. Some individuals may seek revenge or engage in cyber activism, while others aim to extort businesses or individuals for financial gain. The availability of these services has lowered the entry barrier for engaging in cybercriminal activities, making it easier for individuals with limited technical expertise to carry out malicious acts.

Illicit Financial Services

Dark Web markets have also witnessed the emergence of illicit financial services, including money laundering, cryptocurrency exchange, and cashing out services. These services enable cybercriminals to convert their illicit proceeds into traditional currencies or other forms of value while maintaining their anonymity.

Money laundering services on Dark Web markets offer individuals the means to disguise the origin of their ill-gotten funds and make them appear legitimate. These services typically involve complicated financial transactions, including layering, smurfing, and mixing, with the ultimate goal of obfuscating the money trail.

Cryptocurrency exchange services facilitate the conversion of cryptocurrencies into traditional fiat currencies or vice versa. These services play a crucial role in the Dark Web market ecosystem as cryptocurrencies are the primary mode of payment due to their pseudonymous nature. By providing an exchange platform, these services enable users to convert their illicitly obtained cryptocurrencies into more widely accepted forms of value.

Cashing out services, on the other hand, involve converting cryptocurrencies into physical cash or other forms of payment, making it easier for cybercriminals to spend their ill-gotten gains in the real world. These services often use methods such as prepaid cards, money mules, or wire transfers to facilitate the conversion process.

Evolving Trends in Illegal Substances

While the sale of drugs has been a significant part of Dark Web markets since their inception, the types of drugs being traded have evolved. In recent years, there has been an increase in the availability of synthetic drugs, prescription medications, and designer drugs on these platforms. These substances pose significant health risks to users due to their synthetic nature and often unknown composition.

Synthetic drugs, such as synthetic cannabinoids (commonly known as Spice or K2) and synthetic cathinones (commonly known as bath salts), are designed to mimic the effects of illegal substances like marijuana and amphetamines. These substances are particularly dangerous as their chemical composition can vary widely, leading to unpredictable and potentially life-threatening effects.

Prescription medications, including opioids and benzodiazepines, are also commonly traded on Dark Web markets. The availability of these medications without proper prescriptions contributes to the ongoing opioid crisis and poses a substantial risk to public health.

Designer drugs, also known as new psychoactive substances (NPS), are synthetic substances created to replicate the effects of controlled substances while circumventing legal restrictions. The rapid development and constant evolution of designer drugs make it challenging for law enforcement to keep up with the changing market. This poses a significant threat to public health and safety.

Implications and Challenges

The changing landscape of Dark Web markets poses significant implications and challenges for society, law enforcement, and cybersecurity professionals. The availability of digital goods and services, as well as cybercrime-as-a-service offerings, has expanded the threat landscape and increased the potential for cybercriminal activities.

Law enforcement agencies face the challenge of adapting to the evolving nature of Dark Web markets. Traditional investigative techniques and legal frameworks may struggle to keep up with the pace of technological advancements and the increasing sophistication of criminals operating on these platforms. International cooperation and collaboration between agencies are essential to effectively combat the proliferation of illegal goods and services on Dark Web markets.

For cybersecurity professionals, the emergence of cybercrime-as-a-service presents new challenges in terms of threat detection and prevention. The availability of hacking tools, malware, and botnets-as-a-service allows individuals with limited technical skills to engage in cybercriminal activities. Proactive monitoring, advanced threat intelligence, and collaboration with law enforcement agencies are crucial in combating these emerging threats.

In conclusion, Dark Web markets have experienced significant changes in the types of goods and services offered. The shift towards digital goods, emergence of cybercrime services, and the availability of illicit financial services pose serious challenges to society. Efforts from law enforcement agencies, cybersecurity professionals, and public awareness campaigns are necessary to mitigate the risks associated with Dark Web markets and protect individuals and businesses from the growing threats present in this realm.

The role of cryptocurrency in the evolution of Dark Web transactions

Cryptocurrencies have played a significant role in the evolution and growth of Dark Web transactions. These digital currencies offer a high level of anonymity and security, making them the preferred medium of exchange for illegal goods and services on Dark Web markets. In this section, we will explore the role of cryptocurrency in facilitating transactions on the Dark Web, its advantages and risks, and the challenges it poses for law enforcement agencies.

Introduction to cryptocurrency

Cryptocurrency is a digital or virtual form of currency that uses cryptography for secure financial transactions, control the creation of additional units, and to verify the transfer of assets. The most well-known cryptocurrency is Bitcoin, but many others have emerged since its inception, such as Ethereum, Monero, and Litecoin.

Advantages of cryptocurrency on Dark Web markets

The use of cryptocurrency on Dark Web markets offers several advantages for both buyers and sellers:

- **Anonymity:** Cryptocurrencies provide a high level of anonymity as they do not require personal information to complete transactions. Unlike traditional banking systems, which often require identification and verification processes, cryptocurrency transactions can be conducted pseudonymously, protecting the real-world identity of parties involved.

- **Decentralization:** Cryptocurrencies operate on a decentralized network, such as blockchain, which eliminates the need for a central authority like a bank. The absence of a central authority reduces the risk of censorship and interference by governments or financial institutions, making cryptocurrencies an attractive choice for individuals engaging in illegal activities.

- **Security and encryption:** Cryptocurrencies use advanced cryptographic techniques to secure transactions and control the creation of new units. This ensures that transactions on the Dark Web are protected from unauthorized access and tampering. Additionally, the use of encryption further enhances the privacy and security of these transactions.

- **Ease of use:** Cryptocurrencies offer a convenient and user-friendly payment method for Dark Web transactions. The digital nature of these currencies allows for quick and seamless transactions across borders, without the need for intermediaries or the complexities associated with traditional banking systems.

- **Global accessibility:** Cryptocurrencies provide equal access to individuals irrespective of their geographic location. This global accessibility enables Dark Web markets to operate on an international scale, connecting buyers and sellers from different parts of the world. It also facilitates the globalization of illegal activities, creating a significant challenge for law enforcement agencies.

Risks and challenges of cryptocurrency on Dark Web markets

While cryptocurrency offers various advantages for Dark Web transactions, it also presents unique risks and challenges:

- **Volatility:** Cryptocurrencies are known for their price volatility, with values fluctuating rapidly within short periods. This volatility poses a risk to both buyers and sellers on Dark Web markets, as the value of transactions can change significantly before they are confirmed. This uncertainty can make it difficult to determine the actual worth of illegal goods and services.

- **Money laundering:** The anonymity and decentralized nature of cryptocurrencies make them an ideal medium for money laundering. Criminals can exploit the lack of regulatory oversight to convert their illicit proceeds into cryptocurrency and move funds across borders without detection. The use of cryptocurrency in Dark Web transactions further complicates the already challenging task of tracing and recovering illicit funds.

- **Illicit activities financing:** The use of cryptocurrency on Dark Web markets enables the financial support of various illegal activities, such as drug trafficking, weapon trading, and cybercrime. The anonymity provided by cryptocurrencies makes it difficult for law enforcement agencies to track and disrupt these illicit financial flows. The absence of a central authority also hinders traditional methods of financial surveillance and control.

- **Cybersecurity risks:** Cryptocurrencies are not immune to cybersecurity risks. Dark Web markets, where large volumes of cryptocurrency transactions occur, are attractive targets for hackers. These attackers may exploit vulnerabilities in cryptocurrency platforms, wallets, or exchanges to steal funds or compromise user identities. Additionally, the lack of regulatory oversight and the anonymous nature of transactions make it challenging to recover stolen funds or hold the responsible parties accountable.

- **Regulatory challenges:** The decentralized nature of cryptocurrencies and Dark Web markets poses substantial regulatory challenges. Governments and financial institutions struggle to establish legal frameworks and regulatory mechanisms to monitor and control the use of cryptocurrency without hindering technological innovation. The borderless nature of these transactions adds complexity to the regulatory landscape, requiring international cooperation to address challenges effectively.

Law enforcement challenges and responses

The use of cryptocurrency on Dark Web markets presents significant challenges for law enforcement agencies:

- **Anonymity and tracing:** Cryptocurrency transactions are pseudonymous, making it challenging to link specific users to their real-world identities. Law enforcement agencies face difficulties in tracing the flow of funds and identifying the individuals involved in illegal activities. However, advances in blockchain analysis techniques and collaboration between agencies have improved the ability to uncover patterns and connections in cryptocurrency transactions.

- **Regulatory frameworks and legislation:** The dynamic and rapidly evolving nature of cryptocurrencies often outpaces the development of regulatory frameworks and legislation. Governments worldwide are working to address this challenge by introducing regulations to monitor and control cryptocurrency activities. However, creating effective regulations that strike a balance between privacy, security, and oversight remains a complex task.

- **International cooperation:** Dark Web markets operate across national borders, requiring international cooperation among law enforcement agencies to combat their activities effectively. Sharing intelligence, coordinating investigations, and harmonizing legal efforts are critical in dismantling global criminal networks. Collaborative efforts, such as

Europol's Joint Cybercrime Action Taskforce (J-CAT), have yielded notable successes in combating Dark Web markets.

- **Capacity building:** Law enforcement agencies need to enhance their technical capabilities to investigate and prosecute Dark Web market participants effectively. Training programs, specialized units, and collaborations with cybersecurity experts are essential to keep pace with the ever-evolving techniques used by criminals within the cryptocurrency ecosystem.

- **Education and awareness:** Educating the public, particularly individuals susceptible to involvement in Dark Web transactions, is crucial in preventing and reducing the demand for illegal goods and services. Law enforcement agencies, together with educational institutions, can develop outreach programs to inform individuals about the risks, legal consequences, and ethical implications associated with Dark Web market involvement.

Conclusion

Cryptocurrencies have revolutionized Dark Web transactions, providing a high level of anonymity, decentralization, and security. Their advantages and the challenges they pose have far-reaching implications for law enforcement agencies, financial systems, and society as a whole. To effectively combat the criminal activities facilitated by cryptocurrency on Dark Web markets, global cooperation, technological advancements, regulatory frameworks, and public awareness initiatives are essential. The continuous evolution of both cryptocurrencies and Dark Web markets ensures an ongoing battle that demands innovation, adaptability, and the balancing of privacy and security considerations.

Potential impacts of emerging technologies on the fight against Dark Web markets

As the Dark Web continues to evolve, so too must the strategies and technologies used to combat its illicit activities. Emerging technologies play a crucial role in the fight against Dark Web markets, offering both new opportunities and challenges for law enforcement and cybersecurity professionals. In this section, we will explore some of the potential impacts of these emerging technologies on the ongoing battle against Dark Web markets.

Advancements in Artificial Intelligence (AI)

Artificial Intelligence (AI) has the potential to revolutionize the fight against Dark Web markets. Machine learning algorithms can analyze vast amounts of data and identify patterns, enabling law enforcement to proactively detect and monitor illegal activities in real-time. AI-powered tools can assist in automated monitoring of Dark Web marketplaces, flagging suspicious transactions, and identifying potential threats.

For example, AI algorithms can analyze blockchain transactions to detect money laundering activities on Dark Web marketplaces. By tracking and analyzing the flow of cryptocurrencies, law enforcement agencies can identify individuals and organizations involved in illegal activities. This can aid in the identification and prosecution of Dark Web market participants.

However, there are ethical considerations in the use of AI for Dark Web market surveillance. Privacy concerns and potential misuse of AI for mass surveillance need to be carefully addressed to ensure a balance between privacy and security.

Blockchain Technology

Blockchain technology, which underlies cryptocurrencies like Bitcoin, has the potential to disrupt the operations of Dark Web marketplaces. The transparency and immutability provided by blockchain can assist in tracking and tracing illicit transactions on the Dark Web.

Law enforcement agencies can leverage blockchain analysis tools to link transactions to specific individuals or entities. By analyzing the blockchain, investigators can follow the money trail and disrupt the financial infrastructure of Dark Web markets.

Additionally, the integration of blockchain technology into the supply chain of online marketplaces can enhance transparency, making it more difficult for illegal goods to be traded on Dark Web platforms. Blockchain-based provenance systems can provide a verifiable record of a product's origin and legitimacy, reducing the risk of counterfeit goods making their way onto Dark Web markets.

However, the decentralized nature of blockchain technology also presents challenges for law enforcement. It can be challenging to attribute transactions to specific individuals due to the pseudonymous nature of cryptocurrencies. Innovations in blockchain privacy protocols, such as zero-knowledge proofs, may further complicate the task of tracking illicit activities.

Big Data Analytics

The exponential growth of data generated on the internet offers both opportunities and challenges in combating Dark Web markets. Big data analytics can help in identifying patterns and trends, enabling law enforcement agencies to make informed decisions and prioritize their efforts.

By analyzing massive amounts of data from various sources, such as social media, forums, and marketplaces, law enforcement can uncover connections between Dark Web market participants and identify potential threats. Advanced data mining techniques can reveal hidden relationships and networks operating within the Dark Web ecosystem.

Moreover, big data analytics can aid in proactive detection and prevention of Dark Web activities. By analyzing data in real-time and using predictive analytics, law enforcement agencies can anticipate and respond to emerging threats more effectively.

However, the scalability of big data analytics presents challenges. Processing and analyzing vast amounts of data in real-time require robust computational resources and sophisticated algorithms. Additionally, privacy concerns arise when accessing and analyzing user data, necessitating the implementation of appropriate safeguards and legal frameworks.

Collaboration and Information Sharing

Emerging technologies not only improve the efficiency and effectiveness of individual law enforcement agencies but also facilitate collaboration and information sharing among agencies on a global scale. The fight against Dark Web markets requires international cooperation and knowledge sharing to overcome jurisdictional boundaries.

Secure communication protocols and information-sharing platforms enable law enforcement agencies to collaborate, exchange intelligence, and coordinate operations. By combining resources and expertise, agencies can take down Dark Web marketplaces more effectively and apprehend individuals involved in illegal activities.

However, challenges related to data privacy and national security hinder seamless collaboration. Balancing the need for information sharing with the protection of sensitive information is crucial. Standardized protocols and secure platforms are necessary to ensure the confidentiality and integrity of shared data.

Conclusion

Emerging technologies have tremendous potential in the fight against Dark Web markets. The advancements in artificial intelligence, blockchain technology, big data analytics, and collaboration platforms enable law enforcement agencies and cybersecurity professionals to stay one step ahead of criminals operating in the hidden corners of the internet.

However, ethical considerations must be taken into account when deploying these technologies. Balancing privacy and security, ensuring fairness in law enforcement actions, and addressing potential misuse are essential. Moreover, continual innovation and collaboration are necessary to keep up with the ever-evolving landscape of Dark Web markets.

As we move forward, it is crucial for law enforcement agencies, governments, and the cybersecurity community to embrace emerging technologies responsibly, effectively disrupt Dark Web activities, and safeguard the security and privacy of individuals both online and offline.

In the next section, we will delve into the ethical implications of surveillance on the Dark Web and discuss the importance of striking the right balance between privacy and security.

Ethical Considerations in Combating Dark Web Markets

Balancing privacy and security in Dark Web investigations

Balancing privacy and security is a critical aspect of conducting investigations on the Dark Web. While law enforcement agencies need to gather evidence and take action against illegal activities, they must also respect privacy rights and protect the anonymity of individuals not involved in criminal activities. Striking the right balance between privacy and security requires careful considerations and specialized techniques. In this section, we will explore the challenges and ethical implications involved in maintaining this delicate balance.

The tension between privacy and security

Privacy and security are two fundamental rights that often find themselves in conflict, particularly in the realm of Dark Web investigations. On one hand, individuals have the right to privacy and the expectation that their online activities remain confidential. On the other hand, law enforcement agencies have a duty to protect society from criminal activities, which sometimes necessitates invading privacy in order to gather evidence.

The Dark Web, with its encrypted communication channels and anonymity features, provides an environment where individuals can engage in illegal activities away from prying eyes. As a result, law enforcement agencies face the challenge of balancing their need for security with the need to respect individual privacy.

Legal frameworks and regulations

To strike a balance between privacy and security, law enforcement agencies need to operate within a clearly defined legal framework. This framework sets the boundaries for conducting investigations, ensuring that privacy rights are respected while allowing for effective law enforcement.

Different countries have different legal frameworks to govern Dark Web investigations. For example, in the United States, law enforcement agencies often require a court-issued warrant to conduct surveillance or gather evidence on the Dark Web. The warrant process involves demonstrating probable cause to a judge, who then authorizes the investigation. This legal safeguard ensures that privacy is not violated without reasonable justification.

International cooperation is also crucial in Dark Web investigations. Law enforcement agencies from different countries need to collaborate and respect the privacy laws of each jurisdiction involved. Mutual legal assistance treaties and information-sharing protocols help facilitate this cooperation while maintaining privacy safeguards.

Encryption and anonymization challenges

One of the biggest challenges in Dark Web investigations is dealing with encryption and anonymization techniques used by criminals. Encryption ensures secure communication by encoding messages, making it difficult for law enforcement to intercept and decipher them. Anonymization tools, such as Tor, further complicate investigations by obfuscating the identities and locations of Dark Web users.

While encryption and anonymization are essential for protecting privacy and security in legitimate contexts, they also create challenges for law enforcement. Decrypting encrypted messages and de-anonymizing users can be time-consuming and technically demanding. Moreover, the use of encryption and anonymization raises ethical questions about the extent to which privacy can be invaded in the pursuit of security.

Balancing investigative measures

Law enforcement agencies must carefully consider the investigative measures they employ to strike a balance between privacy and security. The use of intrusive techniques should be proportional to the severity of the potential harm to society and should be guided by legal constraints.

Techniques such as monitoring online communications, conducting undercover operations, and infiltrating Dark Web marketplaces are commonly used by law enforcement. However, these techniques should only be employed when there is sufficient evidence to justify them and when less intrusive methods have been exhausted. The principle of strict necessity should guide investigators to minimize the invasion of privacy while still achieving their security objectives.

Transparency, accountability, and oversight

Transparency, accountability, and oversight play crucial roles in maintaining the delicate balance between privacy and security in Dark Web investigations. To ensure that investigative activities are conducted ethically and within legal boundaries, there should be mechanisms in place for independent oversight and review.

Oversight bodies, such as internal affairs divisions or external review boards, can provide independent assessments of the justification and proportionality of investigative actions. These bodies help ensure that privacy rights are respected and that law enforcement agencies are held accountable for their actions.

Transparency is also essential in building public trust. Law enforcement agencies need to be open about their Dark Web investigation activities to the extent allowed by law. Publicly disclosing the legal framework within which investigations occur and providing general information about the types of investigative techniques employed enhances accountability and helps allay concerns about privacy invasion.

Ethical considerations in the use of collected data

In Dark Web investigations, the collected data contains sensitive and private information about individuals. It is essential to treat this data ethically and responsibly. Law enforcement agencies should only use the data for legitimate investigation purposes and ensure that it is protected from unauthorized access and use.

The ethical considerations extend to data retention as well. Holding onto collected data for longer than necessary poses a risk to privacy and security. Strict policies and protocols should be in place to ensure that data is securely disposed of once it is no longer required for investigative purposes.

Ethical dilemma: the trade-off between privacy and security

The balancing act between privacy and security in Dark Web investigations raises an ethical dilemma. On one hand, privacy is a fundamental human right that should be respected and protected. On the other hand, security is crucial for protecting society from harm.

Resolving this dilemma requires a comprehensive approach that takes into account the wider societal impact. It involves considering the severity of criminal activities, the effectiveness of alternative investigative techniques, and the potential consequences of invading privacy or compromising security. Ultimately, striking the right balance requires a nuanced understanding of the ethical implications and a commitment to upholding the rule of law.

In conclusion, balancing privacy and security in Dark Web investigations is a complex and multifaceted task. Law enforcement agencies must navigate legal frameworks, encryption challenges, and ethical considerations to effectively combat illegal activities while respecting individual privacy. The ongoing evolution of technology and the changing landscape of the Dark Web present ongoing challenges, requiring ongoing vigilance and adaptability in striking this delicate balance.

The ethical implications of surveillance on the Dark Web

The rise of Dark Web markets has prompted increased surveillance efforts by law enforcement agencies and cybersecurity professionals. While this surveillance is aimed at combating illegal activities and ensuring the safety and security of individuals, it raises several ethical concerns. This section explores the implications of surveillance on the Dark Web, discussing the balance between privacy and security, the ethics of surveillance, and the potential consequences of surveillance for individuals and society as a whole.

Privacy vs. security

One of the key ethical dilemmas in the context of Dark Web surveillance is the trade-off between privacy and security. The Dark Web was originally designed to provide anonymity and privacy to its users, allowing individuals to protect their identity and communicate securely. However, the increase in criminal activities on the Dark Web has led to the need for surveillance to protect individuals and society from harm. This tension between privacy and security raises questions about the extent to which surveillance should be allowed and how it should be conducted.

From a privacy standpoint, individuals have the right to protect their personal information and autonomy. The surveillance of Dark Web activities, which involves monitoring online communications and tracking user behavior, intrudes upon this privacy. It raises concerns about the potential abuse of surveillance powers, the creation of a surveillance state, and the erosion of civil liberties.

On the other hand, maintaining security is crucial in combating illegal activities and protecting innocent individuals from harm. By monitoring and intercepting Dark Web activities, law enforcement agencies can identify and apprehend criminals involved in activities such as drug trafficking, weapon sales, and cybercrime. Surveillance can also serve as a deterrent, discouraging individuals from engaging in illicit activities on the Dark Web.

Ethics of surveillance

The ethical implications of Dark Web surveillance extend beyond the privacy and security debate. They touch upon broader questions about the justification, transparency, and accountability of surveillance practices. Ethical considerations related to Dark Web surveillance include:

1. Proportionality: Is the surveillance proportional to the threat? It is important to assess whether the level of surveillance is appropriate given the risks posed by Dark Web activities. Excessive surveillance can infringe upon individuals' rights and create a chilling effect on freedom of expression.

2. Informed consent: Do individuals participating in Dark Web activities have knowledge of the surveillance and the potential consequences? Ensuring that individuals are aware of the surveillance taking place allows them to make informed decisions about their online behavior and take necessary precautions.

3. Minimization of harm: Are surveillance activities designed to minimize harm to innocent individuals? It is important to consider the potential collateral damage of surveillance, such as the exposure of sensitive personal information or secondary consequences for individuals not involved in criminal activities.

4. Transparency and accountability: Are surveillance activities conducted in a transparent manner? Law enforcement agencies and cybersecurity professionals should be accountable for their surveillance practices and subject to oversight to prevent abuse of power.

Consequences of surveillance

The ethical implications of Dark Web surveillance extend to the potential consequences for individuals and society as a whole. While surveillance aims to protect individuals from harm, its widespread and indiscriminate use can have unintended consequences and lead to negative outcomes.

1. Unintended chilling effect: Extensive surveillance can create a climate of fear and inhibit freedom of expression and exploration of ideas. Individuals may self-censor their online activities, limiting the exchange of diverse opinions and impeding technological innovation.

2. Surveillance creep: Once surveillance mechanisms are in place, there is a risk of their expansion and use beyond their original purpose. Mission creep refers to the gradual broadening of surveillance activities to include activities unrelated to criminal investigations, potentially leading to the monitoring of innocent individuals.

3. Stigmatization and guilt by association: The indiscriminate nature of surveillance can result in innocent individuals being flagged as potential criminals based on their online behavior or associations. This guilt by association can lead to reputational harm, social isolation, and the erosion of personal freedom.

4. Effectiveness and efficiency: Surveillance efforts may not always yield the desired outcomes. The resources invested in extensive surveillance could be better allocated to prevention, education, and addressing root causes of criminal activities. Additionally, surveillance can be circumvented by those engaging in illegal activities, rendering the effort less effective.

Case study: The Silk Road

The Silk Road, one of the most notorious Dark Web marketplaces, provides a case study in the ethical implications of surveillance. Ross Ulbricht, the founder of the Silk Road, was apprehended and the marketplace shut down by law enforcement agencies after an extensive investigation. While the closure of the Silk Road mitigated illegal activities, it also raised ethical concerns about the surveillance techniques employed.

The investigation involved sophisticated surveillance methods, including the infiltration of the Silk Road's administration team and the use of tracking techniques to identify illegal transactions. Critics argue that the surveillance conducted during the investigation crossed ethical boundaries, infringing upon privacy rights and potentially setting dangerous precedents for future investigations.

Furthermore, the closure of the Silk Road led to the displacement of illegal activities to other Dark Web marketplaces, highlighting the need for a comprehensive strategy that addresses the root causes of such activities rather than solely relying on surveillance.

Conclusion

The ethical implications of surveillance on the Dark Web are complex and multifaceted, touching upon issues of privacy, security, transparency, and accountability. Balancing the need for surveillance to combat illegal activities with the preservation of individual rights and freedoms is a challenge for law enforcement agencies, cybersecurity professionals, and society as a whole. It is crucial to engage in ongoing dialogue, establish clear guidelines and oversight mechanisms, and pursue alternative approaches to addressing the root causes of criminal activities on the Dark Web. Only through a comprehensive and ethical approach can we strike an appropriate balance between privacy and security in the fight against Dark Web markets.

Ensuring fairness in law enforcement actions against Dark Web market participants

In the fight against Dark Web markets, law enforcement agencies play a crucial role in identifying and apprehending individuals involved in illicit activities. However, it is essential to ensure fairness in these law enforcement actions to protect individual rights and maintain the integrity of the legal system. This section examines the ethical considerations and challenges associated with ensuring fairness when dealing with Dark Web market participants.

Presumption of Innocence

One of the fundamental principles of justice is the presumption of innocence, which holds that an individual is innocent until proven guilty. This principle should guide law enforcement actions against Dark Web market participants, ensuring that they are treated fairly and have the opportunity to defend themselves in a court of law.

Maintaining the presumption of innocence becomes even more critical in the context of the Dark Web, where individuals may engage in illegal activities but remain anonymous. Law enforcement agencies must carefully investigate and gather evidence to establish guilt beyond a reasonable doubt before apprehending any suspects. It is crucial to avoid preconceived notions or biases that may unfairly influence the investigation or subsequent legal proceedings.

Proportional Use of Force

Another ethical consideration in law enforcement actions against Dark Web market participants is the proportional use of force. While it is essential to apprehend individuals involved in illegal activities, the level of force employed by law enforcement should be commensurate with the threat posed by the suspect.

In situations where suspects are found to be involved in non-violent crimes, law enforcement should prioritize non-violent apprehension methods to minimize harm and ensure fairness. Overzealous use of force can undermine the integrity of law enforcement actions and result in unnecessary harm to individuals being apprehended.

Respect for Privacy and Data Protection

Law enforcement actions against Dark Web market participants often involve collecting and analyzing vast amounts of data, including personal information and online communications. While this data is crucial for investigations, it is essential to respect privacy rights and adhere to legal frameworks governing data protection.

Investigators must obtain proper legal authorization, such as search warrants, before accessing and analyzing individuals' data. Additionally, procedures must be in place to prevent misuse or unauthorized access to sensitive information unrelated to the investigation. Respecting privacy rights and data protection principles ensures that law enforcement actions remain fair, transparent, and compliant with the law.

Transparency and Accountability

Maintaining transparency and accountability is crucial in ensuring fairness in law enforcement actions against Dark Web market participants. It is vital for law enforcement agencies to operate within the bounds of the law, following established procedures and adhering to ethical guidelines.

To ensure transparency, law enforcement agencies should document their investigative processes, including the methods used to collect evidence and the decision-making processes leading to an arrest. This documentation can be subject to review by independent bodies, promoting accountability and helping to identify and address any potential abuses or unfair practices.

Securing Legal Representation

Fairness in law enforcement actions against Dark Web market participants also necessitates ensuring their access to legal representation. Individuals accused of crimes, regardless of the context, have the right to be represented by competent legal counsel throughout the legal process.

Law enforcement agencies should facilitate the provision of legal aid to Dark Web market participants who may lack the resources to secure legal representation independently. This ensures that accused individuals have access to the necessary resources and expertise to defend themselves effectively.

Avoiding Collateral Damage

In the pursuit of Dark Web market participants, law enforcement actions should aim to minimize collateral damage to innocent individuals. The nature of the Dark Web often makes it challenging to trace criminal activities accurately. Investigative efforts should focus on identifying and targeting individuals involved in illegal activities while minimizing harm to innocent parties.

This requires thorough investigative techniques and the appropriate allocation of resources to ensure that only those individuals directly involved in Dark Web marketplaces are targeted in law enforcement actions. Unfair or indiscriminate targeting of individuals not directly involved in illegal activities can have severe consequences and erode public trust in law enforcement agencies.

Collaboration with Legal and Judicial Systems

Ensuring fairness in law enforcement actions against Dark Web market participants requires close collaboration with legal and judicial systems. Law enforcement agencies should work within the existing legal frameworks and respect the independence of the judiciary.

By engaging in legal proceedings and presenting evidence in a transparent manner, law enforcement agencies maintain the integrity of the legal system. This collaboration allows for rigorous scrutiny of the evidence and safeguards against unfair treatment or bias during the legal process.

Conclusion

In the battle against Dark Web markets, law enforcement agencies play a vital role in apprehending individuals involved in illegal activities. However, it is crucial to ensure that these law enforcement actions are conducted with fairness and respect for individual rights. Upholding principles such as the presumption of innocence, proportional use of force, respect for privacy and data protection, transparency and accountability, securing legal representation, avoiding collateral damage, and collaboration with legal and judicial systems are essential to ensure fairness in law enforcement actions against Dark Web market participants. By adhering to these principles, law enforcement agencies can maintain public trust, protect individual rights, and contribute to a fair and just legal system.

Ethical challenges faced by cybersecurity professionals in countering Dark Web market activities

As cybersecurity professionals work to counter the activities of Dark Web markets, they face a number of ethical challenges. These challenges stem from the unique nature of the Dark Web and the practices of its users. In this section, we will explore some of these ethical challenges and discuss possible strategies for addressing them.

One of the primary ethical challenges faced by cybersecurity professionals is the balance between privacy and security in Dark Web investigations. While it is important to uncover illegal activities and protect the online community, it is also crucial to respect individuals' right to privacy. The nature of Dark Web activities often involves anonymity and encryption, making it difficult to identify and track individuals engaged in illegal activities. Cybersecurity professionals must navigate this challenge by ensuring that their investigative practices are both effective in countering Dark Web markets and respectful of individuals' privacy rights.

To overcome this challenge, cybersecurity professionals can rely on established legal frameworks and principles. They should work within the boundaries set by the law and obtain proper authorization for their investigative activities. Collaboration with law enforcement agencies is crucial in ensuring that investigations are conducted lawfully. Ethics training and ongoing education are also essential for cybersecurity professionals to have a clear understanding of their ethical responsibilities and the legal framework within which they operate.

Another ethical consideration is the potential for unintended consequences when countering Dark Web market activities. While the primary goal is to disrupt illegal trade and protect individuals from harm, there is a risk of collateral damage. For example, taking down a Dark Web marketplace can also result in unintended consequences such as the displacement of users to other platforms or the creation of new, more resilient marketplaces. Cybersecurity professionals must carefully weigh the potential risks and benefits of their actions, considering the broader implications for the online ecosystem.

To address this challenge, cybersecurity professionals should adopt a comprehensive approach that goes beyond simply targeting individual marketplaces. They should work in collaboration with other stakeholders such as law enforcement, policymakers, and research institutions to develop strategies that address the root causes of Dark Web activities. This may involve initiatives focused on raising awareness, improving cybersecurity measures, or providing support for individuals who may be vulnerable to exploitation on the Dark Web. By taking a holistic approach, cybersecurity professionals can minimize the unintended consequences of their actions while still effectively countering Dark Web markets.

Additionally, cybersecurity professionals must grapple with the ethical implications of surveillance on the Dark Web. Monitoring Dark Web activities often requires invasive techniques, such as the use of malware or the collection of personal information without consent. While these techniques may be necessary to gather intelligence and disrupt illegal activities, they raise significant ethical concerns related to privacy and consent. Cybersecurity professionals must ensure that their surveillance practices are proportionate, targeted, and conducted with appropriate legal authorization.

To address this challenge, cybersecurity professionals should adopt a principle of transparency and accountability. They should clearly communicate the purpose and scope of their surveillance activities to relevant stakeholders, such as law enforcement agencies and judicial authorities. Regular audits and reviews of surveillance practices can help ensure that they are aligned with legal and ethical standards. Additionally, cybersecurity professionals should actively engage in the development of policies and regulations that govern surveillance activities on the Dark Web, advocating for safeguards that protect privacy rights while still enabling effective investigations.

In conclusion, cybersecurity professionals face significant ethical challenges in countering Dark Web market activities. Privacy concerns, unintended consequences, and the ethics of surveillance are just a few of the complex issues they must navigate. By adhering to legal frameworks, adopting a comprehensive approach, and promoting transparency and accountability, cybersecurity professionals can effectively address these challenges and contribute to the fight against Dark Web markets while upholding ethical standards.

Conclusion

Conclusion

Summary of key points discussed in the book

Throughout this book, we have explored the fascinating world of Dark Web markets, delving into various aspects of their operation, the participants involved, the challenges faced, and the measures taken to combat them. In this final section, we summarize the key points discussed in each chapter, providing a comprehensive overview of the content covered.

Chapter 1 introduced the concept of Dark Web markets, starting with an understanding of the Dark Web itself. We explored the definition of the Dark Web and its differences from the Surface Web, as well as the anatomy of the Dark Web and various access methods. The different layers of the Dark Web were examined, shedding light on the complexity of this hidden ecosystem. Additionally, we discussed various types of Dark Web markets, their evolution over time, the popular goods and services offered, and highlighted examples of famous Dark Web marketplaces. Finally, we examined the impact of Dark Web markets on society.

Chapter 2 explored the various participants involved in Dark Web markets. We focused on buyers and sellers, understanding their motivations and demographics. Buyer personas and their preferences were analyzed, along with the risks and precautions associated with using Dark Web markets. We also delved into the characteristics of Dark Web market sellers, the process of becoming a seller, the types of goods and services sold, pricing strategies, and the techniques sellers employ to ensure anonymity and security. Additionally, we highlighted the crucial role of law enforcement and cybersecurity professionals in combating Dark Web markets.

Chapter 3 delved into the Dark Web market ecosystem, focusing on the infrastructure that enables their operation. We examined the role of hosting services and the challenges they face in supporting Dark Web marketplaces. Emphasis was placed on the use of encryption and anonymous communication tools to maintain security and privacy. In addition, we explored the security and trust mechanisms employed in Dark Web markets, such as escrow systems, reputation and feedback systems, and the role of market moderators in maintaining trust. We also discussed the tools and technologies used on Dark Web markets, including cryptocurrencies, privacy-enhancing technologies, and law enforcement tools for tracking activities.

Chapter 4 explored the various forms of cybercrime prevalent on Dark Web markets. We focused on the illicit drug trade, discussing its rise and the popular drugs sold on these platforms. The challenges faced by law enforcement in combating the online drug trade were analyzed, along with the impact of drug marketplaces on drug policies. We also examined the weapons and firearms trade on Dark Web markets, highlighting the availability of weapons and the challenges in regulating online weapon sales. The connection between Dark Web markets and real-world violence was brought to light, along with efforts to combat illicit weapon trade. Additionally, we explored the underground economy of cybercrime services and the types of services available on Dark Web markets. The impact of cybercrime-as-a-service on the digital landscape was examined, alongside strategies for countering these offerings.

In Chapter 5, we delved into the fight against Dark Web markets from both law enforcement and technological perspectives. We explored global strategies and initiatives aimed at dismantling Dark Web marketplaces, highlighting successful law enforcement operations. The challenges faced by law enforcement in prosecuting Dark Web market participants were discussed, emphasizing the role of international cooperation. We also examined technological solutions for Dark Web market surveillance, including advances in monitoring and data analysis, machine learning and artificial intelligence, tools for proactive detection and prevention, and emerging technologies for market investigation. Additionally, we focused on the importance of education and awareness campaigns, discussing strategies for raising awareness about the dangers of Dark Web market involvement and engaging communities, schools, and law enforcement in prevention efforts.

Chapter 6 explored the future trends and ethical considerations surrounding Dark Web markets. We discussed emerging technological advancements shaping the future of Dark Web markets, changes in the types of goods and services offered, and the role of cryptocurrency in their evolution. Ethical considerations were addressed, including the balance between privacy and security in Dark Web investigations, the implications of surveillance on the Dark Web, ensuring fairness in law enforcement actions, and the ethical challenges faced by cybersecurity professionals in countering Dark Web market activities.

In conclusion, this book has provided a comprehensive exploration of Dark Web markets, covering topics ranging from their definition and operation to the challenges faced by law enforcement and the future trends in this underground ecosystem. By examining the various aspects of Dark Web markets, we have gained a deeper understanding of their impact on society and the measures taken to combat them. It is clear that collaboration, innovation, and education are essential in the ongoing battle against Dark Web markets, ensuring a safer digital landscape for all.

The ongoing battle against Dark Web markets

The fight against Dark Web markets is an ongoing battle that requires collaboration and innovation from various stakeholders. Law enforcement agencies, cybersecurity professionals, and technological experts are continuously working to combat the illicit activities that take place in these hidden online marketplaces. This section will discuss the challenges faced in this battle, the strategies employed by law enforcement, and the importance of international cooperation.

Challenges in combating Dark Web markets

The battle against Dark Web markets is a complex and constantly evolving challenge. There are several key challenges that make it difficult to effectively crack down on these platforms:

- **Anonymity and encryption:** Dark Web markets provide a high level of anonymity to buyers and sellers, making it difficult for law enforcement to trace their activities. Encryption technologies further enhance the security and privacy of transactions, preventing interception and monitoring.

- **Global nature:** Dark Web markets transcend geographical borders, operating in multiple jurisdictions. This creates challenges for law enforcement agencies as they must navigate legal frameworks and jurisdictions to take action against participants in these markets.

- **Evolving technology:** As technology evolves, so do the methods and tools used by Dark Web market operators. They constantly adapt their operations to counteract law enforcement efforts. Staying ahead of these developments requires continuous technological and investigative updates.

- **Growing user base:** Dark Web markets continue to attract a growing number of users, making it challenging to keep up with the sheer volume of illicit activities taking place. The scale of the problem requires significant resources and coordination among law enforcement agencies worldwide.

- **Revenue generation:** Dark Web markets generate substantial revenue through the sale of illegal goods and services. This financial motivation enables them to invest in security measures and make it more difficult for law enforcement to infiltrate their operations.

Addressing these challenges requires a multifaceted approach that combines the efforts of law enforcement agencies, cybersecurity professionals, and technological advancements.

Law enforcement strategies and initiatives

Law enforcement agencies play a crucial role in the battle against Dark Web markets. They employ various strategies and initiatives to dismantle these illicit platforms and bring perpetrators to justice. Some of the key approaches include:

- **Undercover operations:** Law enforcement agencies establish undercover identities to infiltrate Dark Web marketplaces and gather evidence against sellers and buyers. These operations help gather intelligence and build cases against individuals involved in illegal activities.

- **Collaboration and intelligence sharing:** International cooperation among law enforcement agencies is vital to combatting Dark Web markets. Sharing intelligence, expertise, and resources enhances the capability to take down major marketplaces and apprehend individuals involved in criminal activities.

- **Targeted enforcement actions:** Law enforcement agencies conduct targeted operations to arrest key individuals and seize assets involved in Dark Web market operations. These actions disrupt the operations and financial infrastructure of these illicit platforms.

- **Legislative measures:** Governments enact legislation to address the challenges posed by Dark Web markets. Laws may cover aspects such as cryptocurrencies, encryption, and international cooperation to empower law enforcement agencies in their battle against these platforms.

- **Training and capacity building:** Law enforcement agencies invest in training programs to enhance their capabilities in investigating and prosecuting Dark Web market participants. These programs ensure that investigators and prosecutors are equipped with the necessary skills to tackle the complexities of online crime.

While significant progress has been made in dismantling Dark Web markets, continued efforts are needed to stay ahead of the criminals operating on these platforms.

The importance of international cooperation

International cooperation is pivotal in the fight against Dark Web markets. Since these platforms transcend geographical boundaries, collaboration among law enforcement agencies from different countries is crucial. Some key aspects of international cooperation include:

- **Information sharing and joint investigations:** Interpol and other international law enforcement organizations facilitate the sharing of intelligence and coordination of joint investigations. These efforts help identify the global reach of Dark Web market operators and enable targeted actions across multiple jurisdictions.
- **Legislative harmonization:** Countries around the world must align their legal frameworks to address the challenges of Dark Web markets effectively. Harmonization of legislation related to cybercrime, cryptocurrencies, and encryption ensures that there are no safe havens for criminals operating on these platforms.
- **Training and capacity building:** International cooperation involves sharing expertise and best practices in tackling Dark Web markets. Training programs, workshops, and information exchange platforms help build the capabilities of law enforcement agencies worldwide.
- **Public-private partnerships:** Collaboration between the public and private sectors strengthens the fight against Dark Web markets. Technology companies, financial institutions, and cybersecurity firms can contribute their expertise and resources to support law enforcement efforts.

By working together, international stakeholders can enhance their collective ability to combat Dark Web markets and protect society from their harmful consequences.

Innovation and the future

Innovation plays a vital role in the ongoing battle against Dark Web markets. As criminals continuously adapt their methods, law enforcement agencies and cybersecurity professionals must stay one step ahead. Some emerging areas of innovation include:

- **Advancements in data analysis:** Law enforcement agencies are increasingly leveraging machine learning and artificial intelligence to sift through massive amounts of data and identify patterns related to Dark Web activities. These advancements enable proactive detection of illicit marketplaces and their participants.

- **Technological tools for investigation:** Innovative tools are being developed to aid law enforcement in investigating and monitoring Dark Web market activities. These tools utilize advanced techniques such as network analysis, data visualization, and natural language processing to uncover insights and identify key actors.

- **Education and awareness:** Educating the public about the dangers of Dark Web markets is crucial in prevention efforts. Innovative awareness campaigns leveraging social media, interactive workshops, and community engagement can empower individuals to protect themselves and their communities from the influence of these illicit platforms.

- **Collaborative platforms and knowledge sharing:** The development of collaborative platforms that enable law enforcement agencies, cybersecurity professionals, and researchers to share intelligence and expertise is essential. By fostering a collective approach, these platforms can drive innovation and enhance the effectiveness of efforts against Dark Web markets.

In conclusion, the battle against Dark Web markets is complex, but ongoing efforts by law enforcement agencies, cybersecurity professionals, and technological innovators are making a difference. International cooperation, the use of advanced technologies, and innovative strategies are crucial in disrupting the operations of these illicit platforms. By staying vigilant, adaptive, and collaborative, we can continue to tackle the challenges posed by Dark Web markets and protect society from their harmful effects.

Now I will end the document.

The importance of collaboration and innovation in addressing the issue

Collaboration and innovation play a crucial role in addressing the complex challenges posed by Dark Web markets. As the nature of illicit activities on the Dark Web continues to evolve, law enforcement agencies, cybersecurity professionals, and other stakeholders must come together to develop effective strategies and solutions. In this section, we will explore the importance of collaboration and innovation in the fight against Dark Web markets, highlighting their impact on law enforcement operations, technological advancements, and societal awareness.

1. Collaboration among stakeholders in combating Dark Web markets

The battle against Dark Web markets requires a coordinated effort among various stakeholders, including law enforcement agencies, government bodies, private sector organizations, and research institutions. By collaborating and sharing resources, expertise, and intelligence, these entities can significantly enhance their ability to combat the proliferation of illegal goods and services on the Dark Web. Collaboration can take various forms, such as information sharing partnerships, joint operations, and specialized task forces.

For example, the collaborative efforts of international law enforcement agencies, such as the FBI, Europol, and Interpol, have led to successful operations that have disrupted major Dark Web marketplaces and apprehended key individuals involved in illicit activities. The sharing of intelligence and operational support among these agencies enables them to counter the global nature of Dark Web markets effectively.

Furthermore, collaboration between law enforcement and cybersecurity professionals is essential in developing proactive strategies to detect and prevent criminal activities on the Dark Web. By sharing knowledge and expertise, these two groups can stay ahead of the techniques and tools employed by cybercriminals, leading to more effective investigations and prosecutions.

2. Innovation in technology for Dark Web market surveillance

Innovation in technology is crucial for addressing the issue of Dark Web markets. As criminals continually adapt and evolve their methods, law enforcement and cybersecurity professionals must leverage cutting-edge technologies to detect, monitor, and deter illegal activities on the Dark Web.

Advances in data analysis, machine learning, and artificial intelligence have the potential to revolutionize Dark Web surveillance. These technologies can enable the automated monitoring of Dark Web marketplaces, analyzing patterns, and detecting suspicious transactions or behaviors. By leveraging these tools, law enforcement agencies can prioritize their resources and focus on high-value targets, increasing the chances of successful operations against Dark Web markets.

Moreover, the development of tools for proactive detection and prevention is critical in staying ahead of emerging threats on the Dark Web. Innovative solutions that can identify new forms of illicit activities, detect vulnerabilities in Dark Web infrastructure, or track the movement of cryptocurrency transactions provide invaluable support for law enforcement agencies and cybersecurity professionals.

3. Societal awareness and education

Collaboration and innovation extend beyond law enforcement and cybersecurity professionals. Societal awareness and education also play a crucial role in addressing the issue of Dark Web markets. Educating the public about the risks and dangers associated with using or supporting Dark Web marketplaces can help reduce demand and limit the reach of these illicit activities.

Information campaigns aimed at the general public, schools, and communities can raise awareness about the potential consequences of engaging with Dark Web markets. By emphasizing the links between Dark Web activities and real-world harm, such as drug addiction, violence, and the funding of criminal organizations, it is possible to discourage individuals from getting involved in illicit transactions.

Collaboration between law enforcement agencies, educational institutions, and community organizations can be instrumental in spreading awareness and educating individuals about the dangers of the Dark Web. These efforts can empower individuals to protect themselves from the influence of Dark Web markets and make informed decisions to ensure their own safety and security.

In conclusion, collaboration and innovation are essential components in addressing the issue of Dark Web markets. By working together and embracing technological advancements, stakeholders can develop effective strategies to combat the proliferation of illegal goods and services on the Dark Web. Furthermore, societal awareness and education initiatives help reduce demand and limit the impact of Dark Web activities on individuals and communities. The fight against Dark Web markets requires a multi-faceted approach that combines the collective efforts of law enforcement, cybersecurity professionals, and the general public. Only through collaboration and innovation can we hope to make significant progress in countering the threats posed by Dark Web markets.

Final thoughts on the future of Dark Web markets and cybersecurity

The future of Dark Web markets and cybersecurity is a constantly evolving landscape, shaped by advances in technology and the ever-changing strategies of cybercriminals. As we conclude our exploration of this topic, it is important to reflect on the potential outcomes and considerations for the future.

One aspect that is likely to shape the future of Dark Web markets is the continuous development of new technologies. Advancements in areas such as blockchain, artificial intelligence, and decentralized networks are expected to have a significant impact. These technologies have the potential to enhance both the security measures employed by Dark Web markets and the capabilities of law enforcement agencies and cybersecurity professionals.

Cryptocurrencies, which have played a pivotal role in the operations of Dark Web markets, are also expected to undergo significant changes. As governments and regulatory bodies continue to scrutinize cryptocurrencies, we may witness the emergence of alternative methods of conducting secure and anonymous transactions on the Dark Web. Privacy-enhancing cryptocurrencies, decentralized exchanges, and other innovations aim to address concerns about the illicit use of cryptocurrencies, while still providing a level of anonymity.

Another key trend that is likely to shape the future of Dark Web markets is the diversification of goods and services offered. While illegal drugs and weapons have been the predominant focus, other types of illicit activities, such as human trafficking, stolen data trading, and hacking services, are expected to gain prominence. As criminals adapt to the changing market demands, the fight against Dark Web markets must keep pace by developing new strategies and tools to combat emerging cybercrime trends.

One area that requires continued attention is the role of law enforcement and global cooperation. Collaborative efforts among international law enforcement agencies have yielded significant successes in the fight against Dark Web markets. However, the decentralized nature of these markets presents unique challenges. Keeping up with the technological advancements of criminals necessitates not only adequate funding and resources but also effective information sharing and coordination among law enforcement agencies worldwide.

Technological solutions, such as Dark Web monitoring and data analysis, will continue to play a crucial role in the fight against Dark Web markets. Machine learning and artificial intelligence algorithms can assist in identifying patterns, detecting suspicious activities, and proactively preventing cybercrimes. With the exponential growth of data generated on the Dark Web, advanced analytical approaches will be essential in extracting actionable intelligence and targeting key individuals and marketplaces.

Education and awareness campaigns will also remain vital in combatting the influence of Dark Web markets. These efforts should focus not only on informing the general public about the dangers associated with Dark Web involvement but also on empowering individuals to protect themselves from cyber threats. Engaging communities, schools, and law enforcement in prevention efforts can foster a culture of cybersecurity awareness and resilience.

Ethical considerations will continue to be a topic of debate in the fight against Dark Web markets. Balancing the need for privacy and security is a complex challenge that requires careful thought and consideration. Law enforcement agencies and cybersecurity professionals must navigate a fine line between conducting necessary investigations and infringing on individual privacy rights. Ensuring fairness, transparency, and accountability in law enforcement actions against Dark Web market participants is paramount.

In conclusion, the future of Dark Web markets and cybersecurity is an ever-evolving battleground. Technological advancements, changes in the illicit goods and services offered, and developments in law enforcement strategies will shape this landscape. Vigilance, collaboration, innovation, and continuous education will be crucial in addressing the challenges posed by Dark Web markets. By staying ahead of cybercriminals and adapting to emerging trends, we can work towards a safer and more secure digital future.

Index

9 781778 906008